STRUCTURED SET
A Practical Guide

EDITORS-IN-CHIEF

**Iain S Goldrein MA (Cantab) and
Margaret R de Haas LlB (Hons)**

Barristers, 12 King's Bench Walk, Temple,
London, and the Corn Exchange Chambers,
Fenwick Street, Liverpool

Authors and Editors of the Butterworths
Personal Injury Litigation Service

With a foreword by
The Honourable Mr Justice Michael Wright

Butterworths
London, Dublin, Edinburgh
1993

United Kingdom	Butterworth & Co (Publishers) Ltd, 88 Kingsway, LONDON WC2B 6AB and 4 Hill Street, EDINBURGH EH2 3JZ
Australia	Butterworths, SYDNEY, MELBOURNE, BRISBANE, ADELAIDE, PERTH, CANBERRA and HOBART
Belgium	Butterworth & Co (Publishers) Ltd, BRUSSELS
Canada	Butterworths Canada Ltd, TORONTO and VANCOUVER
Ireland	Butterworth (Ireland) Ltd, DUBLIN
Malaysia	Malayan Law Journal Sdn Bhd, KUALA LUMPUR
New Zealand	Butterworths of New Zealand Ltd, WELLINGTON and AUCKLAND
Puerto Rico	Equity de Puerto Rico, Inc, HATO REY
Singapore	Butterworths Asia, SINGAPORE
USA	Butterworth Legal Publishers, AUSTIN, Texas; BOSTON, Massachusetts; CLEARWATER, Florida (D & S Publishers); ORFORD, New Hampshire (Equity Publishing); ST PAUL, Minnesota; and SEATTLE, Washington

A CIP Catalogue record for this book is available from the British Library.

ISBN   0 406 02056 6

Printed and bound in Great Britain by Mackays of Chatham plc, Chatham, Kent

Foreword

Every English judge is well accustomed, when assessing the value of a claim for future loss in a personal injuries case under our present system, to peering into a crystal ball in an attempt to foresee the course of events, sometimes many years into the future. It is a regrettable but undeniable fact that, notwithstanding the intellectual effort that frequently goes into the process, the result that emerges is, in the light of subsequent events, almost bound to be wrong. The plaintiff will undoubtedly be likely to live for a longer or shorter period than the exact figure given at trial as his expectation of life; the deterioration in his condition so confidently forecast by the medical experts called on his behalf may be much delayed or never occur; inflation may produce an unexpected increase in the cost of providing the services that a severely disabled plaintiff needs.

In almost every case the effect of such variables will show, with the benefit of hindsight, either that the lump sum of money awarded to the plaintiff to cover such losses and expenses has been insufficient for the purpose, or that the plaintiff (or his estate) has received an undeserved windfall.

When, in 1987, an agreement negotiated between the Association of British Insurers and the Inland Revenue produced the concession that a payment by instalments of an antecedent debt in the form of an annuity, subject to certain conditions, would be treated as capital in the hands of the recipient and not income, and thus non-taxable, the opportunity opened to remove from the process of calculation of fair and proper compensation for future loss a major element of guesswork presently inherent in it, without at the same time penalising the plaintiff by exposing him to a liability to income tax on his damages.

This development was quickly recognised as being of great potential benefit both to plaintiffs, and to the insurance community at large, and much interest has been generated in it. Numerous conferences and seminars have been held around the country, attended by underwriters, claims managers and members of both wings of the legal profession. Within two years the first settlement of a major personal injuries claim to be structured on the basis of this new approach was approved by the Court, and many more have followed and will follow.

In the circumstances, the need for a clear and comprehensive guidebook to the principles underlying the structuring of a settlement of a personal injuries or fatal accidents claim, and the technical problems attendant upon its negotiation and implementation, is obvious, and our authors have been quick to recognise and fill that need.

I fully expect this book to become a standard and valued work of reference in the library of every set of chambers and firm of solicitors whose members wish to be regarded as serious practitioners in the personal injuries field, and, perhaps even more so, in the offices of every indemnity insurer with a significant exposure to these risks. While, perhaps regrettably, there is still no power in the Court to impose a structure upon the parties, nor is it yet possible to incorporate a structure into an award made by way of judgment rather than settlement without forfeiting the tax advantages, the benefits of structures in large claims are by now sufficiently well-recognised on both sides to make them an increasingly frequent device.

The authors have provided a most useful tool for the hands of the various labourers in this particular field. I wish their book every success.

The Hon Mr Justice Michael Wright

Preface

The Index to Halsbury's Law of England, under the word 'Settlement', inter alia recites the following:

> 'Marriage settlement, equitable interests, gift made by settlement, settlement of property . . . etc.'

Under 'Structure' one finds:

> 'Power to deal with dangerous structure, structure plan, removal of unauthorised structure . . . etc.'

Structured settlements? Nothing!

This work is designed to help plug that gap. In the field of personal injury litigation, 'structured settlements' are new legal technology.

Such settlements are of course a means whereby the plaintiff, who would otherwise recover a very substantial lump sum in damages, instead receives sums of money payable by regular instalments guaranteed for life.

To explain what structured settlements achieve is simple. But what does the litigator have to do, to bring this 'technology' into the action? When does he do it? How does this technology work? What are its component parts and how are they put together, and by whom?

These are the questions this book is designed to answer. The answers, however, can represent no more than the present state of this new and rapidly developing field: it would be to mislead the reader to suggest that the concept of the structured settlement has reached a final stage. In the jurisprudence of the United Kingdom, the concept is barely off the starting blocks. Indeed, after this book went to print, the interest rates fell further. The consequences for structured settlements can only be guessed at. In contrast, such settlements have been part of the legal machinery on the other side of the Atlantic for over a decade (despite their very low interest rates). Hence the text provided in Chapter 8 by David Gross and Cynthia Maner Campbell. By explaining the US experience, they afford to us a perspective of the route down which we in the United Kingdom may be expected to pass as the 1990s unravel.

In explaining the nuts and bolts of structured settlements, we have sought to address the issues from different perspectives: from the viewpoints of the victim, of the victim's legal adviser, the 'Exchequer' (as Neil Harris from the Royal Insurance engagingly expresses the position), the Bar, and last but by no means least, the forensic accountant whose role in the field of structured settlements is recognised in the relevant Practice Direction.

This bringing together of a number of disciplines looking at a litigation problem from different angles (each representing perhaps different interests) has a bearing on the significance of structured settlements in the overall setting of personal injury litigation: such settlements cannot be imposed by the courts, they can only be achieved by consent. They benefit both sides. Thus, there is an incentive to both sides to work, if possible, in harmony with each other rather than contentiously at arm's length.

Trial by battle has long since been abolished, together with trial by ordeal. Contemporary reviewers of the court scene may be forgiven for thinking that such spirit of confrontation has survived formal abolition into modern times. That is certainly the view of Alastair Graham, the father of a brain-damaged victim who has provided a text for this work.

We live, however, in an era of paper presentation of litigation, cards on the table, a greater awareness of the need to resolve issues before arriving at the court door rather than in court corridors or in the courtroom itself. Structured settlements, with their implicit need for co-operation, thus perhaps reflect, and certainly are consistent with, the spirit of the times.

This work would not have been possible without assistance from so many others. We acknowledge the generous help provided by those listed on page xi for their having provided us with source material. John Frenkel of Frenkel Topping inevitably and properly stands out for special mention, having done so much to create the 'machinery' of the structured settlement.

Valerie Bannister of DYP (Insurance and Re-Insurance Research Group) also stands out for special mention, guiding our attention to sources of information around the world.

Finally, it gives us particular pleasure to express appreciation to Mr Justice Wright for providing the Foreword. It is entirely appropriate that he should. He chaired one of the first conferences held nationally on the topic of structured settlements. He also chaired the Bar Conference Workshop in this discipline in 1991. And, of course, he was good enough to pen the original chapter on the subject for the Butterworths Personal

Injury Litigation Service as long ago as 1989. His chapter set the agenda
for this book.

Iain S Goldrein
Margaret R de Haas

12 King's Bench Walk
Temple
London

The Corn Exchange Chambers
Fenwick Street
Liverpool

Valentine's Day 1993

Acknowledgements

Ann Alexander, Alexander Harris
John Bogue, Bogue & McNulty
Christopher Butler, Finers
John Couch, Pattinson & Brewer
John Frenkel, Frenkel Topping
Penelope Graham
Dennis Hulls, Structured Compensation
Dennis Jarvis, L Watmore & Co
Alan A Meyer, Halsey Lightly
David McIntosh, Davies Arnold Cooper
Adrian Parkhouse, Farrer & Co
Mr Peniston, Moorish & Co
Julian Radcliffe, Hogg Robinson Insurance
Andrew Richards, David Yablon Minton Ellis
D Rutter, Metcalfe Copeman & Pettefar
Arnold Simanowitz, Association for Victims of Medical Accidents
Brian Wheatley QC, Wheatley Macpherson Daley & Sugar

The publishers would like to thank European Study Conferences for permission to reproduce Chapter 7, The Law Society for permission to reproduce its guidance notes as Appendix IV, and John Frenkel of Frenkel Topping for permission to reproduce the schedule of damages appearing at Appendix V.

List of chapters

Contents

Chapter 3
The Plaintiff's Solicitor's Approach 65

Chapter 4
Defendants' Perspectives 83

1 General Principles

Stephen Worthington

1 THE NATURE OF A STRUCTURED SETTLEMENT

A structured settlement normally consists of a conventional lump sum payment to the plaintiff together with an annuity or series of annuities paid to the plaintiff.

The word 'structured' denotes both the flexibility of the arrangement and the fact that it can be individually tailored to the specific plaintiff. The use of the word 'settlement' emphasises that as the law stands at present structured damages require the agreement of both the plaintiff and the defendant. Neither party can be forced into a structured settlement. (*Burke v Tower Hamlets Health Authority* (1989) Times, 10 August.)

The lump sum element of the settlement is calculated so as to cover both the cost of purchasing some capital item which the plaintiff may require, eg a suitable home and to provide a 'nest egg' or contingency fund against unforeseen eventualities.

The annuity payments take on the character of a pension for the plaintiff and commonly continue for life or for a specified period, whichever is longer. The method of arranging the annuities is flexible and can be determined according to the needs of each plaintiff. So rather than having a single annuity which pays the same sum each year (usually on a monthly basis) it is possible to have a smaller basic annuity with a deferred annuity to cater for some foreseeable future expense and a step annuity which provides lump sum payments at fixed yearly intervals to pay for the cost of replacement of capital items.

In addition to their flexibility, structured settlements confer two principal advantages upon a plaintiff. Firstly, the Inland Revenue treats the annuities as capital rather than income payments so that they are non-taxable. Secondly, the annuity payments can be index-linked so that they carry an inbuilt hedge against inflation.

2 THE HISTORY OF STRUCTURED SETTLEMENTS

2.1 The USA and Canada

It seems that the origin of the use of annuities for the payment of personal injury damages may derive from German practice. However, the movement towards structured settlements as we know them really started in the USA in the 1960s. Since then a number of States have initiated legislation either permitting or requiring certain forms of damages awarded for a tort to be paid in instalment or annuity form. Recent federal legislation has provided that any party to an action involving a claim for future loss may require that those damages be paid by instalments. It is too early to say whether that legislation will be adopted by more individual States.

Canada followed the USA in the early 1980s. In Ontario the Courts now have power to impose a structured settlement in cases where the plaintiff requests one subject to the Court's jurisdiction to determine that a structured settlement is not in the plaintiff's best interests. Elsewhere in Canada, where no such legislation exists, the Supreme Court has held that the Court has no power to impose a structured settlement where either or both parties do not consent (and see *Fournier v Canadian National Railway Co* (1972) AC 167 PC).

2.2 England and Wales

The parties to an action have always been able to enter an agreement whereby the damages are paid by the defendant to the plaintiff as an annuity (see *Metcalfe v London Passenger Transport Board* (1938) 2 All ER 352). However, until the advent of the modern structured settlement such arrangements were extremely rare because there was no perceived tax advantage to the plaintiff in accepting an annuity.

Prompted by the success of structured settlements in the USA, discussions took place between the Association of British Insurers and the Inland Revenue between 1984 and 1987 leading to a concession by the Inland Revenue in mid-1987 that structured settlements would have tax free status.

The Revenue's concession was based upon an analysis of a line of authority (particularly *Dott v Brown* [1936] 1 All ER 543) which decided that a series of payments or annuities which constituted instalments of an antecedent debt were to be treated as capital and not income and were therefore non-taxable.

3 HOW A STRUCTURED SETTLEMENT WORKS

The agreement to enter a structured settlement is an agreement between the plaintiff and the defendant's insurer in which the insurer agrees to take over and become responsible for the debt, ie the damages payable by the defendant to the plaintiff. The arrangement between the Association of British Insurers and the Inland Revenue envisages that an insurer will 'reinsure' its liability to make instalment payments to the plaintiff by purchasing the annuity or annuities from a life insurance company.

However, it is vital that there be separate contracts governing the payment by the life insurer to the defendant's insurer and the payment by the defendant's insurer to the plaintiff. If the payment is made directly by the life insurer to the plaintiff then the payment will be treated by the Inland Revenue as a payment of income and it will lose its tax-free status. In the normal case the defendant's insurer will purchase an annuity from the life insurer which annuity will be used to make the instalment payments to the plaintiff.

The life insurer is obliged to deduct tax from the payments it makes to the defendant's insurer. However, the defendant's insurer is required under its separate contract with the plaintiff to pay the gross amount to the plaintiff. Thus, the defendant's insurer must gross up the payments it makes to the plaintiff to cover the deduction made by the life insurer.

The defendant's insurer can recover the cost of that grossing up exercise as a deduction from its corporation tax liability to the Inland Revenue.

Illustration

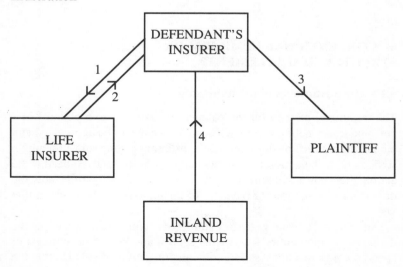

The plaintiff and the defendant's insurer agree that £300,000 of the damages to which the plaintiff is entitled will be used for a structured settlement. Various quotations are obtained from different life insurers. The best quotation will entitle the plaintiff to a gross annuity of £25,700 for life with guaranteed increases for inflation linked to the retail price index.

The diagram shows:

(1)   the payment of the lump sum of £300,000 by the defendant's insurer to the life insurer to purchase the annuity;

(2)   the payment of £20,700 pa (ie the annuity of £25,700 net of tax) by the life insurer to the defendant's insurer, with a ten-year minimum guarantee period, RPI-linked;

(3)   the payment of £25,700 pa (the grossed up annuity) to the plaintiff by the defendant's insurer for life guaranteed for a minimum of ten years and RPI-linked;

(4)   the recovery by the defendant's insurer from the Inland Revenue of the sum of £5,000 pa being the sum expended by the defendant's insurer to gross up the payment from the life insurer before payment to the plaintiff.

In this example the payments continue during the life of the plaintiff and are subject to increase by reference to the Retail Price Index.

4   CONVENTIONAL LUMP SUM OR STRUCTURED SETTLEMENT?

4.1   The advantages of the lump sum

The traditional method for the payment of damages to a plaintiff in a personal injury action is for each head of damage to be aggregated and paid to the plaintiff by the defendant's insurer as a lump sum either upon settlement of the action or at the conclusion of the trial.   Indeed if the action proceeds to judgment then it is the plaintiff's right and the defendant's obligation for payment of the damages to be made in that way.

The principal advantage to the plaintiff of a lump sum award is that the damages are then entirely under his control and he is free to invest or spend them as he chooses.   For some plaintiffs the knowledge that the damages award represents a determinable amount which is readily accessible or is available for distribution to their beneficiaries when they die is an important psychological feature.

The lump sum award also removes any risk associated with the subsequent insolvency of a defendant or a defendant's insurer.

For the defendant's insurer the lump sum award brings finality to the litigation. The insurer's file and the reserve can be closed.

4.2 The disadvantages of the lump sum

4.2.1   The principal disadvantage of the lump sum award flows from the manner in which it is calculated. The award of general damages for pain, suffering and loss of amenity is calculated by reference to a notional tariff for the injury sustained which tariff is then adjusted for the disabilities of the individual plaintiff. The award of general damages may also include an amount to represent future contingencies. However, a future contingency must be assessed at present value and there is a substantial risk that the plaintiff will be under-compensated if and when the contingency becomes manifest.

Illustration

The plaintiff is a 22-year-old male who sustains a knee injury from which he has made an excellent recovery. The agreed medical evidence is to the effect that the plaintiff is certain to develop osteoarthritis in his fifties. The fact that the deterioration in the knee is a certainty rather than a chance precludes a claim for provisional damages. The uplift in the award of general damages for the osteoarthritis in 30 years' time is likely to be trivial after it has been discounted for accelerated payment.

4.2.2   When assessing future losses the courts have traditionally adopted the multiplier/multiplicand approach. This may cause unfairness to the plaintiff. The multiplicand must be assessed at present value and the Court is not permitted to take into account inflation. In times of high inflation this may be seriously detrimental to the plaintiff, when even prudent investment of the lump sum does not provide adequate compensation against the effects of inflation. The multiplier is calculated after taking into account the contingencies of life and discounting for the fact that the plaintiff is receiving an accelerated benefit. The theory underlying the concept of damages for future loss is that the lump sum damages will be prudently invested such that the interest from the investment and the capital sum when used up gradually will be adequate to last out the period required (*Taylor v O'Connor* (1971) AC 115). The reality of the situation is that the multiplier/multiplicand approach to future loss is unlikely to achieve that result.

Illustration

A 25-year-old tetraplegic has an agreed expectation of life to aged 65. The experts agree that the average nursing costs for the plaintiff throughout his life will be £25,000 pa. The Court adopts this figure as the multiplicand and applies a multiplier of 16 giving a total award for future nursing costs of £400,000. At first sight this is a considerable sum which should provide a good return if prudently invested. However:

(i)   a return of 10% pa on the investment would produce £40,000 pa. If (which is likely because of the investment of the rest of his damages) the plaintiff is taxed at the rate of 40% then the investment return falls to £24,000 pa;

(ii) the plaintiff will have to supplement the investment return by £1,000 pa out of capital to fund his care;

(iii) the erosion of the capital is likely to increase substantially as the cost of care increases with inflation. The greater the erosion of capital the lower the annual return on the investment;

(iv) if the plaintiff survives to the end of his expectation of life then he will, in fact, have nursing costs of £25,000 for 40 years irrespective of inflation, ie total nursing costs of £1,000,000;

(v)   on any view the initial sum of £400,000 will be exhausted long before the end of the plaintiff's life.

4.2.3   The tax implications of a lump sum award have already been mentioned. The lump sum is not taxable in the plaintiff's hands because the tax which the plaintiff would have had to pay in any event is taken into account when calculating the lump sum (*British Transport Commission v Gourley* (1956) AC 185). However where the lump sum is invested then the interest which the lump sum carries is taxable. In the case of the seriously injured plaintiff where the lump sum award is substantial a large part of the investment income will be taxed at the higher rate of 40%. In the ordinary course of events the Court is not permitted to take into account the incidence of future taxation when assessing future loss (*Hodgson v Trapp* [1989] AC 807).

4.2.4 The risk of dissipation of a lump sum award is the corollary to the benefit achieved in granting to the plaintiff the freedom to choose what to do with the award. The problem of dissipation applies not only to the profligate plaintiff who spends immediately what is intended to last for many years but also to the plaintiff who invests unwisely. Moreover, even the wise plaintiff who receives professional investment advice will suffer a cost penalty in paying for that advice which cost will not have been included in the lump sum. The risk of dissipation has wider consequences than those inevitably affecting the plaintiff. The seriously injured plaintiff whose damages are dissipated becomes a substantial burden on the taxpayer.

4.3 The advantages of the structured settlement

4.3.1 *The advantages for the plaintiff*

4.3.1.1 The principal advantage of a structured settlement from the plaintiff's point of view is the knowledge that the damages will never run out. The majority of structured settlements are guaranteed at least for the life of the plaintiff and are index linked to cater for inflation.

Illustration

In the illustration above concerning the 25-year-old tetraplegic with a life expectancy to 65 and annual care costs of £25,000 pa a structured settlement consisting of the purchase of an annuity with a lump sum payment to the life company of £300,000 might produce:

(i)   an annuity of £25,000 pa, which is
(ii) index-linked, and
(iii) guaranteed for the plaintiff's life.

4.3.1.2 Structured settlements also have the advantage of flexibility. The arrangement and elements of the structure concentrate on the individual plaintiff's needs both present and future. The structure will involve an annuity or series of annuities tailored to provide for the income and capital requirements of the plaintiff.

Illustrations

(i) Where a young paraplegic plaintiff has minimal care costs at the time of trial but those care costs are projected to increase substantially in later life the structure can provide for a deferred annuity which will commence payment when the future care costs are projected to increase.

(ii) Where the same plaintiff requires aids and equipment which will need to be replaced at regular intervals during his life the structure can provide for a further annuity to make capital payments at a fixed interval of years.

(iii) In the case of a plaintiff whose care needs are projected to increase gradually with age an annuity can be purchased which will step up the annual payments at determined intervals to cater for the increased cost of care.

(iv) In certain cases, particularly involving the older plaintiff or the plaintiff whose life expectation is uncertain or low, the interests of the plaintiff and of his beneficiaries can be protected under the structured settlement by building into the annuity a guaranteed period during which the annuity will be paid irrespective of the earlier death of the plaintiff.

4.3.1.3   The tax advantages of the structured settlement are obvious. The seriously injured plaintiff who receives a substantial lump sum may well be liable to higher rate tax on the bulk of the investment income. The annuity or annuities under a structured settlement are non-taxable in the plaintiff's hands. In those circumstances the structured settlement may represent a saving of 40% on the annual return to the plaintiff.

4.3.1.4   It has already been noted that the wise plaintiff with a large lump sum to invest will obtain professional advice upon the investment regime and will be obliged to pay for that advice. The proper planning of a structured settlement should ensure that the plaintiff's financial needs are catered for as and when they arise thereby obviating the necessity for continuing and costly investment advice.

4.3.2   *The advantages for the defendant's insurer*

The principal advantage of the structured settlement to an insurer is a commercial one. Because a structured settlement requires the consent of both parties the defendant's insurer is entitled to exact a price for its consent. The majority of structured settlements are agreed between the parties after the plaintiff and the defendant's insurer have negotiated and agreed the damages on the conventional lump sum basis. In those circumstances the price exacted by the defendant's insurer for agreeing to a structured settlement normally involves a discount on the lump sum amount before structuring. It will be seen in Chapter 2 that an analysis of the published information concerning cases which have led to a structured settlement suggests that the average discount agreed between plaintiffs and defendants' insurers is in the range of 9–17.5% of the net sum structured. Other information suggests that the discount frequently approximates to 10% of the conventional lump sum award.

Illustration

The plaintiff and the defendant's insurer negotiate a 'settlement' of the plaintiff's claim on the basis that the plaintiff's claim is worth £800,000 on a conventional basis. The negotiations are conducted on the footing that both parties are agreeable, in principle, to a structured settlement. The defendant's insurer then requests a discount on the lump sum before they will consent to a structured settlement. The parties negotiate a discount of 10%. The plaintiff is then left with a figure of £720,000 which is available for the structured settlement.

The rationale behind the insurer's claim for a discount is the administration and financial cost of being the middleman between the life insurer and the plaintiff. Because the annuity must be paid through the defendant's insurer that insurer incurs the administration cost of receiving the payments from the life insurer and transmitting them to the plaintiff. Such payments are usually made on a monthly basis. Moreover the defendant's insurer also has to bear the financial cost of grossing up the payments received from the life insurer before transmission to the plaintiff during the period between payment to the plaintiff and reimbursement by the Inland Revenue.

However, experience of structured settlements does not suggest any compelling evidence of a true correlation between the discounts obtained by insurers and the cost to those insurers of being involved in the structured settlement. In the circumstances, it is not clear whether the correlation is real or illusory.

4.4   The disadvantages of the structured settlement

4.4.1   *The disadvantages for the plaintiff*

4.4.1.1   Although the advantage of the structured settlement is the flexibility which can be achieved when the structure is being set up, the disadvantage is the inflexibility of the structure once it has been established. The plaintiff cannot unravel the structure once it has come into existence and this may result in hardship to the plaintiff if some unforeseen eventuality should occur. This potential problem makes it imperative to ensure that the structure of the scheme is comprehensively considered and analysed at the outset. In normal circumstances it will usually be wise for those advising on the structure to recommend that a suitable contingency fund be set aside for investment in the conventional way before the balance is used to purchase the annuity so that the plaintiff has a 'cushion' against unforeseen financial problems.

Illustration

The parties negotiate a conventional settlement at £800,000. The plaintiff's needs may require the immediate expenditure of a capital sum of £100,000 for a car and for adaptations to his home. This will reduce the sum available for structuring to £700,000. It may then be considered prudent to set aside a contingency fund of £100,000 for investment in the conventional manner leaving £600,000 available for the purchase of the annuity or annuities (subject to the amount of discount negotiated with the insurer).

4.4.1.2   The fact that the plaintiff has, in effect, to give back some of his damages to the insurer as the insurer's discount for agreeing to the structured settlement may be perceived as an unfair disadvantage by some plaintiffs.

4.4.1.3   Even in circumstances where the structure includes a guarantee period during which the annuity will continue to be paid in the event of the death of the plaintiff the premature death of the plaintiff may deprive his beneficiaries of an inheritance which would have been available to them if the lump sum award had been conventionally invested. This may be a major disadvantage to those plaintiffs for whom the provision of an estate on death for division between their beneficiaries is an important social or psychological factor.

Illustration

The plaintiff has a life expectation of 30 years from the date the structured settlement is established. The sum of £400,000 is used to purchase an index-linked annuity which is guaranteed for ten years even in the event of the supervening death of the plaintiff during that period. If the plaintiff fulfils his life expectation then the annuity return index-linked over 30 years will be very substantial. However, if the plaintiff dies 11 years after the structure is established the annuity will cease and the return on the structure will be relatively small by comparison with the capital sum invested.

4.4.1.4   A plaintiff cannot pursue a claim for provisional damages if he wishes to enter a structured settlement. This is because a provisional damage award necessarily involves a judgment and any judgment will extinguish the antecedent debt which is a vital factor in preserving the tax-free status of the structured settlement.

4.4.1.5   A structured settlement removes any problems in relation to the future insolvency of the defendant because the defendant's liability to pay damages is assumed by and devolves upon the defendant's insurer. However it raises a new concern in relation to the potential insolvency of the life insurer or the defendant's insurer. This is a matter of some relevance to the advisers of a plaintiff with a long life expectation since it is impossible to predict the strength or weakness of the insurance market or any particular insurer 20 or 30 years hence.   The potential insolvency of the life insurer is not a particularly significant risk because the plaintiff is protected by the Policyholders Protection Act 1975. However, that legislation would not protect a plaintiff if the defendant's insurer became insolvent and this is relevant because the plaintiff's entitlement to the annuity is an entitlement vis-à-vis the defendant's insurer and not the life insurer.

The fact that it has tended to be the larger insurers who have been at the forefront of structured settlements has provided comfort to most plaintiffs. On the other hand the prudent plaintiff's adviser may wish to consider obtaining contingency insurance to cover the insolvency of the defendant's insurer.   Unfortunately at the present time such insurance is not easy to obtain and tends to be expensive but as structured settlements become more widespread and begin to represent the norm rather than the exception the cost and availability of such insurance may improve.

4.4.2   *The disadvantages to the defendant's insurer*

4.4.2.1   Insurers with a large volume of personal injury claims like to see finality to each claim so that they may close their books. This is one of the reasons why insurers have, understandably, been resistant to provisional damages. The same may be said for structured settlements. Where a structure has been set up the defendant's insurer has a responsibility which does not normally cease until the death of the plaintiff.

4.4.2.2   The second disadvantage is allied to the first and it concerns the additional administrative burden and expense which a structured settlement imposes on the defendant's insurer.   The position of the defendant's insurer as middleman between the life insurer and the plaintiff involves the establishment of new administrative systems and may require more staff.   For the large insurers who are involved in a number of structured settlements this problem may not be difficult to overcome but it has proved a major stumbling block with small insurers, some of whom will not countenance involvement in a structured settlement for that reason.

4.4.2.3   The cost of grossing up the payments from the life insurer before onward transmission to the plaintiff imposes a further financial burden on the defendant's insurer. The extent to which this is a disincentive to involvement in a structured settlement for any particular insurer may depend upon the nature and timing of the arrangement for reimbursement by the Inland Revenue.

5 THE CRITERIA FOR A STRUCTURED SETTLEMENT

There is no doubt that it is the professional duty of the lawyers involved in personal injury cases to consider and advise upon structured settlements whenever they may be appropriate. Indeed there is a view that to fail to do so in an appropriate case may amount to professional negligence.

5.1 When to consider a structured settlement

5.1.1 As well as being available in ordinary personal injury actions structured settlements may be established in medical negligence cases and also for the benefit of the dependents in a fatal accident.

5.1.2 It is impossible to lay down any hard and fast rules about the level of damages required before a structured settlement becomes viable or attractive. As a rule of thumb damages below £75,000 are unlikely to provide a sufficient return on the annuity to make structuring an attractive option. However even below that figure a structured settlement may be viable depending on the facts of a particular case.

Illustration

The plaintiff is a 55-year-old spinster with no immediate family and no dependents. She owns her own home. As a result of the relevant accident she has sustained a serious leg injury and will not be able to work again. She is in receipt of income from an accident insurance policy which is sufficient for her immediate needs. Unfortunately she has an illness unconnected with her injury which is likely to mean that she will need the assistance of a part-time carer in three to five years' time. The damages for her injury are likely to be in the region of £50,000. This plaintiff may wish to consider a structured settlement consisting of a deferred annuity to pay for help towards her future care costs. This may well be preferable to a lump sum since she has no particular need of the capital and nobody she would wish to provide for after her death. (See also the case of WB in Chapter 2.)

5.1.3 In severe or catastrophic cases where the damages will be substantial then a structured settlement should always be considered and investigated.

Illustrations

(i)   Young paraplegics frequently have few care needs or expenses but the medical evidence normally predicts that those needs will become substantially greater and more expensive with age. If the projected increase is not for 20 years or more then a structured settlement by way of a deferred or step annuity or a combination of them may be the only sure way of protecting the damages against inflation until the care expense becomes a reality.
(ii) In many serious injury cases the plaintiff is cared for by parents. It is often the case that the parents express great anxiety about the possibility that the plaintiff will have to go into an institution when the parents die or become infirm. A structured settlement can be tailored in such a way as to cater for this event.
(iii) If the deceased in a fatal injury accident leaves a young family then part of the damages may be structured so as to provide an annuity or series of annuities to pay for the cost of educating the children or other specific eventuality.

5.2   Who can and cannot enter a structured settlement

5.2.1   Any plaintiff who is sui juris may enter a structured settlement.

5.2.2   As a matter of principle there is no reason why cases involving infant plaintiffs or infant dependents in a fatal accident case cannot be structured. Such cases will, of course, require the approval of the Court. Where a structured settlement is proposed the Court will be asked to approve the arrangement in two stages (although usually at one hearing).

The Court will first of all be asked to approve the conventional lump sum settlement figure negotiated between the parties. Then the terms of the proposed structure will be explained to the Court and it will be asked to approve the structured settlement, including the amount of the insurer's discount.

5.2.3 Structured settlements are also available in the case of adult plaintiffs under a disability, eg as a result of brain damage sustained in the relevant accident. In such cases the Court of Protection will frequently be involved with the result that the proposed structured settlement will require the approval of the Court of Protection as well as the Court. In cases involving the Court of Protection the conventional lump sum award is calculated to include the Court of Protection costs of administering the fund. Until recently there was lack of clarity about how the Court of Protection fees should be levied upon moneys derived from a structured settlement. On 14 August 1992 the Lord Chancellor's Department issued a Press Notice concerning the implementation of the Court of Protection (Amendment) Rules 1992 which came into force on 24 August 1992. The rules determine that 50% of the moneys arising under a structured settlement are deemed to be income for the purposes of calculating clear annual income for Court of Protection fee purposes. The result of these rules is that there will be savings in those cases that are structured. The defendant's insurers will be the ultimate beneficiaries under the new rules since plaintiffs will have less Court of Protection costs recoverable against them. It follows that in comparing any conventional award with a structured settlement the savings in Court of Protection costs now need to be taken into account.

5.2.4 *Insurers*

5.2.4.1 Because the defendant's insurer is obliged to gross up the payment received from the life insurer before payment to the plaintiff, the defendant's insurer will only be prepared to enter a structured settlement if it can reclaim the tax from the Inland Revenue. As matters stand at present the defendant's insurer can only do this by setting off the tax paid as to the plaintiff against its own corporation tax liability to the Inland Revenue.

5.2.4.2   Non-corporation tax payers cannot reclaim those sums. It follows that mutual insurance companies which are not trading companies and do not pay corporation tax can only enter a structured settlement with a tax loss. This has meant that 'mutuals' will not enter structured settlements although there has been a move on the part of some of the mutual insurers to 'de-mutualise' in order to overcome this problem.

5.2.4.3   In cases involving road traffic accidents where the defendant's insurer may be entitled to avoid the defendant's insurance policy the insurer may, none the less, be obliged to satisfy any judgment the plaintiff obtains against the defendant by virtue of the provisions of s 151 of the Road Traffic Act 1989. The insurer's obligation to pay the damages does not arise until seven days after the judgment is obtained. If the plaintiff and the defendant's insurer strictly observe their rights and obligations in such cases then a structured settlement is not possible because a judgment destroys the antecedent debt principle upon which the Inland Revenue tax concession is based. If, however, the defendant's insurer indicates its willingness to negotiate a settlement of the action before a judgment then a structured settlement can be considered.

5.2.4.4   There are a number of large corporations which are self-insured. There seems no reason in principle why a self-insured company cannot enter a structured settlement but in such cases it would be necessary to obtain the individual approval of the Inland Revenue for each settlement so as to ensure that it meets the requisite criteria.

5.2.5   *Public authorities*

There are a variety of public authorities against whom personal injury claims are frequently made. Because those authorities do not pay corporation tax it is not practicable, at present, for them to enter structured settlements.

5.2.6   *Area Health Authorities*

Area Health Authorities are usually the ultimate payer of damages in medical negligence cases. They do not pay corporation tax. However the Inland Revenue has agreed that Area Health Authorities can reclaim the income tax required to make the gross payment to the plaintiff (see *Field v Hertfordshire Health Authority* (1991) PMILL vol 7 no 9 p 22). This is a significant move forward in the field of structured settlements. The concession does not apply to cases in which the damages are payable by a medical defence union on behalf of an individual medical practitioner because the medical defence unions are non-profit-making and do not pay corporation tax. Fortunately since the re-organisation of responsibility for meeting claims for medical negligence the number of claims which are met by medical defence unions has substantially decreased.

5.2.7 *The Motor Insurers Bureau*

There are three types of case in which the Motor Insurers Bureau ('MIB') are liable to pay damages to a plaintiff:

(i) where the negligent driver is untraced and MIB is obliged to deal with the plaintiff's claim under the Untraced Drivers Agreement 1972;

(ii) where there is no insurance to cover either the defendant or the vehicle being driven by the defendant in which case MIB is obliged to pay the plaintiff's judgment under the Uninsured Drivers Agreement 1988;

(iii) where the defendant is uninsured but there is an insurer in the background in relation either to the defendant or the vehicle being driven by the defendant which insurer will be obliged to satisfy any judgment obtained by the plaintiff against the defendant under the Uninsured Driver Agreement because of the domestic agreement between insurers and MIB.

In the first two types of case a structured settlement is not possible because the damages are payable by MIB but MIB is a non-corporation tax payer. Even if the Inland Revenue were, in due course, to permit MIB to reclaim the income tax paid to the plaintiff it is uncertain whether MIB would be amenable to structured settlements because of the administrative burden and expense they impose.

In the third type of case the fact that the damages are payable by an insurer rather than MIB makes a structured settlement possible provided it is negotiated and agreed before the plaintiff obtains judgment against the defendant.

5.2.8   *The Criminal Injuries Compensation Board*

At the present time the CICB cannot enter into a structured settlement for two reasons. Firstly, an award by the CICB is an ex gratia payment such that there is no antecedent debt sufficient to satisfy the Inland Revenue criteria for tax-free status. Secondly, and in any event the CICB does not pay corporation tax. It is understood that the CICB is currently studying the feasibility of structured settlements, but it is almost certain that if the CICB is to be given the power to enter structured settlements then this will require legislative intervention.

6   THE NEGOTIATION, ARRANGEMENT AND APPROVAL OF A STRUCTURED SETTLEMENT

6.1   The negotiation

6.1.1   As soon as the amount of damages likely to be recovered by a plaintiff can be provisionally estimated then consideration should be given to a structured settlement.

6.1.2   At that stage the other party ought to be approached for a decision whether, in principle, it would be amenable to a structured settlement. Conventionally the initial approach has tended to come from the plaintiff's solicitors but there is no reason (tactical or otherwise) why it should not come from the defendant's insurers.

6.1.3   There is a common misconception that consideration of a structured settlement is only appropriate where liability has been admitted or is clear cut. This is not correct. In serious or catastrophic cases even a finding of substantial contributory negligence can result in a large award to the plaintiff. Moreover in cases involving potentially large damages the fact that primary liability may be hotly contested with a real risk that the plaintiff's claim will fail completely may not deprive the claim of a substantial settlement value. In such cases there is no reason why a structured settlement cannot be mooted. The benefits to the plaintiff of the structure and the potential discount to the defendant's insurer may enable issues of liability and quantum to be negotiated to an outcome acceptable to both sides.

6.1.4 There are two possible approaches to the negotiation of a structured settlement.

6.1.4.1 The first approach ignores the conventional method of assessing damages and concentrates solely on the plaintiff's needs.

Illustration

The plaintiff is a 25-year-old paraplegic. He requires alternative accommodation which will cost £100,000 and needs a variety of aids and appliances. The medical and nursing evidence suggests that his present care needs will cost £7,500 pa, rising to £15,000 pa at 50 and £25,000 pa at 60. It would be possible for the plaintiff and the defendant's insurer to negotiate a structured settlement which provided an immediate capital payment of £100,000 for accommodation, a series of stepped or deferred annuities for the plaintiff's care needs, living expenses and capital requirements and a sum by way of a contingency fund for conventional investment. This approach ignores what the plaintiff would be entitled to by way of a lump sum award and concentrates solely on the future with, perhaps, some provision for expenses already incurred.

This method has not found much favour with plaintiffs or their advisers because of the fear that the plaintiff may be sold short on the overall settlement. Moreover, it is an approach which causes difficulty in advising a plaintiff about the comparative benefits of the structured settlement because there is no conventional lump sum against which to measure it.

6.1.4.2 The second and by far the most common approach is for the parties to negotiate settlement on a conventional basis before considering the terms of the structured settlement. The attraction of this approach is that those involved in the negotiation know precisely what sum is available for the structure and there is an agreed figure to which both parties may fall back if, for any reason, the structured settlement does not proceed.

6.1.5 The time at which the negotiations take place is not critical provided the action does not proceed to a final judgment. An interlocutory judgment, eg a judgment under Order 14 RSC, will not prevent a structured settlement (*Everett v Carter* (1991) PMILL vol 7 no 8 p 63) but any final judgment will destroy the antecedent debt owed by the defendant to the plaintiff and so deprive the structured settlement of its tax-free status.

6.1.6   None the less there are a number of matters to consider in relation to the timing of the negotiations towards settlement.

6.1.6.1   The guiding principle ought to be 'the sooner the better'. From the insurers' point of view there may be a considerable incentive to enter a structured settlement if the negotiations can be concluded in advance of the trial so that brief fees and the other immediate pre-trial costs may be saved. This is likely to mean that both parties will need to advance their trial preparations to ensure that experts' reports, schedules and counter-schedules are finalised at an early stage so that negotiations towards settlement of the conventional award can take place on an informed basis.   When that stage has been reached it will often be sensible for the parties and their legal advisers to meet at a round table conference in the hope of completing the negotiations.

6.1.6.2   If, for any reason, it does not prove possible to negotiate a settlement of the conventional sum before trial then there is no reason why this cannot take place at the Court door.   In that event it will be necessary to ask the Court to adjourn the trial or stay the action on terms agreed between the parties on the basis that the parties intend to investigate the possibility of a structured settlement. Experience suggests that judges are generally amenable to that course of action.

6.1.6.3   Even in cases where there is a contested trial on liability or quantum or both a structured settlement is still possible provided the Court does not give judgment.   In such a case the parties may agree that a structured settlement is sensible but be unable to agree what the correct figure for quantum should be or even whether the defendant is liable to the plaintiff at all.   In this event the trial proceeds in the normal manner but the parties can agree that at some suitable point before judgment is given the Court be informed that if the claim is successful the parties would like to consider structuring and the judge can then be invited to give his decision on liability and quantum without actually entering judgment.   Thereafter the trial will be adjourned or stayed whilst a structured settlement is considered.

6.1.7 When the conventional damages have been agreed with a view to a structured settlement it is essential that the parties consider and agree various ancillary matters which will or may have a bearing upon the terms of the final agreement. In a number of cases the failure of the parties to agree these ancillary matters at this stage has led to disputes during the period between successful negotiation of the lump sum and the final structured settlement. It is beyond the scope of this chapter to deal with every conceivable problem which may arise but a number of the major areas of conflict can be considered so that they may be avoided.

6.1.7.1 It is important that the parties attempt to agree how the insurers discount is to be calculated. It may be possible to conduct the negotiations towards the lump sum settlement on the basis that those negotiations and final figure actually take into account that discount, ie so that the agreed figure is somewhat lower than would otherwise have been the case but there is no further discount. If that course is not followed then there ought at least to be some agreement as to whether the insurers discount will be calculated as a specific percentage or lump sum deduction from the whole of the conventional award or only the amount of the award used to purchase the annuity.

Illustration

The conventional award is agreed at £500,000. The plaintiff needs an immediate capital sum of £100,000 to buy a house and anticipates requiring a contingency fund of £75,000. This will leave £325,000 available to purchase an annuity or annuities. The defendant's insurers request a discount of 10%. The parties would be well advised to agree, at that stage, whether the discount is to be calculated at 10% of the total sum of £500,000 or 10% of the annuity sum of £325,000.

6.1.7.2 The question of interest should also be addressed and agreed.

Illustration

The parties negotiate a settlement at the door of the Court in the conventional basis and agree a figure of £800,000. The trial is then adjourned to investigate a structure. If the trial had proceeded to judgment on that day the plaintiff would have been entitled to interest at the judgment rate of 15% on the whole of that sum until payment. The structured settlement may take some weeks or months to investigate and establish. An impasse may develop if the plaintiff insists upon interest at the judgment rate on the whole sum of £500,000 until the date when the structure is established or, conversely, the insurers refuse to pay any interest at all as part of their price for agreeing to structure. There is a middle ground, which has found favour in a number of cases, in which the parties agree that the plaintiff be entitled to interest only on the amount which is not used to purchase the annuity on the basis that he has been 'kept out' of that money and the defendant's insurer has been able to earn interest on it but that the plaintiff has not been deprived of the lump sum to purchase the annuity since it will not come to him in any event.

6.1.7.3   There should be clear agreement about who is to be responsible for the costs associated with investigating and establishing the structure. The plaintiff will need to engage the services of accountants to advise about the precise arrangement of the structure, obtain quotations from various life insurers and may need to liaise with the Inland Revenue. The placing of the business with a life insurer results in the payment of commission (usually 2% or 3%) and it is sometimes the case that the accountants waive any fees associated with their work in return for an entitlement to receive that commission. Other accountants will charge their ordinary fees for the work they undertake. Whichever approach is adopted, there should be a clear agreement between the various parties as to the payment of the accountant's charges. If, for any reason, the structured settlement is not concluded then the accountants may agree to waive those fees. Alternatively, the defendant's insurers may agree to be responsible for them. What is important is that these eventualities be considered and agreed at the outset. In fact it has become common for the defendant's insurers to insist upon being responsible for arranging and establishing the structure in which event they become responsible for the accountancy fees in return for the plaintiff's agreement that the insurers be entitled to retain the commission received for placing the annuity with the life insurers. This is perfectly acceptable provided the plaintiff's legal advisers ensure that they have independent advice to enable them to evaluate the proposed structure. Generally the defendant's insurer is prepared to be responsible for the reasonable cost of that independent advice but it is as well to settle this point in advance. The same principles apply to the determination of responsibility for the increased legal costs which are likely to be generated by a structured settlement. They are commonly considered to be costs in the cause recoverable in the normal way but since there is no certainty that a Taxing Master would take that view it is wise for the parties specifically to agree how they shall be dealt with.

6.1.7.4 Finally it is essential that the agreement reached before investigating the possibility of a structured settlement be a concluded agreement conditional upon the terms of the structure. It is possible that a structured settlement will prove unviable or ultimately unattractive to the plaintiff. If that happens then it is obviously undesirable from the point of view of both parties that one of them might wish to re-open the settlement agreed on the conventional basis. This problem can be avoided by the plaintiff agreeing to accept either the agreed lump sum or a structured settlement based on that figure and the defendant's insurer agreeing to hold that sum open for acceptance by the plaintiff until such time as the structured settlement is agreed.

7 THE ARRANGEMENT OF THE STRUCTURE

7.1 Constructing the package

The essential requirement in constructing the package which will form the structured settlement is an assessment of the plaintiff's needs both present and future.

The plaintiff's legal advisers, with the assistance of accountants experienced in structured settlements, should ask themselves a variety of questions.

(a) What are the plaintiff's immediate capital needs? How much should be set aside to cater for those needs?
(b) What are the plaintiff's future capital needs? When will they arise and how should they be provided for?
(c) What are the plaintiff's immediate requirements by way of income both for specific expenditure, eg care, mortgage, transport, etc, and also for ordinary living expenses?

(d) Will those income requirements increase (or decrease) in the future and, if so, how and when?

(e) Does the plaintiff have any dependents? If so then how are they presently being supported, how will they be supported in the future and what are their present and future needs?

(f) What contingency sum will it be necessary to set aside to provide a financial cushion against unforeseen eventualities?

(g) What sum will the defendant's insurers require as their discount?

The resolution of these questions will determine:

(i) how the structure ought to be arranged to provide for the needs of the individual plaintiff;

(ii) how much money will be available to purchase the annuity or annuities;

(iii) whether a structured settlement is viable at all.

Illustration

(a) A conventional lump sum award of £1,000,000 has been negotiated between the parties. A discount of 10% on that sum has been agreed as appropriate for the defendant's insurers co-operation in agreeing to a structured settlement. The plaintiff has immediate capital needs of £200,000 for the provision of suitable accommodation (together with the costs of adaptation) and the purchase of a suitable vehicle. A contingency sum of £100,000 is considered appropriate. There is, therefore, available for the purchase of an annuity, or a series of annuities, the sum of £600,000.

(b) The sum of £500,000 is the agreed conventional award with an agreed discount of 10%. The plaintiff has immediate capital needs of £200,000. This leaves £250,000 available for the purchase of annuities. The plaintiff requires an income of at least £20,000 per annum net to meet his needs. The best quotation obtainable from a life insurer indicates that the cost of an annuity of £20,000 guaranteed for ten years or life whichever occurs later and index-linked to the retail price index will cost £250,000 or that the same annuity without the guarantee period will cost £220,000. In this case the plaintiff may have to forgo setting aside a contingency fund at all if he wishes to have the security of the guarantee period or forgo the guarantee period or reconsider the entire viability of a structured settlement.

7.2 Obtaining the quotation

Once the requirements of the structure have been determined and the amount available for the purchase of the annuities is known the structure is then presented to various life insurers for them to quote the cost of purchasing the package of annuities. This is normally done by accountants instructed either by the plaintiff or the defendant's insurers.

The package of annuities may include one or more of the following categories of annuity which have been approved by the Inland Revenue.

(i) Periodic payments for life or some other fixed period which may be with or without a guaranteed minimum period and with or without index linking.

(ii) Periodic payments of lump sums at fixed intervals, eg payments of a lump sum every five years to provide for the cost of replacing capital items.

(iii) Periodic payments which step up in value at pre-determined intervals, eg to provide for increased care costs in later life.

(iv) Periodic payments the commencement of which are deferred to a specified date, eg to pay for the future educational expenses of a child.

When the life insurance quotations are available the accountants or other retained financial advisers will explain and advise upon the quotations and provide advice as to which quotation provides the best return.

7.3 The structured settlement

The conclusion of the structured settlement involves the plaintiff and the defendant's insurer entering into a written agreement.

The Association of British Insurers and the Inland Revenue have agreed a draft agreement ('the Model Agreement') for use in structured settlements.

If the parties adopt and follow the Model Agreement then it is unnecessary to obtain specific Inland Revenue approval for the settlement.

It is possible to amend or expand upon the Model Agreement if that proves necessary in any particular case but in that event it will be necessary to obtain Inland Revenue approval of the agreement before it is concluded so as to ensure that its tax-free status is recognised and accepted.

The Model Agreement is included at Appendix III.

The essential features of the Model Agreement are that:

(i)   the defendant's insurer assumes a direct contractual liability to the plaintiff in substitution for the liability of the defendant;

(ii) the liability of the defendant's insurer is crystallised as a debt of a fixed amount;

(iii) the method of settlement of the debt by the defendant's insurer is the making of the payments specified in the Schedule to the agreement.

There are four schedules which may be attached to the Model Agreement:

(i)   *The Basic Terms Schedule*
This Schedule is for use where the payments to the plaintiff will continue only for a pre-determined period (not life) and in fixed amounts.

(ii) *Indexed Terms*
This is the Schedule used where the payments are for a pre-determined period as in (i) but are to be indexed to the Retail Price Index.

(iii) *Terms for Life*
This is the Schedule to be used in the commonest type of structured settlement, ie where the payments will continue for the life of the plaintiff with or without a guarantee period.

(iv) *Indexed Terms for Life*
This Schedule is used as in (iii) but with index linking of the payments as in (ii).

It is to be observed that although the Model Agreement and the Schedules are legal documents those most familiar with them are the accountants and other financial advisers who regularly advise upon and are involved in the establishment of structured settlements. In those circumstances the legal advisers to the plaintiff and the defendant's insurer will be well advised to elicit the assistance of those professionals when drafting the settlement agreement.

7.4 Court approval

In cases involving persons under a disability or infant dependents in a fatal accident any structured settlement will require Court approval. In the former case the settlement will also require the approval of the Court of Protection.

In *Kelly v Dawes* ((1990) Times, 27 September) Potter J set out the procedure which the Court will expect to be followed when seeking approval of a structured settlement.

A Practice Note of 12 February 1992 (1992 1 WLR 328) now sets out the documents which will be required to be lodged with the Court prior to the approval of a structured settlement. These include:

(a) an opinion of Counsel assessing the value of the claim on a conventional basis (unless approval has already been given) and on the proposed structured settlement;
(b) a report of forensic accountants setting out the advantages and disadvantages of the structured settlement to the plaintiff;
(c) a draft agreement approved by the Inland Revenue;
(d) any necessary consent from the Court of Protection.

8 THE FUTURE

The structured settlement may be in its infancy within the English legal system but it is a thriving child.

The Law Commission has recently published Consultation Paper No 125 which includes a detailed analysis and critique of structured settlements and invites comments upon improvements for the future.

In the unreported case of *O'Toole v Mersey Regional Health Authority* (21 August 1992) the infant plaintiff and the Health Authority obtained Court approval for what was the first self-funded structured settlement. Instead of purchasing annuities from a life insurer the Health Authority, with the support of the Department of Health and the Treasury, agreed to be responsible for making annual payments to the plaintiff, index-linked and tax-free.

This case illustrates the momentum behind the concept of structured settlements and their capacity for expansion and redefinition.

2 Case Law

Rodney Nelson-Jones

1 *FOLEY V FLETCHER AND ROSE*[1]

Lady Emily Foley is the first reported recipient of a structured settlement. It was set up in 1854.

She and Sir F Scott each sold a half share in various buildings lands and mines to Messrs Fletcher and Rose. The purchase price was £99,000. £6,770 was paid as a lump sum. The balance of £92,230 was payable in half yearly instalments over 30 years.

Undoubtedly the purchase price included an enhancement in respect of interest. When paying early instalments, Mr Fletcher and Mr Rose deducted £236 as income tax.

It was held that the instalments were payments of money due as capital. Therefore they were not liable to income tax.

This case presents the classic features of a structured settlement. Lady Foley received immediately part of the sum due to her. The rest was converted into tax-free instalments to be paid on a basic terms basis.

Notes
1   1858 2 H&N 769.

2 *INLAND REVENUE COMMISSIONERS V RAMSAY*[1]

The same principle was applied to the purchase of a professional practice in 1932.

Mr Ramsay agreed to buy the practice of a dentist in Wimpole Street. The primary price was £15,000, which was subject to increase or decrease as the agreement provided. £5,000 was payable immediately. Mr Ramsay was to pay to the vendor in respect of the balance of the purchase price, each year for ten years, 25% of the net profits of the practice. Such sums were to be paid to the vendor as capital sums paid in respect of the purchase price. If the total paid during the ten years amounted to more or less than £10,000, the primary price of £15,000 was to be increased or decreased accordingly.

When making a return of the income for supertax purposes, Mr Ramsay deducted the £886 payable by him under the agreement for the tax year in question.

The Court of Appeal held that under the agreement the sum of £15,000 was made the purchase price from beginning to end. The mere fact that in the result the amount paid might be greater or less than the primary price did not alter the legal position. Therefore the instalments were repayments of capital. The £886 was not deductible from income for tax purposes.

With the substitution of the concept of damages for the purchase price, the basic outline of a structured settlement emerges. Part of the debt was payable in an immediate lump sum, and the balance by periodic payments on a sort of indexed terms basis.

Notes
1   (1936) 154 LT Rep 141.

3   *DOTT V BROWN*[1]

This is the seminal case that paved the way for the modern structured settlement. It arose out of bankruptcy proceedings.

Mr Brown owed Mr Dott between £9,000 and £10,000. This debt was the subject of proceedings in bankruptcy which eventually came before the Court of Appeal in February 1933. A compromise consent order was made whereunder Mr Brown covenanted to pay £1,000 on 31 March 1933, £1,000 on 31 March 1934 and £250 on each succeeding 31 March, so long as Mr Dott should live, such covenant to bind Mr Brown's estate after his death.

The terms of this agreement were carried out until the spring of 1935. Then Mr Brown, instead of paying £250 as provided, deducted income tax amounting to £56.5s and sent a cheque for £193.15s.

The Court of Appeal held that all the payments were capital payments, instalments of the capital consideration, payable in discharge of the pre-existing debt. Accordingly the payment fell outside the Income Tax Acts. Mr Brown had been wrong to make the deduction.

What the Court of Appeal had sanctioned in 1933 was, in effect, a structured settlement. After the first two payments totalling £2,000, the balance of the debt was to be discharged by periodical payments on the terms for life basis. As in the preceding two cases, these payments were tax free because they were discharging a capital debt.

Notes
1   (1936) 154 LT 484.

4 *STACHNIK V MITCHELL*[1]

A structured settlement in a UK personal injury case was first reported as long ago as 1981.

It involved Miss Stachnik, a young Canadian woman who resided with her parents in Ontario. Whilst on holiday in England in 1973, she sustained severe injuries in a road accident when a car driven by Douglas Mitchell, in which she was a passenger, collided with a bus in Hertfordshire. Mr Mitchell admitted negligence. She became a spastic quadriplegic with a gross speech defect and limited mobility. Her intellect was substantially impaired, and she became incapable of managing her own affairs. She had no prospects of marriage.

In June 1981, when she was 30 years old, Lawson J approved a settlement of £300,000. Out of this the insurers used 425,000 Canadian dollars to purchase from a Canadian life company two annuities:

i) $1324.95 per month, increasing at 3% pa compound, for a term certain of seven years, payable to Stella's parents who were caring for her;

ii) $2,500 per month, increasing at 4% pa compound, for a period of 40 years and thereafter during any remaining part of Stella's life, payable into the Ontario Health Insurance scheme which would look after her needs by means of non-taxable payments.

In addition, a substantial saving was achieved for the insurers (Legal and General).

This case demonstrates the relative ease with which structured settlements in UK cases may be enjoyed by foreigners of states whose tax laws are favourable to them. The converse applies to foreign plaintiffs resident in states where the annuity income would be taxable.

Notes
1   (1981) CLY 586.

5 *KELLY V DAWES*[1]

A feature of the landmark case of *Kelly v Dawes*, the first structured settlement involving an injured British plaintiff to be approved by the court, is the way in which the receipt of a capital sum from another source diminished the need for lump sum damages.

In July 1986 Catherine Kelly, a recently married nurse aged 22, suffered serious injuries in a road accident. Her husband Andrew Kelly was killed. The driver of the other vehicle was wholly to blame. His insurers, KGM Motor Policies, settled her claim arising out of her husband's death.

As a result of her injuries, Catherine Kelly was transformed into a bedridden invalid with grossly impaired neurological functions, almost wholly unaware of her surroundings, and totally dependent on skilled nursing care and the devoted attention of her loving parents and family. Her condition would not improve for the rest of her life, and her uncertain life expectancy was reduced to around 20 years.

In November 1988 it was agreed that the sum payable on a conventional basis was £427,500. It was further agreed that, under a structured settlement, the total would be £410,000. £110,000 of this was to be paid as a lump sum. The insurers would use the balance of £300,000 to purchase an annuity for the rest of Catherine Kelly's life. The annual sum to be provided under the quotation obtained was £25,562 index linked, guaranteed for a minimum period of ten years. Thus the payments were to last for ten years or her life, whichever is the longer.

In July 1989 Potter J approved this pioneering structured settlement. There had been an increase in nursing costs and loss of earnings between the provisional reaching of the settlement and its final approval. Instead of the damages being increased, the ostensible discount was reduced. In reality, it was £27,000 (9%) out of the structured sum of £300,000.

Notes
1   QBD transcript, 14 July 1989.

6   *EVERETT V EVERETT AND NORFOLK COUNTY COUNCIL*[1]

This was another famous structured settlement, yielding headlines such as 'Record £8.9 million award for brain damaged teenager'. It arose out of a road accident in 1981 in which Heidi Everett, then aged 13, suffered a serious head injury.

In consequence, she suffered neurological disorder with impaired voluntary movement, unsteadiness and abnormal movements. Her comprehension was at the level of a five- or six-year-old, and she was unable to talk. She was left with severe loss of vision, constant dribbling and epilepsy controlled by drugs. Her life expectancy was reduced to approximately 65.

In March 1991 her case was provisionally settled on the basis that the appropriate lump sum award would have been £950,000 plus Court of Protection fees which turned out to be £31,000, a total of £981,000. This was broken down as follows:

Interim payments	£ 36,000
Payments to parents for pre-trial care	£ 30,000
Contingency fund	£138,622
Structured sum	£706,378
Insurer's discount	£ 70,000
Total	£981,000

The structured sum was applied to purchase three annuities:

i)   an immediate annuity of £17,000 pa, increasing at 6% pa compound, payable for life;
ii) deferred annuity of £18,735 pa, to commence after five years, increasing at 6% pa compound, payable for life;
iii) a greatly deferred annuity of £29,186 pa, to commence after 20 years, increasing at 5% pa compound, payable for life.

Morland J approved the settlement in June 1991. If Heidi lives to the age of 65, she will have received payments totalling around £9 million.

Notes
1   (1991) PMILL Vol 7 No 6 p 41.

7   *PAYNE V THACKRAY*[1]

Similar headlines, such as '£13 million damages for Bradford boy', arose in another road accident case involving a three-year-old child. In August 1982 John Payne was mown down by a motor cycle.

He sustained severe head injuries and was unconscious for some weeks. He suffered permanent spastic quadriplegia with generalised ataxia. He is often incontinent. He will almost certainly need 24 hours-a-day supervision for the rest of his life. He required specialist purpose-built accommodation. His life expectancy is virtually normal. Specialist treatment at St Andrews Hospital in Northampton may assist him when he reaches the age of 18.

A contested trial on quantum took place before Mr Justice Waller who in July 1991 assessed the damages at £959,210. He was asked not to make any further order, and the case was adjourned to allow a structured settlement to be arranged.

£70,000 was payable in respect of past care. It was agreed that a contingency fund of £359,000 be invested with the Court of Protection: £233,500 of this was to be spent on purchasing and equipping the special accommodation, leaving £125,000 available for investment. The structured sum of £463,000 was used to buy a single annuity of £18,207.48 pa net, Retail Price Index linked, payable for life subject to a minimum period of ten years. The discount to the insurers (Norwich Union) was £67,210.

Payments for past care	£ 70,000
Contingency fund	£359,000
Structured sum	£463,000
Insurers' discount	£ 67,210
Total	£959,210

His Honour Judge Donald Herrod QC approved the settlement in August 1991. The case demonstrates how a structured settlement may follow a contested trial, provided that the trial judge refrains from awarding damages even when he assesses them.

Notes
1   (1991) PMILL Vol 7 No 8 p 60.

8   *MOXON V SENIOR*[1]

Just as structured settlements may be reached when the quantum of damages has been contested, so also can they be arranged in cases in which there is substantial contributory negligence.

An example is the claim brought by Barry Moxon which was settled in May 1991 on the basis of a one-third reduction for contributory negligence.

Mr Justice Judge approved a full liability valuation of £975,000 which would have resulted in lump sum damages of £650,000. He adjourned the case to allow the parties to structure the settlement.

Barry Moxon had a continuing need for substantial attendance, which would continue for the rest of his life. The various assessments of his life expectancy ranged from 12 to about 20 years. His elderly parents were providing much of his care, but when they ceased to be able to do this the need for professional care would increase.

Interim payments of £107,500 had already been ordered. It was agreed that £92,500 be paid to the Court of Protection as a contingency fund and that the insurers should receive a discount of £50,000 (12.5%) on the sum structured of £400,000.

Interim payments	£107,500
Contingency fund	£ 92,500
Structured sum	£400,000
Insurers' discount	£ 50,000
Total	£650,000

The £400,000 was to be paid out to GA linked Life Assurances to buy two annuities:

a) from August 1991, an annuity yielding £25,000 pa, indexed at 5% pa compound, paid by way of monthly instalments for 5 years or for Barry Moxon's life, whichever is the longer;

b) from August 1993, £12,058 pa, again indexed at 5% pa compound, for 5 years or for life, whichever is the longer.

The total tax saving achieved by the scheme was calculated at £111,743. This formed the basis of the insurers' discount of £50,000.

When approving the agreement in July 1991, Judge J observed: 'The great advantage of a structured settlement is that both sides benefit.' An additional feature of the settlement was the way in which the indexed terms for life basis of the annuities resolved the dispute over life expectancy without requiring the issue to be litigated.

Notes
1   QBD transcript, 10 July 1991.

9   *HEELEY V BRITTON*[1]

The capacity of structured settlements not only to absorb contributory negligence discounts but also to resolve major life expectancy problems is further illustrated by this case. It came before Mr Justice Rougier for approval in December 1990.

In May 1982 Paul Heeley, then aged 21, had spent the evening drinking with Simon Britton. At 1.05 am the next morning he was a passenger in a car driven by Britton which went off the road. Liability was never disputed, and contributory negligence was agreed at 10%.

Paul Heeley was treated at Pinderfields Hospital until December 1985. Thereafter his mother nursed him at home with the assistance of professional nurses. He improved to the point where he could be up in a wheelchair, but he remained brain damaged and could not speak clearly. One medical expert assessed his life expectancy at 1–15 years; another put it at 20 years.

Rougier J accepted that the appropriate traditional assessment, net of contributory negligence, was £900,000.

Interim payments of £107,500 had been paid. It was agreed that £237,500 was to be paid into the Court of Protection as a contingency fund. The insurers (Holdsure Motor Policies at Lloyds) were then to apply £452,700 to purchase an annuity. The tax saving was substantial, and so was the insurers' discount of £102,300.

Interim payments	£107,500
Contingency fund	£237,500
Structured sum	£452,700
Insurers' discount	£102,300
Total	£900,000

The structured sum purchased a single large annuity of £50,000 pa, index-linked, payable for life subject to a minimum of five years.

'a) After one year's payments have been made and at the end of every 12 (Twelve) months thereafter up to and including the end of the twelve month period ceasing in the year 2023, the amount will be increased (or decreased) in the General Index of Retail Prices (all items) for the year ending 3 (Three) months prior to the date of the alteration. From the anniversary of the policy in the year 2024, and in subsequent years, payments will continue to increase (or decrease) similarly, provided that at the time in the opinion of the Insurer suitable British Government Index Linked Stocks still exist to support the continuation of such increases (or decreases). Should the Insurer deem on any subsequent anniversary that suitable Stocks no longer exist, the increase due then and in each subsequent year would be 7 per cent of the amount of the annuity payable immediately prior to the date of increase.

b) A minimum of 60 (Sixty) payments shall be made under this Schedule, regardless of the date of the death of the Claimant, but subject to this no amounts shall be payable after the date of death of the Claimant.'

In approving the settlement, Rougier J remarked: 'The sooner it is possible to award damages on this infinitely less hit and miss basis the better.'

Notes
1   QBD transcript, 19 December 1990.

10   *GRIMSLEY V GRIMSLEY AND MEADE*[1]

Structured settlements may also take place in cases in which liability has been contested. If the plaintiff succeeds in a split trial on liability, his damages may be dealt with in a subsequent structure.

In February 1985 Garylee Grimsley, then aged 9, was a rear seat passenger in a car driven by his father which collided with a vehicle driven by Mr Meade. At a split trial, his father was held 90% liable and Mr Meade 10% liable.

Garylee had suffered a serious head injury resulting in permanent brain damage. At the age of 15 he had the mental age of a 10-year-old. He was permanently wheelchair-bound, although his disabilities were not as severe as those of a paraplegic. He would never be able to work. He was expected to live to the age of 65.

The value of his claim on a conventional basis was agreed at £825,000. Interim payments of £186,000 had already been made. It was agreed that a contingency fund of £200,000 be paid to the Court of Protection. The future costs that it was desired to structure, assessed on the traditional multiplier/multiplicand basis, consisted of:

Nursing care	£300,560
Rehabilitation costs after age 19 (£932 x 14)	£13,048
transport annual cost after age 19 (£2,246 x 14)	£31,444
Accommodation: increased running costs after age 19	£14,700
Total	£359,752

The cost to the insurers of purchasing the annuities to provide this was £337,000, a saving of about £22,000. In addition, it was calculated that the scheme produced substantial tax savings of £160,000 and agreed that the insurers should receive half the benefit of this; namely £80,000. Therefore the insurers, the Lion Insurance Company, enjoyed a total discount of £102,000 (30.27%) on the sum structured of £337,000.

Interim payments	£186,000
Contingency fund	£200,000
Structured sum	£337,000
Insurer's discount	£102,000
Total	£825,000

The annuities purchased with the structured sum produced the following sums:

a)   £4,500 pa payable immediately, increasing at 5% pa compound, guaranteed for life or 30 years, whichever is the longer;
b)   £15,683 pa, payable in three years' time, increasing at 5% pa compound, guaranteed for life/27 years;
c)   £15,540 pa, payable in ten years' time, increasing at 5% pa, guaranteed for life/20 years.

Before approving the settlement in January 1991, McCullough J expressed considerable concern about the size of the insurer's discount. He eventually accepted the reasoning that it was justified by Garylee's relatively long life expectancy of another 50 years during which the insurers would have to administer the structured scheme and be out of pocket each year through receiving annuities net of tax, paying them gross and only recovering the difference at the end of the year.

Notes
1   (1991) PMILL Vol 7 No 9 p 67.

11   *EVERETT V CARTER*[1]

Another route to a structured settlement is summary judgment under RSC Order 14.

This was followed in the case of Raymond Everett who, when aged about 24, sustained a severe head injury in a road traffic accident in December 1985. An Order 14 judgment was obtained in April 1989.

Raymond Everett's intellect was much impaired, he had severe problems with his memory and he was aggressive and threatening to those outside his family. He could walk, dress slowly and feed slowly. He will be permanently dependent upon the care and support of others and will never be able to work.

The value of the claim on the conventional basis was agreed at £1,200,000 plus £100,000 Court of Protection management costs, a total of £1,300,000. Interim payments of £130,000 had already been made. A further payment of £46,314 was set aside for the family in respect of past care, losses and expenses. Interest of £59,141 was payable from the date agreement was achieved over the conventional sum up to the date of the Court Order. This went into a contingency fund of £273,144. It was agreed that the capital cost of the structured settlement was £799,683 with a discount to the insurers, the Prudential Assurance, of £110,000 (13.76%).

Interim payments	£130,000
Other lump sums (including interest)	£319,458
Structured sum	£799,683
Insurer's discount	£110,000
Total (including interest)	£1,359,141

The structured sum was used to establish four annuities:

a) an immediate annuity of £25,000 pa, payable monthly, to increase at 5% pa compound, guaranteed for life or 15 years, whichever be the longer;

b) a deferred annuity of £22,500 pa, payable monthly after six years, to increase at a fixed rate of 5% pa compound, again guaranteed for life/15 years;

c) a further deferred annuity of £37,500 pa, payable monthly in 12 years' time, increasing at 5% pa compound, guaranteed for life with no minimum period;

d) a lump sum payment or 'step annuity' of £25,000, payable in two years' time, thereafter to be paid at the end of every 5 years, to increase at 5% pa compound.

Macpherson J approved the settlement in July 1991. When reporting it, Raymond Everett's solicitor (Bryan Neill) expressed some concern at the size of the insurer's discount and commented that it was undesirable that the ability to have damages structured should depend upon the whim of insurers.

Notes
1   (1991) PMILL Vol 7 No 8 p 63.

12   *BECK V PLASTICISERS LTD*[1]

Most structured settlements to date have resulted from road accidents. However they may also arise in other types of accident or even in cases of disease.

The first reported structured settlement in an industrial accident case was arranged for Albert Beck who in May 1990, when aged 42, was injured in the course of his employment by the defendants as a truck driver. He was marking up bales when two substantial ones dislodged and fell on him.

Following the accident he was confined to a wheelchair as a paraplegic. His 41-year-old wife gave up work to care for him. He would continue to be dependent on others to some extent for his care and welfare. The prospects of his finding gainful employment were negligible. He was expected to live to the age of 67.

Liability was not in dispute. Damages on the conventional basis were agreed at £517,500. There had already been interim payments of £150,000. £115,000 was to be paid as a lump sum. This left a sum available for structuring of £220,000, after taking into account the Eagle Star's discount of £32,500.

Interim payments	£150,000
Lump sum	£115,000
Structured sum	£220,000
Insurer's discount	£32,500
Total	£517,500

The structure was designed to produce a net income of £17,734 pa increasing in line with the Retail Price Index. In addition, Mr Beck would receive State benefits of £13,939 pa. The resultant total of £31,673 pa exceeded his needs which had been calculated at £25,000 pa. The structure was guaranteed for 20 years so that Mrs Beck would be provided for until the age of 61 should Mr Beck die within his reduced life expectancy.

His Honour Judge Donald Herold QC approved the settlement in January 1992.

Notes
1   (1992) PMILL Vol 8 No 6 p 45.

13   *FIELD V HEREFORDSHIRE HEALTH AUTHORITY*[1]

Structured settlements may also be reached in certain medical negligence cases. The first and largest is that of Rebecca Field.

She was born in November 1984. Forceps were negligently used during the birth. There was no sign of spontaneous breathing at the time. She had to be supported by artificial respiration. She remains extensively paralysed and receives continuous artificial respiration via a tracheostomy. She can only speak a few words to her parents who have provided her with constant care. Life expectancy was extremely uncertain. She would probably live into her twenties and possibly into her thirties.

The Health Authority admitted liability. The level of conventional damages was agreed at £1,700,000. When the case came to court on 4 June 1991, it was adjourned for a structure to be considered.

It was agreed that a lump sum of £550,000 be paid. The original cost of the structured programme was £1,042,000, but subsequently a lower quote enabled this to be reduced. The saving to the Department of Health on behalf of the Treasury exceeded £100,000 in any event. After allowing for the advantage to them of paying around £1,600,000 almost 5 months later than otherwise, their total saving approximated to £200,000.

The structured sum purchased the following payments to Rebecca:

a) an immediate amount of £59,000 pa, payable monthly, increasing every year at the rate of 5% pa compound, and guaranteed for her life or ten years, whichever be the longer;

b) a deferred amount of £15,315 pa, starting in five years' time, payable monthly, increasing at 5% pa compound, and guaranteed for her life or ten years from the first payment, whichever be the longer;

c) a deferred amount of £32,578 pa, starting in ten years' time, payable monthly, increasing at 5% pa compound, and guaranteed for whichever proves to be longer of her life or five years from the first payment;

d) a lump sum payable at the end of every five years, based on the sum of £50,000, to be increased in line with the Retail Price Index, only to be paid while she is alive.

Phillips J approved the settlement on 31 October 1991. The Treasury's approval in this case does not mean that every medical negligence claim against a Health Authority can be structured in future. Both the Department of Health and the Treasury stated that any such structured settlements must provide savings to them as well as to the plaintiff, in that their total costs associated with the case must be less than they would have been in a conventional settlement.

Notes
1   (1991) PMILL Vol 7 No 9 p 72.

14 *TOMBS V MERTON AND SUTTON HEALTH AUTHORITY*

The largest single annuity to date has been purchased in the tragic medical negligence case of Alan Tombs.

In August 1987, when aged 27, he was treated at Sutton General Hospital for anal dilation and infection of haemorrhoids. In the process of administering anaesthesia, carbon dioxide was given by mistake. He suffered very severe brain damage in consequence.

Damages on the conventional basis amounted to £1,644,252. Interim payments of £244,252 had been made. £273,000 was paid over immediately for the purchase and adaptation of accommodation for Mr Tombs. £17,300 was paid to his wife and the balance to the Court of Protection. £950,000 was placed into the structure. The defendants received a discount of £100,000.

Interim payments	£244,252
Other lump sum payments	£335,000
Structured sum	£965,000
Defendants' discount	£100,000
Total	£1,644,252

A single annuity was purchased of £85,075 pa, Retail Price Index linked, payable for Mr Tombs' life or for ten years, whichever is the longer. This was considered sufficient to cover not only annual expenses but also the replacement cost of the capital items.

Mr Justice Macpherson approved the settlement in February 1992.

15 *O'TOOLE V MERSEY REGIONAL HEALTH AUTHORITY*

This is the first medical negligence case to be resolved through a structured settlement that is self-funded.

Sian O'Toole was born in January 1982 and was ten years old when his case was settled on a conventionally assessed basis of £675,000. Just over £225,000 was paid as a contingency sum to the family and into the Court of Protection. In addition, Mersey Health Authority agreed to pay regular sums of:

i)   £20,000 pa, Retail Price Indexed linked, payable for life with a
      guaranteed minimum payment period of 20 years;
ii)   £5,000 every five years, Retail Price Index linked, payable for life.

Sian's solicitor was given very specific instructions as to what was
required in terms of periodic payments. Accordingly the agreement to
structure was based directly on the requirements, rather than negotiated
on the basis of a discount for the defendants.

The novel feature of the case was the agreement of the Mersey Health
Authority to make payments under a structured settlement without
purchasing an annuity to match its obligations. This followed detailed
discussions with the Department of Health and the Treasury. A significant
cash saving for the National Health Service was achieved.

In August 1992 the settlement was approved by Mr Justice May.

16   *LOVELL V SOUTHAMPTON AND S W HAMPSHIRE HEALTH AUTHORITY*

Another self-funded structured settlement has been reached in the case
of Victoria Lovell.

In June 1984, when she was $3^3/4$ years old, she was admitted to
Southampton Eye Hospital to undergo a routine operation to correct a
squint. Hospital staff were aware that she had been suffering from a cold.
Whilst she was in the recovery room after the operation a plug of phlegm
entered her windpipe and she stopped breathing. Cardiac arrest occurred,
and Victoria suffered severe irreversible brain damage.

Damages on the conventional basis were agreed shortly before trial at
£875,000. Mr Justice Otton approved this on 30 March 1992 and
adjourned the case to allow investigation of a structured settlement.
Negotiations were protracted, as the defendant Health Authority was
directed by H M Treasury and the Department of Health to put forward
a self structure.

£287,000 was paid as interim payments and other lump sums. A further
£76,000 plus £37,306 interest since 30 March was payable immediately
of which £50,000 is being paid into the Court of Protection as a
contingency fund and £63,306 is being paid to the Receiver. The
structured sum is £465,000 from which the Health Authority is to make
periodic payments. Their discount was £47,000.

Lump sums	£363,000
Interest from 30 March 1992	£37,306
Structured sum	£465,000
Health Authority discount	£47,000
Total (including interest)	£912,000

Under the structure, the Health Authority will pay £24,114.96 pa, increasing annually in line with the Retail Price Index, payable for life subject to a guaranteed minimum period of ten years whether Victoria survives or not. These payments are guaranteed by the Department of Health in the event of the Health Authority ceasing to exist. Indeed the payments to be made by the Health Authority will be provided by the Department of Health.

The case came again before Mr Justice Otton on 27 November 1992 when he approved the structured settlement and the arrangements relating to it.

17   *BOOBBYER V JOHNSON*[1]

Structured settlements can also be arranged in fatal cases. The first was set up for Mrs Marie Louise Boobbyer whose husband Geoffrey was a surgeon.

On 4 November 1984 Mr Boobbyer was driving a Metro car along a country road in Kent when he was involved in a collision with a Datsun driven in the opposite direction by Anthony Johnson. Mr Boobbyer was killed. Liability was apportioned on a 50-50 basis.

The damages due were conventionally assessed at £550,000. £70,000 had been paid as an interim payment. Another £70,000 was payable immediately. It was agreed that £350,000 would be structured, with a discount to the insurers (Highway Motor Policies) of £60,000.

Lump sum payments	£140,000
Structured sum	£350,000
Insurer's discount	£60,000
Total	£550,000

The structured sum was used to provide for Mrs Boobbyer with an annuity of £19,556 pa, payable monthly for life, subject to a guaranteed minimum period of 20 years, Retail Price Index linked as follows.

'After one year's payments have been made and at the end of every 12 (twelve) months thereafter, the amount will be increased (or decreased) in proportion to the increase (or decrease) in the General Index of Retail Prices (all items) for the year ending 3 (three) months prior to the date of the alteration or if the General Index of Retail Prices (all items) no longer exists such other published Index of Retail Prices which the Insurer may at its absolute discretion deem to be appropriate.'

Rougier J approved the settlement in the High Court on 20 January 1992.

Notes
1   The Lawyer, 11 February 1992.

18   *KEARNEY V CALDWELL*

The first structured settlement in Northern Ireland was set up for Jane Kearney. In April 1989, when she was nearly seven years old, she came out from a home and was crossing a road in Belfast when a car driven by Mr Caldwell collided with her.

She sustained very severe brain damage and gross physical disability in her arms and legs. She is incontinent and requires feeding. She has bilateral ptosis. She has behavioural problems, and her arms are splinted to avoid damage to her eyes. Intensive nursing is required.

Owing to risks on liability, her claim was compromised for what on a conventional basis would have been £350,000. £90,000 was payable as a lump sum to provide for Jane's immediate accommodation which had to be specially adapted to her needs. A discount of £25,000 was agreed with the insurers (Provincial Insurance). The balance of £235,000 went into the structure.

The Provincial Insurance agreed to pay an annuity starting at £13,694 pa, increasing at 5% pa compound, payable for the rest of Jane's life subject to a minimum payment period of 20 years.

Lump sum	£90,000
Structured sum	£235,000
Insurer's discount	£25,000
Total	£350,000

McDermott J approved this structured settlement in March 1992.

19   *MARSHALL V WESTMINSTER CITY COUNCIL*[1]

This case resulted in the first structured settlement involving a mutual insurance company.

In June 1982 Andrew Marshall, then aged 4, was playing in the balcony of his parents' flat in St Johns Wood when he fell against a plastic infill panel which formed part of the balcony construction. The panel came away from its fixings, causing him to fall some 20 ft to the ground.

Andrew's parents sued on his behalf Westminster City Council which instituted its own proceedings against the architect responsible for the design of the balcony railings, as the Council was obliged to carry out remedial works to a substantial number of similar properties for which it was liable. Eventually, the architects' insurers agreed to accept responsibility for 85% of the Council's claims including that of Andrew Marshall.

Settlement of Andrew's claim was agreed for what on a conventional basis would have been £620,000. £285,000 was payable as lump sum damages. £300,000 was set aside to be structured. The insurer's discount was £35,000.

Lump sum	£285,000
Structured sum	£300,000
Insurer's discount	£35,000
Total	£620,000

The structured sum of £300,000 was applied to purchase two annuities from Aetna Life Insurance Company:

i)   for a premium of £220,000, an immediate annuity of £12,664 pa,
     increasing at 5% pa compound, with a guaranteed period of 30 years;
ii) for a premium of £80,000, a deferred annuity of £8,390 pa, increasing
     at 5% pa compound, with a guaranteed period of 23 years.

Some doubt was expressed about the viability of this arrangement, given
the mutual status of Municipal Insurance, the insurers of Westminster
City Council. Although 85% of the settlement was to be funded by the
architect's insurers, they were not a party to Andrew Marshall's action.
Whereas if Municipal Mutual Insurance were to be made party to the
structured settlement, most of the tax advantages would be lost.

It was therefore arranged that the settlement should be reached in the
name of the City of Westminster itself. The City of Westminster would
incur a temporary loss of cash flow by virtue of the fact that it would be
receiving annuity payments from the life insurers net of tax whilst
making gross payments to the plaintiff, until the balance could be
recouped from the Inland Revenue. Consequently the parties agreed that
the City of Westminster should receive a single payment of £7,500 from
the discount figure as compensation for this. The £27,500 balance of the
discount was apportioned between Municipal Insurance and the architect's
insurers in the proportions previously agreed between them in respect of
liability.

Turner J approved this structured settlement in March 1991. It was only
possible because the Court and the Inland Revenue were prepared to
permit the city council to take the place of the mutual insurers in order
to obtain the tax benefits and guarantee future payments.

Notes
1   QBD transcript, 8 March 1991.

20   *RE A. M.*

In suitable cases a structured settlement can be used to purchase annuities
for members of a plaintiff's family.

The plaintiff was a lorry driver who was aged 25 when he was injured
in a road accident. He sustained a severe head injury and could hardly
speak. His mobility was greatly restricted.

He was married with two young children. His wife was unable to meet his future care needs, and his family moved to a nearby house. He received care from his mother. The conventional level of damages was assessed at around £745,000. Just over £243,500 was paid as a cash sum. The structure cost £452,000, leaving the defendants with a saving of about £50,000.

Lump sum payment	£243,500
Structured sum	£452,000
Insurer's discount	£50,000
Total	£745,500

The structured sum was used to buy the following annuities:

i)   £20,000 pa immediate, Retail Price Index Linked, payable for life with a guaranteed minimum of 20 years. It was split between his mother, who was now caring for him, and his wife. This allowed his wife to take out a mortgage with a building society which accepted her share of the annuity as income when calculating how much she could borrow. The deposit was met out of the damages for her past care;

ii) two term certain annuities for £2,600 pa each, increasing in line with the Retail Price Index, to cease when each child reaches the age of 18 years;

iii) an annuity of £8,545 pa, to commence ten years from trial when the plaintiff's mother would probably have to pay for assistance to help her, increasing in line with the Retail Price Index, payable for his life subject to a guaranteed minimum period of 20 years;

iv) an annuity of £26,222, payable at the end of every five years to help replace capital equipment, increasing in line with the Retail Price Index.

This case is significant for the flexible and innovative nature of the annuities purchased with the structure. The settlement was approved by the Court of Protection.

21   *WICKENS V J & J STEEL ERECTION LTD*

The lowest known insurer's discount is 7.5%. This was negotiated in the case of Silice Karito Wickens.

On 9 February 1985, when he was 21 years old, Wickens was working as a steel erector at the third floor level on a construction site when he slipped and fell about 25 ft. The place and the system of work were unsafe, and the defendants were convicted under section 2(1) of the Health and Safety at Work Act 1974.

The accident left him paraplegic at the level T7: he had no sensation or movement below the level of his chest. His life expectancy was normal, but it was anticipated that he would need greater care and attention 10–15 years after settlement.

This occurred when he was aged 26 on a conventionally assessed basis of £500,000. It was allocated as follows:

Interim payments	£35,000
Cash contingency fund	£100,000
Fund to purchase house/car	£150,000
Structured sum	£200,000
Insurer's discount	£15,000
total	£500,000

The structure was used to buy two annuities:

i)   an annuity of £6,500 pa, increasing at 5% pa compound, payable for life subject to a guaranteed minimum payment period of 30 years;
ii) a deferred annuity of £26,572 pa, to start in ten years' time, increasing at 5% pa compound, payable for life subject to a minimum payment period of 25 years.

The settlement was reached well before the court hearing date which enabled the defendant's insurers (General Accident) to agree a lower discount than otherwise. The substantial deferred element matched the expected increase in the plaintiff's care needs.

22   *RACKSHAW V STALLARD*[1]

Structured settlements are not only to be found in large cases. They may also be appropriate where the conventionally assessed value is around £250,000 or less.

When aged 7, Sarah Rackshaw was crossing the road when she was knocked over by a motor vehicle driven by Mr Stallard.

Liability was eventually agreed with a 25% deduction for contributory negligence.

She suffered a head injury which immediately rendered her unconscious. A CT scan showed her major injury to be bi-fronted extradural haematoma with resulting damage to the large vein lying between the global hemispheres. She developed epilepsy which was only controlled by medication. There was substantial spasticity in her left arm which became largely useless. She walked with a very noticeable limp. She suffered intellectual impairment, so that she needed to be taught in a special learning unit within her state school. She was unlikely to become independent and would always need supervision (as distinct from care). Her life expectancy was unaffected. She was 14 by the time of the hearing.

The parties agreed a full liability assessment of £350,000 which, net of contributory negligence would have yielded a conventional settlement figure of £262,500.

Interim payments of £12,000 had to be deducted. The Court of Protection insisted on a contingency fund of £55,000. The Eagle Star's discount was agreed at £20,500 (11.71%). This left £175,000 for purchase of annuities.

Interim payments	£12,000
Contingency fund	£55,000
Structured sum	£175,000
Insurer's discount	£20,500
Total	£262,500

The structured total of £175,000 provided for two annuities:

a)   £100,000 was to purchase an immediate annuity of £5,269 pa, indexed at 5% pa, payable for life, guaranteed for a minimum of 30 years;

b) £75,000 was to purchase a deferred annuity of £6,460 pa, commencing in 5 years' time, indexed at 5% pa, payable throughout her life, guaranteed for a minimum period of 25 years from commencement.

Annuity (b) was designed to start at a time when she would have become independent, had she not been injured in the accident.

Mr Justice Potts approved the settlement in June 1991.

Notes
1   (1991) PMILL Vol 7 No 6 p 42.

23 *SMITH V J R PEMBROKE*[1]

Structured settlements are now being arranged in certain cases worth between £100,000 and £200,000.

In August 1984, a vehicle driven by the defendant careered through a tent in which Susan Smith was camping. She sustained a brain injury which diminished her ability at work.

In July 1992, when she was 24 years old, she accepted the defendant's insurers' overall offer of £175,000 of which £145,000 could be used to fund a structure if she so required. No insurer's discount was separately calculated by means of agreeing an overall lump sum and then a reduction from it. Instead the insurers simply offered what they were prepared to pay, a £30,000 lump sum plus £145,000, and it was for the plaintiff and her advisers to decide whether to structure the £145,000 or to take it as a further lump sum.

Susan Smith chose to structure it. Her agents obtained for her an annuity of £6,694 pa, payable quarterly for life, linked to the Retail Price Index up to the year 2023. After that date, if gilts linked to the RPI are not available to support the index linking, the annuity will increase by 7% pa.

When approving the award in July 1992, Mr Justice Otton commented: 'This is the lowest figure I have ever contemplated for a structured settlement, but it shows how damages have become more sophisticated with the introduction of structuring'.

Notes
1   The Lawyer.

24 *RE L.O.M.*[1]

A structured settlement of even more moderate value was set up following a collision between two horse riders at a cross-country event.

The plaintiff suffered a broken back and quadriplegia and sued the other rider for negligence. Liability was very much in dispute. The defendant made a compromise offer of £130,000. The plaintiff rejected it. The defendant then offered a lump sum of £30,000 plus £8,000 pa for life, increasing at the rate of 5% pa compound. The plaintiff accepted this.

Thus a contested trial on liability was avoided. The total cost to the defendants remained at £130,000.

Notes
1   Kemp & Kemp 6A–048.

25 *RE W.B.*[1]

The smallest reported structured settlement was arranged for a lady who was 78 years old when she was injured crossing the road.

In consequence, she lost her mobility and was confined to a residential home which cost £10,920 pa.

The conventional award would probably have been between £80,000 and £85,000. The case was settled on the basis that the plaintiff be paid £12,500 immediately plus £10,920 pa, Retail Price Index linked, for the rest of her life, with no guaranteed minimum number of payments.

The total cost of the settlement was £65,749. This implies a substantial saving of between £14,251 and £19,251 on a structured sum of £53,249.

The plaintiff's reward for agreeing to this was the capacity to remain in her chosen residential home for the rest of her life.

Notes
1   Kemp & Kemp 6A–049.

26   *FOURNIER V CANADIAN NATIONAL RAILWAY COMPANY*[1]

Annuities cannot be *awarded* as damages. A Canadian jury's brave attempt to achieve this in 1924 was brusquely rejected by the Privy Council.

Around 2 am one morning in September 1922, Adelard Fournier was driving his wife and their young child towards their home in Quebec. When they came to a level crossing, their car was struck by a train moving backwards. Fournier was killed instantly, and his wife died of her injuries a few days later. The child was less severely injured.

Fournier had six children in all, aged between 3 and 10. Their 'tuteur' sued the Canadian National Railway Company and elected jury trial. The jury found negligence to be proved.

They proceeded to award an annuity of $300 to be paid annually to each of the children until he or she should reach the age of 18. The judge attempted to legitimise this by capitalising the annuities at a value of $15,000 and awarding this sum.

The Privy Council held that the jury's award of annuities was illegal and that the judge had erred by converting it into a capital sum which the jury had never awarded.

Whether the jury is to be regarded as rash or heroically ahead of its time, the ban reflected by this decision on annuities as awardable damages has remained in force to the present.

Notes
1   (1927) AC 167.

27   *METCALFE V LONDON PASSENGER TRANSPORT BOARD*[1]

The unavailability of annuities as a form of award was judicially regretted in this English case.

Frederick Metcalfe was a bus conductor employed by London transport. In July 1937 a tram belonging to London Transport and driven by one of their employees collided with a stationary bus in which he was standing on the platform. He sued for his severe personal injuries. Macnaghten J held that the doctrine of common employment applied, so he was not entitled to recover.

Nevertheless he assessed damages in case of appeal. Metcalfe, aged 32 at trial, had had his left leg amputated below the knee, and his right foot would always be deformed. He had a wife and one child to support, and a mortgage to repay. He could never resume his old occupation. It was doubtful whether he would work again.

Macnaghten J stated that: 'in such a case as this, a secured pension would seem to be the fairest way of compensating this plaintiff – fair to the employers and fair to the plaintiff – but the court has no power to make such an order except with the consent of the parties, and such consent is not given in this case'.

Accordingly he held that, if liability had been established, he would have awarded damages in a lump sum of £3,715.

Notes
1   [1938] 2 All ER 352.

28   BURKE V TOWER HAMLETS HEALTH AUTHORITY[1]

The limitation that Macnaghten J regretted continues to apply, even after structured settlements were introduced in personal injury cases.

Eileen Burke had sustained brain damage during a Caesarian operation at the London Hospital. She applied for an order that her damages should take the form of periodic payments. The defendant Health Authority objected.

Drake J held that the court had no power to order periodic payments instead of a lump sum, except where both parties consent. The order could not be made in the face of the defendant's opposition.

Therefore, whilst the number of structured settlements increases almost exponentially, it is still not permitted to impose a structured award.

Notes
1   (1989) Times, 10 August.

29   BRAYBROOKE V PARKER AND BICKS[1]

Insurers cannot be compelled to disclose the purchase price of an annuity. It follows that they cannot be forced to specify their discount.

Judith Braybrooke was a plaintiff under disability suing through her next friend. She applied for an order that the defendants disclose to her and the court the annuity purchase cost to the defendants' insurers (Sun Alliance). This was prior to a joint application by her and the defendants that a structured settlement of her claim be approved by the Court.

Moreland J rejected the application. He held that the purchase price of the annuity was irrelevant in deciding what was fair compensation for the plaintiff and whether her reasonable requirements for the rest of her life could be satisfied by the proposed structured settlement. The insurers were entitled to keep their cost confidential.

Notes
1   QBD transcript, 22 October 1991.

30   DISCOUNTS AND DIVERSITY

30.1   Discounts

The case law demonstrates the range of discounts enjoyed by insurers in return for consenting to a structured settlement. It is accepted that some discount is appropriate and necessary in order to compensate insurers for (a) the adverse cash-flow consequences of receiving the annuities net and paying them gross prior to tax recoupment and (b) administrative inconvenience and expense.

A list of the discounts that it has been possible to calculate in 13 cases is given below. These discounts have been expressed as a percentage figure of the net structured sum, ie the sums used to purchase the annuities.

The majority of these discounts fall within an inner range of between 9% and 12^1/2%. The lowest tend to be reached when the structured settlement is arranged at a relatively early stage in the case (eg *Wickens*) or where the structured sum is relatively large so that administration costs are proportionately small (eg *Everett H*).

The cases above reflect the standard approach to structured settlements. Three alternative approaches have been adopted in other cases.

First, in the cases of *Heeley* (case no 9) and *Grimsley* (case no 10), the parties appear to have calculated the total tax saving and then allocated it between themselves in negotiated proportions. This has resulted in relatively high discounts of 22.60% (*Heeley*) and 30.27% (*Grimsley*). It is significant that in the *Grimsley* case McCullough J expressed sustained disquiet about the size of discount before eventually accepting it with reluctance. It is also notable that these were two comparatively early structures reached before any range of discounts had been established.

Case No	Plaintiff	Structured sum	Discount	%age
5	Kelly	£300,000	£27,000	9.00
6	Everett H	£706,378	£70,000	9.91
7	Payne	£463,000	£67,210	14.52
8	Moxon	£400,000	£50,000	12.50
11	Everett R	£799,683	£110,000	13.76
12	Beck	£220,000	£32,500	14.77
14	Tombs	£965,000	£100,000	10.36
16	Lovell	£465,000	£47,000	10.11
17	Boobbyer	£350,000	£60,000	17.14
18	Kearney	£235,000	£25,000	10.64
19	Marshall	£300,000	£35,000	11.67
20	A.M.	£452,000	£50,000	11.06
22	Rackshaw	£175,000	£20,500	11.71

The second alternative approach has been for plaintiffs to concentrate simply on achieving a structured settlement to match their needs. Thus the solicitor for Sian O'Toole (case no 15) was given specific instructions on the level of periodic payments required. And W.B. (case no 25) was satisfied by having the cost of her chosen residential home met for the rest of her life.

The third alternative approach has been for defendants to state firstly what payments they are prepared to offer, without specifying any discount, and leaving the plaintiff to decide whether to accept. This was done in the cases of *Smith* (case no 23) and *L.O.M.* (case no 24). Indeed, Smith was even given the choice of whether to structure the main part of the damages or take it as a further lump sum.

At least two-thirds of the cases summarised in this chapter, however, have been resolved by the standard approach of calculating what the conventional lump sum damages would have been and negotiating from this the defendants' discount. This seems to be the mainstream method, but one that is subject to variations and exceptions.

30.2   Diversity

Another main theme to emerge from the reports is the sheer diversity of cases in which structured settlements have been set up.
They have been arranged where plaintiffs have been resident in:

a)   England and Wales;
b)   Northern Ireland (*Kearney*);
c)   Canada (*Strachnick*).

They have been applied in cases arising out of:

a)   road traffic accidents;
b)   an industrial accident (*Beck*; *Wickens*);
c)   medical negligence (*Field*; *Tombs*; *O'Toole*; *Lovell*);
d)   a fatal accident (*Boobbyer*);
e)   an equestrian accident (*L.O.M.*).

They have been reached:

a)   after a split trial on liability (*Grimsley*);
b)   a contested trial on quantum (*Payne*);
c)   an Order 14 Judgment (*Everett v Carter*).

They are applicable even where:

a)   there is substantial contributory negligence (*Moxon*);
b)   a partial compromise offer is accepted (*L.O.M.*);
c)   there is a major dispute on life expectancy (*Heeley*).

And they have been set up in cases worth:

a)   £250,000 upwards;
b)   £100,000 – £250,000 (*Smith*; *L.O.M.*);
c)   £50,000 – £100,000 (*W.B.*).

What a pity then that:

a)   a jury cannot award annuity damages (*Fournier*);

b)   and nor can a judge (*Metcalfe*);
c)   even after the creation of the structuring facility (*Burke*).

3 The Plaintiff's Solicitor's Approach

Bryan Neill

1 INTRODUCTION

1.1 The object of this chapter is to provide the plaintiff's solicitor with a practical guide as to how he or she might go about establishing a structured settlement for a plaintiff in an appropriate case.

1.2 The conventional approach to an award of damages has been that a plaintiff receives a lump sum. The theory behind this is that the lump sum should enable the plaintiff to live off the interest it generates, plus draw on the capital sum each year, so that the lump sum is finally exhausted at the time he dies. For this reason the Court adopts its traditional approach to discounted multipliers.

1.3 The problem is that the theory is a fiction. It does not work out like that. Practitioners know this, judges know it, insurance industry surveys have confirmed that a large number of plaintiffs have little or nothing left by the latter years of their life, and many former plaintiffs know it to their regret. The theory presents an impossible goal. Scientifically, and mathematically, there are too many variables and unknowns in the equation. In practical terms, it is a sad fact that most plaintiffs, perhaps especially those who are most disabled and whose needs the greatest, are inexperienced and incapable of managing large funds. Market fluctuations can be lethal to their investments. The investment income itself is taxed.

1.4 The concept of structured compensation is seen as an alternative whereby the plaintiff will receive his or her damages by periodic payments from the defendant or his insurers. The history and theory of structured compensation are dealt with elsewhere in this publication. However it is against this background that the plaintiff's solicitor must consider, having regard to his client's needs and wishes, whether a conventional award is appropriate or whether he ought instead to investigate the possibility of structuring his client's damages or a proportion of them. Almost certainly, the position has now been reached in which plaintiff personal injury lawyers who do not understand and advise their clients on the pros and cons of structured compensation, especially in large claims, might subsequently find themselves vulnerable to claims in negligence.

1.5 The trend towards structuring presently seems unstoppable. The concept has been recognised in legislation (Social Security Act 1989,

Sch 4) and the Court of Appeal has spoken out strongly in its support (*Butler v Vann*, unreported, July 1991, Donaldson MR). Barring disasters it would seem that the concept is here to stay.

1.6   At present the Courts have no power to order a tax-effective structuring of damages, so that in general structured compensation in the United Kingdom means settlement of a case on structured terms. Hence the label 'structured settlement'.

2   WHAT CASES MAY BE APPROPRIATE FOR 'STRUCTURING'?

2.1   The object of structured compensation is to provide financial security into the future, and to avoid the vagaries of taxation, investment and the marketplace. Thus the most appropriate cases are likely to be those in which the plaintiff will require a steady and continuing stream of funds, such as the plaintiff who will continue to suffer losses or incur expenditure (eg for care) in the future.

2.2   It would be wrong to attempt to set a figure and say that below that figure structured compensation should not be considered. Tax regimes, interest rates and market conditions fluctuate. The plaintiff's situation will be relevant. For example an elderly plaintiff may find it attractive to structure compensation of, say, £50,000 whereas a younger plaintiff with a much longer life expectancy would find the return from such a sum invested in an annuity to be much less rewarding. If we are to follow the American pattern, then it is likely that as more life assurance companies move into this marketplace we may find smaller and smaller sums being structured. However, a rule of thumb in the present UK environment could probably be reasonably stated by saying that a plaintiff's solicitor ought to have regard to the possible benefits of structuring damages that are likely to be in the region of £75,000 or above. Structuring should certainly be considered where the damages reach or exceed a six-figure sum. With plaintiffs who have shorter life expectancies, such as the elderly, structuring can be considered in respect of lower amounts. In all but a very few instances only a proportion of the conventional damages will be available to purchase an annuity or annuities, and a reasonable capital sum will need to remain outside the structure whether to provide for immediate needs such as converted accommodation or transport, or to provide a contingency fund for future emergencies, or both.

3 ADVISING THE PLAINTIFF

3.1 Let us assume that the case is appropriate for structuring. Clearly the first step, before exploring the prospect with the defendants' representatives, is to advise the plaintiff of the possibility, explaining exactly what a structured settlement is and its practical consequences for him. In particular the plaintiff should understand the potential advantages and disadvantages of applying a proportion of the capital sum in such a way. In the case of a plaintiff under a disability, instructions to explore the prospect of structuring will be sought from the Next Friend, perhaps the Official Solicitor, or more commonly very concerned parents or other relatives.

3.2 The advantages to the plaintiff may be summarised as follows.

(a) The stream of damages will take the form of regular payments for life, thus providing the security that the damages will never run out no matter how long the plaintiff lives. Thus the plaintiff will be guaranteed a regular and certain income for life and will not run the risk of having to fall back upon uncertain, and perhaps inadequate, future state benefits.

(b) There is flexibility in the frequency of the periodic payments. Under any annuity they can be paid at regular intervals that the plaintiff chooses prior to the structure being established. Therefore, for example, payments under any annuity can be made monthly or quarterly or annually, etc.

(c) The payments under the annuity or annuities can have guaranteed growth. Thus they can be index-linked, or they can be geared to increase at a fixed rate, for example 5% per annum compound has been commonly adopted.

(d) In addition to the guarantee that the payments will be made at this increasing rate for the whole of the plaintiff's life, guaranteed minimum periods can be built into each annuity so that should the plaintiff die before the end of the guaranteed period his or her estate may receive the balance of the payments due under that annuity up to the end of the guaranteed minimum period. This may be particularly important where, for example, there is a spouse or children to consider.

(e) The payments are guaranteed to be tax-free and the plaintiff is thus spared the problems associated with changes in tax rates and the tax regime generally.

(f) The plaintiff no longer has to be concerned about managing the investment of the fund, changes in investment return, or stock fluctuations.

(g) The plaintiff will save costs of administering the fund, such as the cost of investment advice.

(h) Only a proportion of the gross damages needs to be applied to purchase the annuity or annuities. Thus a capital sum can remain outside and be available to meet immediate needs (accommodation, transport, aids and equipment etc) and future contingencies. Only the balance needs to be applied to purchase the structure. If a need is identified for regular capital outlays from time to time in the future (eg to replace vehicles) an annuity (known as a 'lump sum' or 'step' annuity) can provide for this. This can provide individual capital payments, for example once every fourth or fifth year. Such payments can also be index-linked or increase at a fixed rate.

'In summary, the risk of financial prejudice to the plaintiff arising from the uncertainties of a conventional award are substantially reduced if not entirely avoided' (Goldrein and de Haas: *Butterworths Personal Injury Litigation Service*).

3.3   There are also disadvantages to the plaintiff which must be clearly understood before the decision is taken, and these can be summarised as follows.

(a) Once established, the structure is not flexible. The capital employed to purchase the annuities is locked away and not available to the plaintiff, and the structure cannot be broken.

(b) There may be a loss of opportunity through no longer having access to this lump sum.

(c) If the plaintiff dies after the expiry of a minimum guarantee period, or if an annuity does not have a minimum guarantee period, there is no residual money due to his estate under that annuity (eg if an annuity, without guarantee, is due to commence payment after 20 years but the plaintiff dies after 18 years, then no payments will be made and the sum invested to purchase that annuity will be lost entirely).

(d) In consideration for agreeing to establish a structured settlement, the defendants' insurance company will require a 'discount' from the plaintiff in the form of a reduction of the conventional damages that he would otherwise receive. 'Discount' will be considered in more detail later in this chapter, but at this stage of discussions with the plaintiff it would be impossible to give him any accurate indication of how much the discount might be.

(e) There is the danger, not to be underestimated in the present economic climate, that the defendants' insurance company, with whom the plaintiff contracts, might become insolvent before the end of the plaintiff's life. This should be mentioned to the plaintiff at this stage, but it ought also to be considered carefully by the plaintiff's advisers before the Agreement itself is signed. There is the possibility for the plaintiff of protection, at least as to the conventional amount invested, from the Lloyd's Central Fund in the case of some insurers, or as a result of the Policyholders Protection Act 1975 in cases of compulsory insurance. There is the possibility (not yet aired before British Courts) that payments from the life company, under the annuity or annuities, might be deemed to be held in trust for the plaintiff by the Trustee in Bankruptcy. It is more likely that they will not but that instead they will be part of the general assets, to which the plaintiff will only be entitled as an unsecured creditor. Enquiries have established that it is not practical (at least at present) to consider insuring against the risk of the general insurer going into liquidation as insurance will not be offered for a period exceeding five years.

3.4   Timing: it is advisable to discuss the possibility of structuring with the plaintiff as early as possible, so that it is not first put to him shortly before trial, and he is not faced with unnecessary and undue pressure to decide.

3.5   Many plaintiffs may be mentally preparing for a large cash sum. Whilst a large cash sum may not seem in their best interests (compared with the returns from a structure) their expectations and those of their family may lead them to reject structured compensation if it is raised too late in the day.

4   APPROACHING THE DEFENDANTS

4.1   The plaintiff's instructions are to investigate the possibility of structuring a proportion of his damages.

4.2   Firstly, it is necessary to sound out the defendants' solicitors (a claim of this value should be litigated and you should not be negotiating with insurers for very long) as to whether, in principle, their insurance clients are prepared to consider structuring a proportion of the plaintiff's damages.

4.3   Timing: as with your client, the earlier this is raised with the other side the better. If it affects nothing else, it will affect the timing of the parties' preparation for trial as will be seen below. It is more likely that a structure will be successfully implemented if it is a common objective of the parties from a fairly early stage.

4.4   The defendants' solicitors will take their insurance client's instructions. If they do not agree then, unless they subsequently change their minds, there being no power for the Court to order a structure, the plaintiff's solicitor will have no option but to proceed to trial in the conventional way. What if they agree?

5   THE DEFENDANTS AGREE IN PRINCIPLE: WHAT NEXT?

5.1   Both the plaintiff's and defendants' solicitors will proceed to prepare and quantify the action exactly as they would have done had it been progressing to trial. There is no guarantee that the parties will reach agreement on the amount of conventional damages. Negotiations on terms for the structure may break down. Either party might change its mind. It is therefore prudent that both parties work to the worst possible option, that is the assumption that the case will go to trial on the date fixed. Therefore both sides will prepare their evidence.

5.2   The one probable exception to this 'nothing changes' approach is in the timetable to trial laid down by the trial directions.

6   TRIAL DIRECTIONS

6.1   Automatic directions will be largely inappropriate in the vast majority of catastrophic claims that will be appropriate for structuring. The number of expert witnesses to be called by the parties will exceed those provided for by the automatic directions. They will mean that a fixed date is necessary for the trial. It is inappropriate to exchange expert evidence shortly after setting down. Instead the timetable will focus on the trial date, and work back from that.

6.2   Whether structuring or not, it is likely that after setting an action down an Application to Fix will be taken out, and subsequently a fixed date obtained. Thereafter a Summons for Directions should be issued to provide the timetable to trial. This should seek Orders for leave to call the appropriate expert witnesses at trial, an exchange date for mutual disclosure of their reports, a date for disclosure of the plaintiff's schedule and the defendants' counter-schedule. (Appendix V provides an example of a specimen Summons for Directions.)

6.3   So far, no change. However, if the parties intend to try to structure, it is desirable to agree an exchange date for reports and disclosure of the plaintiff's schedule (and defendants' counter-schedule) that provides sufficient time for negotiations before the trial. These negotiations between the parties will be to explore whether or not agreement can be reached as to a conventional figure of damages acceptable to both parties, necessary before moving on to structure.

6.4   It may be that the exchange date sought by the plaintiff's solicitor in the Order for Directions will not be any earlier because of the structure, but that he will agree to exchange with the defendants on an earlier date if, by that time, they are still prepared to look at structuring a proportion of the plaintiff's damages. The defendants' solicitors are likely to wish that the earlier exchange date be embodied in the Order. This will be a matter of negotiation and agreement between the parties, or argument before the Master or District Judge.

6.5   In practical terms if, as trial approaches, the defendants are still prepared to structure then the plaintiff's solicitor is likely to agree exchange of reports a little earlier than he otherwise would. He will wish to provide sufficient time (between exchange of the parties' respective cases and the trial) for negotiations to take place, to see if agreement can be reached on a mutually acceptable conventional figure. The defendants' solicitors may be prepared to agree, in consideration of this, to undertake not to take advantage of this earlier disclosure, which is purely for the purpose of negotiations towards structuring, for example by not paying into Court during this time.

6.6   Reports having been exchanged, further views sought from experts and subsequent reports served, and the schedule and counter-schedule delivered, the next step is to make arrangements for a *without prejudice meeting* in order that the issues as now defined between the parties can be discussed.

7   THE WITHOUT PREJUDICE MEETING

7.1   The circumstances of the case will dictate who needs to be present, ie the weight of the case, the issues remaining on liability and quantum, the value of the claim, whether the plaintiff is under a disability, etc. This will be a matter for individual judgment in each case. Structures have been established following meetings between the plaintiff's solicitor and the defendants' insurer alone, solicitors for both parties, solicitors with Counsel, or with Leading and Junior Counsel, Counsel alone, or combinations of the above! In general the defendants' insurers are always likely to wish to be present or nearby. There should be a reasonable balance of representation for each side.

7.2   The more present at the meeting, the greater the costs. Preferably the plaintiff and the defendants' insurers should not be present although they should be capable of being contacted should instructions be required from them. Experts, for example, should not be there. The meeting should not take the form of a 'mini-trial'.

7.3   ADR: although the vast majority, if not all, of these meetings in cases to date have tried to resolve issues between the parties' representatives, there may also be scope for an alternative format being adopted by agreement, such as one of the various types of ADR (Alternative Dispute Resolution), for example mediation by a mutually acceptable independent party.

7.4   At present the most common approach is a meeting between solicitors or solicitors and counsel. This stage will only conclude successfully if both parties approach it in a positive and realistic frame of mind. There are inevitably significant differences between the parties which need to be narrowed. Sensible attitudes must be adopted by both sides towards compromise, but compromise for the purpose of structuring *only*. Delicacy is also required in any concessions that may be made, for example by a party as to the strength of certain of its evidence, as the prospect of a contested trial still looms. It is not infrequently the case that issues are narrowed at a first meeting, but not resolved until a second meeting.

7.5   If no agreement can be achieved between the parties as to a conventional sum then the litigation must proceed to trial in the normal way. On occasions parties have at this stage agreed that the judge hear the action but give no judgment or order as to damages, instead indicating the amount he would subsequently give judgment for.

7.6   Discount is normally sought by defendants' insurers, and conceded by the plaintiff, against that amount of the damages that is to be invested in purchasing the annuities. It is unlikely, when the meeting takes place, that the plaintiff will know how much he will ultimately wish to invest in this way. It is desirable to resolve the question of discount at this stage, so that it does not cause negotiations to break down at a later stage, perhaps (dangerously from the plaintiff's point of view) after lack of time has made it necessary to adjourn the trial in order to implement the structure. In Chapter 2, Rodney Nelson-Jones provides an analysis of discounts on known structures to date, and their relationship in percentage terms to the amounts structured. It is generally considered that, depending upon the size of the sum to be structured, an appropriate 'discount' of between 8% and 15% of that sum is not unreasonable. The greater the amount structured, the lower in percentage terms the discount should be.

7.7   The plaintiff's advisers should try to obtain agreement on the amount of discount, or the percentage amount of the discount in relation to the sum structured, at the without prejudice meeting especially if the meeting is so close to trial that an agreement to structure would mean the trial date would need to be vacated. 'Discount' is bound to be a matter of negotiation. If it is incapable of agreement then the structure may fail. If the plaintiff's solicitor discovers, after the trial date has been vacated, that the defendants' insurers want an unreasonably large discount that he cannot recommend to the plaintiff, so that the structure collapses, he will have lost his trial date and the practical advantages it would have brought. It is likely to be many months before another fixture can be obtained that would be suitable to all expert witnesses. During this period the defendants will have plenty of time to improve their evidence, pay into court, etc. Whether discount can be agreed or not, but particularly if it is not agreed and the trial is to be adjourned, the plaintiff's advisers should seek agreement that a conventional offer will remain open to the plaintiff.

8   INTEREST

8.1   The plaintiff must also consider the question of interest, particularly if the date on which the plaintiff is to receive his damages is to be delayed because of adjournment of a trial date. It is again a matter of negotiation to be dealt with in the without prejudice meeting. Depending upon the strengths of the parties' positions, or the concessions they may have made to achieve agreement in a conventional sum, the plaintiff may seek an agreement from the defendants that they will pay the plaintiff interest at the Judgment Act rate upon the conventional damages between the date on which the trial would otherwise have taken place and judgment been given and the date they are actually paid, or on the amount of the damages that is not structured for the same period. Sometimes interest at the Special Account rate may be agreed. The question of interest on costs might also be raised at this stage.

9   THE CONVENTIONAL SUM AGREED:
THE NEXT STEPS

9.1   There are effectively three steps that now need to be taken.
    As a first stage the plaintiff and his advisers must decide how much of the conventional sum should remain *outside* the structure. Generally this amount will reflect past special damage, provision for immediate needs such as housing, vehicle, etc, and a contingency reserve. The balance,

subject to the discount to be paid to the insurers, is available for investment in a structure.

When deciding the amount to be structured and return that can be achieved through a structure, most careful assessment and planning is required. The object of structured compensation is to provide finance for the plaintiff's anticipated requirements in the future. Structured payments can be moulded to take into account anticipated changes in the plaintiff's circumstances, for example as he or she grows older and needs greater income to provide for such items as increased care requirements. Careful regard must be had to the prognoses opined by the medical and other expert witnesses, and it is important that these matters are discussed with the plaintiff, and the plaintiff's views taken into account. A careful balancing exercise is required. At this stage, and before the market has been approached and the return on annuities investigated, the best that will be achieved will be a rough idea of approximately how much should stay outside the structure, and how much will be available to the plaintiff for investment in a structure.

9.2 *The second stage*, assuming that discount has been agreed, is the brokering. Having regard to the probable sum to be invested, and the desired structure of return sought for the plaintiff, a broker will approach the annuity market and obtain quotes. The market fluctuates rapidly and annuity rates change. The broker must have a fairly clear idea of what he is looking for. The plaintiff and his or her advisers must have planned the structure by assessing the plaintiff's needs and life expectancy. They must have dovetailed the annuity or annuities to fit as much as possible the projected needs, they must have considered when deferred or step annuities should commence, should be paid, and at what date and rate annuity payments should commence and increase. The plaintiff's advisers will need to consider which of the annuities should be guaranteed for a minimum term of years (all will of course be guaranteed for life), and if so for how many years, to provide a return to the estate on an early death. There will be a variety of options available from the market, at a variety of prices. They will need to be carefully considered. It may be that the desired structured return will cost somewhat less than the amount thought available for structuring, in which case the balance can go to the contingency reserve. It might be that it will be more expensive than the funds initially thought available, in which case the plaintiff and his or her advisers will have to consider carefully whether or not to reduce the contingency reserve to provide a greater return through the structured annuities, or whether it is more desirable to retain the contingency reserve and take a lower return through the annuities. This stage will involve fairly intense consideration during a short period as annuity quotes usually only remain open for ten days.

Appendix VI shows the schedule of return under annuities in the substantial case of *Everett v Carter* [(1991) PMILL Vol 7 No 8 p 63].

3.9.3   *The third stage* is the Agreement between the plaintiff and the defendants' insurers which must be drafted in accordance with the Model Agreement. It is recommended that advance approval be obtained from the Revenue before the Agreement is signed. If an infant or patient is involved then Court of Protection approval and Judicial approval will also be required, in that order, reference being had to the guidelines of Potter J in *Kelly v Dawes* (Appendix I). Appendix II contains QBD Practice Direction of Master Topley of 12.2.92, and a copy of the Court of Protection (Amendment) Rules 1992 issued 14.8.92. It is also useful to refer to an interesting article by Master McFarlane, Master of the Court of Protection, and Stephen Jacobi at 33 Law Society's Gazette, 18.9.91, pp 15–16.

3.9.4   On signature of the Agreement, the defendants' insurer will immediately pay the purchase price of the annuities to the life company selected. The insurer will have arranged to sign, at the same time, his own agreement to this effect with the life company. The balance of the conventional damages due to the plaintiff will also be paid.

3.9.5   Payments will then commence from the life company to the insurer, and from the insurer to the plaintiff, in accordance with the terms of the Agreements. For example, the Schedule to the Model Agreement will detail the nature of payments from the defendants' insurer to the plaintiff, ie in respect of each annuity the commencement date, the frequency of payment (monthly/quarterly etc), the amount of each payment, the rate of increase, and any guaranteed periods. Appendix VII is the Agreement and Schedule thereto in *Everett v Carter* and Appendix VIII is the text of the final Order in that case.

10   CASE STUDY: *EVERETT V CARTER*

10.1   As mentioned above a plaintiff is not limited to considering purchase of only one annuity. More than one can be purchased, and they can commence at different times in order to provide a structure that is designed to meet the plaintiff's anticipated requirements. In *Everett v Carter* four annuities were purchased and an illustration of the return from these is (as mentioned above at 9.2) included at Appendix VI, reproduced by kind permission of Frenkel Topping.

10.2   The cost of purchasing the annuities, it can been seen, was just under £800,000 of the plaintiff's damages. All four annuities purchased increase at 5% pa compound. The first two annuities are guaranteed for a minimum period of 15 years. Annuities 3 and 4 are only paid whilst the plaintiff remains alive. All annuities are guaranteed throughout the plaintiff's life. All payments are tax-free.

10.3   *Annuity One* has immediate effect, payable monthly, commencing at an annual rate of £25,000.

10.4   *Annuity Two* commences at the start of the seventh year after the Agreement, also payable monthly, and commences at an annual rate of £22,500.

10.5   *Annuity Three* commences payment in year 13, again monthly, starting at an annual rate of £37,500.

10.6   *Annuity Four* is a 'step annuity' which provides for lump sum payments commencing in year three in the sum of £25,000, increasing 5% pa compound, and subsequently payable every fifth year thereafter.

10.7   The return to the plaintiff's life expectancy of 72 years, under the structured payments, would total £9,237,539, plus of course the conventional contingency sum remaining outside the structure.

11   PAYMENTS INTO COURT

11.1   As with payments made under a judgment or order, payments into Court made *and accepted* cannot be structured. If a payment into Court is made the plaintiff must not state his formal acceptance or attempt to take it out of Court. A payment into Court does not preclude structuring provided that it is not accepted.

11.2   If a payment into Court is made it is still open to the plaintiff to invite the defendant to consider structuring. Alternatively the defendant can accompany a payment into Court with a 'without prejudice' offer to structure. In either case leave can be obtained for the defendant to withdraw the funds from Court (note: they must be withdrawn by the defendant not the plaintiff).

12   THE DISCOUNT

12.1   It is normal for defendants' insurers to seek a discount from the plaintiff's damages in consideration for agreeing to deal with a proportion of his damages by way of structured compensation.

12.2   The justification for the discount is that it is intended to compensate the general insurer for his extra internal administration costs of receiving payments under annuity from the life company, and managing the stream of grossed-up payments to the plaintiff. In addition it will compensate him for his loss of cash flow between receipt of the net payment under the annuity, and being able to recoup through the tax credit, and also against the slight risk that trading losses might prevent him from taking full advantage of the tax credits.

12.3   Depending upon the size of the award, 'discount' seems to be settling down at a figure somewhere between 8% and 15% of the sum structured: 10% seems common.

12.4   The amount of discount sought, and the amount ultimately conceded by the plaintiff, will be a matter of negotiation and agreement between the parties. It must be right that it should bear some relation to the likely cost to the general insurer, and most responsible insurers have approached it on this basis. On a few occasions inordinately high discounts have been extracted, appearing to take advantage of a plaintiff with a gun to his head. Most would consider such a practice undesirable, and certainly it is contrary to the spirit in which structured settlements are approached, in which the general insurer is already likely to have made substantial savings by avoiding the trial costs, and through the positive concessions made by the plaintiff's advisers in the without prejudice meeting to agree the conventional sum. It is not appropriate to swing from a mutual approach to settlement to an adversarial approach as and when it suits a particular party. There are inequalities of bargaining strength in structured settlement negotiations as they must presently be conducted. Should abuse of this increase, it is inevitable that so too will the calls for the Courts to be given power to intervene and perhaps order structured compensation at a plaintiff's application, and adjudicate on matters such as discount.

13 INVOLVEMENT OF ACCOUNTANTS

13.1 Advice should be obtained on the Revenue Law and practice involved, to ensure that nothing is done prior to signing the Agreement that might affect the Revenue's position and prejudice the tax-free nature of the payments to the plaintiff, and to ensure that the Agreement itself complies with the Model Agreement which has been approved by the Revenue.

13.2 At present it remains possible to obtain Revenue approval of these Agreements, but the Revenue cannot be expected to provide this facility forever, particularly as the number of structured settlements increases. Most plaintiffs' solicitors do not have specialist in-house departments to advise on these aspects, and generally accountants will be instructed.

13.3 It is sometimes suggested that a single firm can be appointed to deal with the Agreement, advising both sides about the annuities.The proposition can be properly advanced that such a technique may prove to be insufficient from the plaintiff's viewpoint. The plaintiff should, in the author's view, obtain independent advice.

14 COSTS

14.1 Costs will go in the cause, so that the defendants will meet the plaintiff's standard costs of the action. It is arguable, and in practice has been generally accepted, that these normally include the plaintiff's legal costs and disbursements involved in dealing with the structure. The disbursements extend to the reasonable cost of obtaining reasonable independent advice from accountants. This is in accordance with the general principles of entitlement to costs embodied in RSC Ord 62, r 3. These costs are likely to be but a small fraction of the amount of costs saved through avoiding trial.

14.2   It will be a matter for negotiation in the circumstances of the case, as is the discount. These costs may be linked with the discount negotiations.

15   COMMISSION

15.1   A commission is paid by the life company with whom the business is placed, and at present this is usually a one-off payment to the broker of 3% of the amount invested to purchase the annuities. The question of who takes the commission is bound to come into the equation at some stage. If the broker is instructed by the general insurer, and the general insurer seeks to share the commission with the broker or to pay the broker a flat rate and take the commission, then the plaintiff may argue, with some justification, that there should be some reflection of this additional benefit to the general insurer in the discount sought.

15.2   The converse situation may apply where the plaintiff's representative brokes the annuities, and the commission reverts to the plaintiff.

4 Defendants' Perspectives

Tim Wallis

1 INTRODUCTION

1.1 Benefits and costs to defendants. This chapter concentrates on the benefits and costs which structured settlements have for defendants and their insurers. Such benefits and costs are examined in the context of the key objective of most defendants and insurers: how to dispose of the defendant's liability at the lowest overall cost.

1.2 Practical aspects are then discussed. The individual steps required to arrange a structured settlement are examined, and the role of advisers is discussed. In particular, defendants and their insurance/indemnity arrangements give rise to certain problems, and these will be examined together with the question of the security of structured settlements.

1.3 The wider implications for adversarial litigation are also considered. *Kelly v Dawes* ((1990) Times, 27 September) began the first wave of structured settlements. *Beck v Plasticisers Ltd (Readicut International plc)* (The Personal and Medical Injuries Law Letter vol 8 no 6, 1992) might be regarded as beginning a new wave of co-operative and less adversarial litigation, of which structured settlements form only a part.

1.4 Particular defendants and their insurance/indemnity arrangements give rise to certain problems, and these will be examined separately.

2 THE BENEFITS OF STRUCTURED SETTLEMENTS FOR DEFENDANTS AND INSURERS

2.1 Lower capital cost. The previous chapters make it clear that the capital cost of a structured settlement is less than a conventional settlement. The very essence of a successful structure is that the plaintiff receives a better deal compared with a conventional award, and the insurers pay less. The difference between the value of a conventional award and the cost of a structure is often referred to as the insurer's discount.

2.2   The insurer's discount is flexible. The size of the discount is entirely a matter of negotiation. The table at paragraph 2.25 of illustrates the diversity of the discounts obtained in a number of cases; all of these discounts are of substantial sums. As a proportion of the total value of the case they can vary to take into account, for example, the plaintiff's prospective tax saving and the insurer's administrative costs (which will be increased in a case where there is a long life expectancy). The insurer is in a strong bargaining position here for two reasons. Firstly, the justification for the discount is undeniable: the tax saving and the insurer's administration costs can be clearly demonstrated. Secondly, because a court cannot impose a structure (*Burke v Tower Hamlets Health Authority*, (1990) Times, 10 August) it is open to an insurer to calculate the discount required and offer a structure based on that discount on a 'take it or leave it' basis. If the plaintiff finds the discount unacceptably high his only option is to proceed to court for a conventional award. (Of course, this cuts both ways, and if an insurer seeks to abuse this bargaining position the prospect of a mutually beneficial settlement may be lost.)

2.3   A less adversarial approach is a necessary feature of a structured settlement. One cannot snarl at one's opponent from an entrenched position behind a barricade, and at the same time exercise the degree of co-operation required to achieve a structure. In all probability, a less adversarial approach will result in speedier settlements and reduced costs. This aspect is explored further below.

2.4   Bridging the gap. Whether the gap between the parties is one which relates to liability, quantum or both, a structured settlement can be used to resolve the parties' differences. Insurers are of course familiar with the concept of bridging a gap on contributory negligence by putting arguments about deductions and percentages to one side and getting down to the 'nitty gritty' of the figures, thereby settling the claim. The scope to use structured settlements in this way is very significant.

2.5   Avoiding the sympathy finding. This is a more esoteric but nevertheless real benefit of using a structure to settle. Most insurance claims managers and defendants' lawyers would take the view that in a case involving a disputed life expectancy there is a risk that the trial judge will err towards the side of the badly disabled plaintiff. A structured settlement, centred on the annuity concept, removes that risk.

2.6   Impaired life annuities cost less. With further reference to the annuity concept, a special benefit of using a structure in a case of a plaintiff with an impaired life is that the life office providing the annuity takes the impaired life into account, and the annuity thus costs less than for a person of normal health of the same age.

2.7   Fiscally neutral. For a general insurer structured settlements are neutral so far as taxation is concerned.

2.8   Insurers' and defendants' public image. Undoubtedly the insurer that is seen to provide a badly injured plaintiff with a package providing care and income for the rest of his life will enjoy a higher public regard than the one who adopts an adversarial stance and fights the case to trial. Conversely, the plaintiff's adviser who rejects the structure because of the size of the discount puts his client at peril of being under-funded in later life. Unnecessary aggression by one party can readily undermine a willingness in the other to negotiate.

2.9   Public policy. An oft-quoted Canadian Study (which will it is to be hoped be updated by more recent research by the Law Commission) found that the vast majority of successful plaintiffs dissipated lump sum settlement/awards within a few years of settlement, then to become reliant on the state for support. Thus, to settle on a structured basis may perhaps be in keeping with public policy and some may perceive this to be of some benefit to insurers.

2.10   Settlement moneys remaining within the insurance industry would be regarded by most insurers to be a benefit, if only of a general nature. This benefit is put in sharper focus when it is appreciated that the life company providing the annuity (or annuities) may be a member of the same group of companies as the general insurer, provided it is a separate legal entity.

3   THE COSTS OF STRUCTURED SETTLEMENTS FOR DEFENDANTS AND INSURERS

3.1   Cash flow. It is clear from previous chapters that a structured settlement involves:

(a)   a contract between a life office and the general insurer (the annuity contract) and
(b)   a contract between the general insurer and the plaintiff (the structure contract).

The life office is obliged (Income and Corporation Taxes Act 1988, s 338) to make the payments pursuant to the annuity contract net of tax. The general insurer, however, is obliged by the structure contract to make the payments to the plaintiff without deduction (the tax-free income) and thus has to add the tax back on. The amount added on is reclaimed from the Revenue in due course, usually by deduction from corporation tax, but meanwhile the general insurer has to fund the difference and consequently loses investment income.

3.2   Administering the fund is an extra task for the insurer in every structured settlement, and this is in distinct contrast to the neat finality of a conventional lump sum payment. A structure for an infant plaintiff might be 'on the books' for decades.

3.3   Professional and intermediary fees are another extra. Solicitors and counsel may expend a considerable amount of time in putting a structure together and of course there is no guarantee at the outset that a structure will be successfully negotiated. The question of which party bears the costs, and the payment of intermediaries, will be discussed below.

3.4   Irresponsible media reporting may inflate damages. Sensational press reporting and structured settlements have, regrettably, gone hand in hand. In the recent past a £1 million settlement was a novelty. Now the popular press are reporting '£100 million damages for a girl paralysed by hospital blunder', which perhaps gives the impression of an immediate payment of this sum rather than a lump sum in the region of £$\frac{1}{2}$ million and index-linked annuity payments for the life of the 6-year-old plaintiff. The fear is that such reporting will excite public expectations, assist those already lobbying in this direction, and thus lead to an overall increase in damages.

3.5   Problems associated with reinsurance. Some general insurers reinsure part of their risk with a reinsurer. Where this has happened a problem may arise, and although this problem cannot be described as a cost of a structured settlements it is perceived by some to be a barrier to using structures. The problem is that if a structure is used many of the costs described above are borne by the general insurer, the savings achieved by the structure are enjoyed by the reinsurer, but some reinsurers are proving reluctant to make a contribution to the costs.

4   BENEFITS VERSUS COSTS

4.1   On which side do the scales come down? This is a question for each reader. Before considering the question, however, bear in mind that most people are inherently conservative when it comes to change. Most insurers, solicitors and barristers demonstrate this conservatism, notwithstanding the current pace of change in the personal injury field. They are, nevertheless, reasonably swift to adapt to change when it becomes inevitable. Consider the Civil Justice Review, the initial resistance to some of its recommendations from many quarters, and the way in which reforms (such as earlier disclosure of medical reports and special damages schedules) are now accepted and regarded as beneficial.

4.2   It is easy to make the evidence fit a given point of view. Beware of preconceived notions. Many lawyers and insurers appear to have fixed views on the merits of structured settlements and their relative benefits and costs, and it is not always clear whether such views are based on evidence or research. For example the cash-flow problem and the costs of administration are usually mentioned by those who express themselves to be 'not keen' about structured settlements. Proponents of this form of settlement, on the other hand, will argue that such problems and costs are more than taken care of by the insurer's discount. Neither those in favour (who tend to have been involved in one or more structures) or those against (who tend not to have had any involvement) make it clear that they have actually carried out any costings. The costs of professional advisers and intermediaries in another area where there are arguments, readily to hand, in favour of structures and against. Those in favour may argue that even if substantial additional costs are incurred in achieving a structured settlement, the overall cost of the settlement is likely to be lower than it would otherwise have been because if a structure is used:

a)   the settlement is likely to take place earlier; and
b)   it may not be necessary to devote energy and resources to an adversarial fight.

On the other hand it can be argued that attempting to structure a settlement is to risk incurring considerable extra costs in what may be an abortive settlement attempt, and that risk is better avoided.

4.3 Conclusion: show cause why a structure should not be explored
This, it is submitted, should be the approach in every case where the potential value (£150,000/£200,000) is such that it might be appropriate to structure. The lawyers do not really have a choice: it has frequently been stated (and not only by intermediaries) that failure to give consideration to a structure may amount to negligence. So far as defendants and insurers are concerned, the fact that some insurers have successfully achieved structured settlements on several cases and are continuing to work to that end on other cases makes it imperative that the questions about possible routes to settlement are at least asked. It is suggested that it is important for defendants and insurers to consider a possible structure at two levels.

(a) *The narrow level*
      That is to say, a view of the tangible costs and benefits of a structure in the particular case. It is only logical to carry out some form of costings, even if on a rudimentary basis.

(b) *The broader level*
      By this is meant a value judgement, taking into account the tangible and intangible costs and benefits, about whether a structure is likely to achieve a settlement at a lower overall cost. It is difficult, on this broader level, to carry out any form of meaningful costings, but there is no reason why most insurers could not (and no doubt some already have) monitor the overall cost of several structured settlements and then compare these with the cost of cases previously dealt with on

a conventional basis. (The extra cost of the learning curve would have to be taken into account in such an exercise.) In a case involving reinsurers the evaluation exercise carried out above should be carried out by the reinsurer as well as the general insurer with a view to an agreement between them as to an appropriate sharing of the costs and benefits. The current view, certainly among defendants and insurers who have carried out several structured settlements, is that on the narrower level such settlements have given them a financial benefit, albeit marginal in some cases, and that on a broader level there is an undoubted benefit of significant value. At the present time it seems that structured settlements have already grown out of the pioneering phase of development. With education, and with commitment from lawyers and insurers, they will in all probability shortly become routine.

5   TASK ANALYSIS – WHO DOES WHAT?

5.1   Overlap of functions. In considering the respective roles of defendants/insurers and their professional advisers in connection with structured settlements it should be remembered that these roles vary considerably in cases which are conventionally handled. In a normal personal injury claim, insurance Company A might do virtually all of the work in-house, instruct solicitors only where absolutely necessary to deal with Court procedure and appoint counsel only if the case proceeds to trial in a case where the solicitor does not have a right of audience. At the other extreme insurance Company B might instruct solicitors as soon as the claim is made, take a passive role throughout and instruct forensic accountants to advise extensively on matters relating to quantum. In just the same way there are no hard and fast rules as to who does what in achieving a structured settlement. This section will set out the tasks involved and discuss the role of the advisers.

5.2   He who pays the piper calls the tune. The compensator, be that the defendant or its insurer, ultimately bears the damages and costs. As such the argument can properly be advanced that he has the right to dictate how the case is handled.

5.3   The tasks required to reach a structured settlement

5.3.1   *Preparing to structure*

(a)   *The initial initiative* may come from either party or its representatives and may lead to an agreement in principle to explore the possibilities of a structure or a decision not to.

(b)   *Expert evidence* is then required. The advisers to both parties will need medical and other expert evidence in the usual way.

(c)   *Evaluation of the conventional value and assessment of the plaintiff's needs.* If a structure is envisaged the parties nevertheless need to evaluate quantum in the conventional way, the conventional valuation forming the bench mark against which to test the proposed structure. The same evidence is used to ascertain the financial valuation of the plaintiff's needs upon which the structure is to be based. This task is particularly important bearing in mind that once a structured settlement is made it cannot be varied.

(d)   *Obtaining quotations for the annuity/annuities.* Having ascertained the plaintiff's financial needs the medical evidence and appropriate financial information is submitted to life offices to obtain quotations for the annuity or annuities required. It is important to note that quotations are only good for a certain period (approximately ten days) and this means that all involved have to move at great speed.

5.3.2   *Making the structured settlement agreement (and obtaining Court approval where required)*

(a)   The following are extracts from the Practice Note of the Senior Queen's Bench Master dated 12 February 1992 [see Appendix II] which set out the classes of documents to be lodged with the Court in the case of a settlement where approval of the Court is required. The Practice Note also serves as a useful guide in cases not requiring approval.

(b)   *Counsel's opinion.* 'An opinion of Counsel assessing the value of the claim on a conventional basis (unless approval has already been given) and, if practicable, the opinion of Counsel on the structured settlement proposed;'

(c)   *Draft structure agreement/Inland Revenue approval.* 'A draft of the proposed agreement as approved by the Inland Revenue (and by the

Treasury where the Defendant or the paying party is a Health Authority)'. The Practice Note makes Inland Revenue approval essential in the case of a plaintiff under a disability. In routine cases it will probably suffice to have expert advice to ensure that the model agreement has been adhered to. In practical terms the Revenue are taking a considerable length of time to deal with requests for approval.

(d) *Court of Protection approval.* 'In cases where the plaintiff is under mental disability the consent of the Court of Protection.' The Practice Note gives further details regarding the practicalities of obtaining consent.

(e) *Details of other resources.* 'Sufficient material to satisfy the Court that enough capital is available free of the structure to meet anticipated future capital needs. Particular reference to accommodation and transport needs will usually be helpful in this context'.

(f) *Security.* 'Sufficient material to satisfy the Court that the structure is secure and backed by responsible insurers'.

This issue is discussed separately below.

5.3.3   *Implementing the structure*

(a) *Completing the model agreement.* Parties must either follow the model agreement or exercise great care to ensure that any amendment does not have the consequence of losing the tax advantages.

(b) *Payment of lump sum.* As a rule only part of the settlement will be structured and the agreed lump sum will have to be paid over in accordance with the term of the order.

(c) *Purchase of annuity.* The defendant or general insurer purchases the annuity or annuities from the life office, in accordance with the time scale laid down by the adopted quotation.

(d) *Taxation/payment arrangements.* The general insurer makes the necessary arrangements to receive the annuity instalments net of tax from a life office, gross up those payments to allow for tax, pay the gross instalments to the plaintiff and recover the tax paid.

(e) *Administration of the fund.* The defendant or insurer makes the other necessary arrangements to administer the fund until the conclusion of the settlement.

5.4   Delegation by the defendant/insurer of the above tasks and the role of advisers. Having analysed the above tasks the defendant or insurer will be in a position to instruct advisers and delegate the tasks. The advisers instructed may include an 'intermediary', by which is meant a person, firm or company which has expertise and experience in the field of structured settlements. Other considerations include:

— the in-house expertise and resources of the defendant/insurer
— the expertise and cost effectiveness of solicitors, barristers and other experts known to it.

Tasks(a) – (c) under para 5.3.1 above will no doubt be dealt with in the way in which the defendant or insurers deals with any other personal injury claim. The extremes have been stated above, but the usual procedure in substantial personal injury claim will involve case control by the defendant or its insurer and a team of experts including a solicitor, barrister and medical and possible other experts.

Moving on to task (d) under 5.3.1 and most of the tasks in 5.3.2 most defendants will need to seek expert assistance. In many cases to date, many or all of these tasks have been carried out by an intermediary, and in some cases the intermediary has acted for both sides. It may be that the wholesale delegation of these tasks to an intermediary will not continue in the future in the same way as it has in the past. There are several reasons for this. Firstly, given the number of structured settlements reported, the pool of expertise is now far greater than in the pioneering days of *Kelly v Dawes*. There are already a handful of solicitors who, if acting for defendants or insurers with some experience, would need little or no assistance from either an intermediary or counsel. Secondly, the role of the intermediary acting for both sides has been questioned in the context of the need for each party to receive independent advice (see 'Guidance from the Law Society on Structured Settlements – Practical and Ethical Considerations', The Law Society's Gazette, 28 October 1992, reproduced in Appendix IV, and The Law Commission's consultation paper no 125 'Strucutred Settlements and Interim and Provisional Damages', published in November 1992). Thirdly, there may be a change in the way in which intermediaries are paid. At the present time some intermediaries work on a contingency basis and, if the structure proceeds, are paid a commission on the annuity purchased. On the face of it this is attractive, particularly the contingency element. There may, however, be a move to paying intermediaries on a fee basis rather than a commission basis for the following reasons:

(a) Payment of professional advisers in personal injury cases is traditionally on a fee basis.

(b) The commission is paid from the fund to be used to purchase the annuity, and thus the commission eats into the structure and reduces that payments under the annuity.

The question here appears to be whether the overall cost to the insurer of advice on a fee basis will be less than the cost of advice on a commission basis. On the basis of 'he who pays the piper . . .', that is a question for insurers to answer .

5.5 Professional costs generally. As mentioned above structured settlements do involve additional advisers costs, whether or not an intermediary is used, over and above the costs of a conventional settlement. Where do those costs fall?

(a) **Negotiation.** It is axiomatic that all of the terms of any settlement voluntarily agreed between two parties are negotiable. If an intermediary is instructed on the contingency and commission basis, part of the extra costs may not be immediately apparent in the sense that neither party receives a fee invoice. (As mentioned above the commission in effect comes out of the structure.) If each side obtains independent advice, fee notes or invoices will follow and the question arises as to who pays. It is understood that in some cases which have been structured it has been agreed that although the defendant will pay the plaintiff his usual costs in the usual way the costs directly referable to the structure will be borne by the plaintiff. The argument is that, notwithstanding any discount, the plaintiff is receiving a considerable benefit from the structure and can afford to pay the additional fees.

(b) **Taxation of costs.** If no agreement was reached regarding the plaintiff's additional costs the question would be determined pursuant to the usual rules on costs by a taxing master or district judge. The rules of the Supreme Court provide that the winning party shall be allowed a reasonable amount in respect of all costs reasonably incurred, and any doubts which the taxing officer may have as to whether the costs were reasonably incurred or were reasonable in amount shall be resolved in favour of the paying party (Order 62, r 12, standard basis taxation). To date there are no reports of the question of the costs of the structure having been addressed on a taxation of costs.

6   PARTICULAR DEFENDANTS

6.1   Mutual insurance companies are not liable for corporation tax on trading profits. They are not, therefore, able to recover the tax which a life office would deduct prior to paying instalments pursuant to an annuity contract. The net effect is, quite simply, that it makes no financial sense for a mutual to offer a structured settlement. One way round this problem was found in a recent case, in which a mutual insurance company insured a defendant local authority. The structured settlement agreement was made between the plaintiff and the local authority direct (instead of between the plaintiff and the insurer). One of the snags with this route is that the model agreement cannot be used and so it is necessary to seek (and wait for) the specific approval of the inland revenue.

6.2   Health Authorities and National Health Service Trusts are usually self-insured, and are tax-exempt (NHS and Community Care Act 1990, s 61). Health Authorities are reported as having used structured settlements on a number of occasion, the first case being *Field v Herefordshire Health Authority* ((1991) Personal and Medical Injuries Law Letter, vol 7, no 9) (see Chapter 2, para 13). Health Authorities can fund a structure:

(a)   by the purchase of an annuity in the usual way, or
(b)   by self financing, and paying the periodic payments out of revenue.

Both methods give rise to problems. The purchase of an annuity has to be approved by the Department of Health and the Treasury. This is cumbersome and time-consuming, and some may feel prohibitively so. With self-financing the long-term administration of the fund is seen as a problem with Health Authorities, particularly against the background of constant change in the health service. So far as NHS Trusts are concerned, there is a question as to whether the budget of any particular trust is of sufficient size to deal with a large claim in this way. It is understood that the NHS management executive are exploring the concept of structures in greater depth. Further, it has recently been reported that the Department of Health is looking into the possibility of the Secretary of State for Health guaranteeing self-funded structured settlement payments by Health Authorities. Such a guarantee should remove any fears which plaintiffs may have about a structured settlement agreement with a Health Authority.

6.3 Medical defence organisations are mutuals and, following the introduction of Crown Indemnity, are no longer as heavily involved in litigation as hitherto. The current wisdom appears to be that they are unlikely to use structures.

7 SECURITY

7.1 The key question. The plaintiff needs to be assured that if he accepts a structured settlement the arrangement will be secure. Indeed, in a case requiring Court approval the Practice Note of 12 February 1992 (referred to above and reproduced in Appendix II) provides that the parties should lodge with the Court sufficient material to satisfy the Court that the structure is secure and backed by responsible insurers. In addressing this issue questions have often been asked about the security of the life office. It is submitted, however, that the key question is the security of the party with whom the plaintiff makes the structured settlement agreement. That party is usually the general insurers. It is that party which has the obligation to make the payments. The annuity merely provides the general insurer with the income stream to comply with the structured settlement agreement. Thus, if the life office becomes insolvent the general insurer remains under an obligation to make the payments pursuant to the structured settlement agreement. In most cases, therefore, it will be a matter of satisfying the plaintiff's advisers that the plaintiff's agreement will be with an insurer that is financially sound. Nothing in life is without risk, and it is fair for the insurance industry to argue that its track record proves that an investment placed with it is as safe as it would be with most financial institutions.

7.2 Policyholders Protection Act 1975. Section 10 of the Act provides substantial protection in the event of the failure of the life office.

More relevant, in the context of the key question above, is s 7. The
Policyholders Protection Board has indicated that in the event of a failure
of a general insurer the sums owed by that insurer to a plaintiff pursuant
to s 151 of the Road Traffic Act 1988, and pursuant to a structured
settlement conforming to the ABI model agreement, would be expected
to qualify for protection under s 7 provided that:

(a) all applicable eligibility criteria were met, and
(b) the settlement was contained in a consent order in the usual
way.

This interpretation by the Policyholders Protection Board is based on the
hypothesis that a consent order qualifies as a judgment for the purposes
of of the Road Traffic Act 1988 s 151.

7.3 Lloyd's Syndicates. It is understood that prior to the settlement in
Kelly v Dawes ((1990) Times, 27 September) (see Chapter 2, para 5) a
concern was expressed about security on the grounds that the defendant
was a Lloyd's Syndicate. What would happen to the structured settlement
if the names comprising the Syndicate agreed to bring the Syndicate to
an end? The answer, which apparently satisfied the plaintiff and the
Court, was for Lloyd's Central Funds to confirm that a cessation of the
Syndicate would be covered by the normal transfer of liability to the next
Syndicate but ultimately, if necessary, Lloyd's Central Fund would meet
any valid claim.

8 NEW ENVIRONMENT

8.1 Are structured settlements a one-day wonder? NO, it is submitted
is the emphatic answer to that question. In this section it will be
demonstrated that there are powerful arguments to support the proposition
that the development of structured settlements is merely one of many
changes taking place in the landscape of litigation. There is dissatisfaction
with the present system, particularly its delays and costs, and that has
become a force for change the pace of which will probably not decrease
for some time. The full picture begins to emerge only when structured
settlements are looked at alongside other developments such as Alternative
Dispute Resolution, the Civil Justice Review, other changes concerning

the conventional lump sum and rehabilitation. These developments are explored below.

8.2   A truly remarkable case. The first wave of structured settlements tended to concern cases which had been running for some time (although the parties and their advisers in the trail-blazing *Kelly v Dawes* were hardly slothful between the road traffic accident on 5 July 1986 and the Court approval of the structure on 14 July 1989). Further up the learning curve it has become clear that the earlier a structure is contemplated and discussed the greater the benefits to both parties. The case referred to above as remarkable, and referred to at the beginning of this chapter as probably beginning a new wave of co-operative litigation, is *Beck v Plasticisers Ltd (Readicut International plc)* (The Personal and Medical Injuries Law Letter, vol 8, no 6, 1992).

The facts: On 7 May 1990 the plaintiff, 42, suffered an industrial accident and was consequently confined to a wheelchair as a paraplegic. *Eighteen months* later the conventional value of the claim was agreed at £517,500, a discount was agreed and a structured settlement was achieved.

Many of us who deal with personal injury claims are probably still dealing with pre-May 1990 claims. It is not, however, only the time span from accident to settlement that is remarkable. The following is an extract from the report in The Personal and Medical Injuries Law Letter:

> 'At an early stage the defendants' insurers, the Eagle Star Group, and solicitors Messrs Hammond Suddards approached the plaintiff's solicitors Messrs Morrish & Co with the unusual suggestion that counsel and expert witnesses should be instructed on a joint basis, thereby avoiding the usual adversarial elements in litigation of this type and with the intention of ensuring that a settlement occurred within approximately 18 months of the date of the accident.'

Perhaps this is food for thought when considering whether there are wider benefits to structured settlements and whether or not such settlements are part of developments on a wider scale.

8.3   ADR. The following definition is given in ADR Route Map published by the Centre for Dispute Resolutions:

> '"ADR". The letters stand for "Alternative Dispute Resolution", a new approach that can improve the efficiency and effectiveness of

business and public disputes, negotiation or litigation. Initiated in the United States some ten years ago in response to the problems of litigation, ADR has proved a powerful force for business-like solutions to disputes across the international and legal world. Despite its name, ADR can be used in addition to or along side litigation proceedings as well as an alternative.'

By its very nature ADR is non-adversarial or at least less adversarial than litigation. It is used 'to make settlement negotiations more powerful, more creative and more efficient and to provide a realistic and commercially oriented alternative/ additional technique to arbitration or litigation' (ADR Route Map). In the context of structured settlements the proponents of ADR would say that its particular features include:

— lower costs than litigation
— quicker resolution than litigation
— the maintenance and preservation of a relationship between the parties, eg by concentrating on interests rather than positions, and by constructive negotiations rather than adversarial battles
— a search for a 'win/win' result of the type amply demonstrated by most structured settlements
— flexible procedure.

ADR may have considerable scope for the resolution of personal injury claims. It is not mentioned here for that reason but:

(a) to demonstrate that it is one of the developments arising as a result of dissatisfaction in the system of litigation in its present form, and
(b) to stress the move away from the adversarial approach.

Structured settlements are an imaginative conclusion to a problem-solving exercise. They did not arise as a result of ADR, but they might have done so.

8.4   Civil Justice Review. To some, litigation is all about the great battle of the trial following numerous interlocutory skirmishes, and to others it is about narrowing issues and ensuring the focus is on disposing of the claim at the lowest overall cost. The CJR supported the latter approach with its general emphasis on 'cards on the table' and openness in litigation.

Take the following reforms which have arisen from the CJR:

— more particularity in pleadings
— exchange of witness statements
— early disclosure of medical report and schedule of special damages
  with the plaintiff's pleading
— greater use of interrogatories, and notices to admit facts.

These moves are part of the changing face of litigation. They are not of themselves sufficiently important or powerful to lead immediately to greater co-operation between the parties or to lead to structured settlements, but they do represent a change in atmosphere. Further the overall effect of these procedural reforms is that more work is done early in the case, on paper, and there is less emphasis on trial itself. Once again the adversarial approach is weakened.

One thing about structured settlements is quite clear, and that is that such settlements cannot be reached without a high degree of openness and co-operation. The approach required for structured settlements and the approach required to follow the reforms are similar and are mutually self supporting.

8.5   Changes to the conventional lump sum. It is not necessary to hark too far back to find the days when the single lump sum was the only method of providing for the tortfeasor to compensate the victim. The deficiencies of this method are obvious: an estimate of, say, future nursing care will almost always prove to be wrong, in hindsight, thus leaving the plaintiff over-compensated or still in need of care after the money has run out. Many concerns about the lump sum approach are expressed by The Law Commission in its consultation paper no 125 'Structured Settlements and Interim and Provisional Damages' published in November 1992. The way in which structured settlements solve many of the problems created by the lump sum approach, in a totally equitable manner, is a major contribution to society; if that is an overstatement it is only marginally so. In *Heeley v Britton* (1990, QBD, unreported, Chapter 2, para 9) Rougier J referred to structured settlements as being an ' infinitely less hit and miss basis' on which to deal with damages.

8.6   Interim payments. Structured settlements, however, are not the only way in which the lump sum method of compensation has been varied by a more sophisticated approach. Interim payments are now an established tool of case management and, as will be seen below, can be used as part of the rehabilitation programme. An interim payment can be used (providing the liability situation is appropriate) to assist in establishing the plaintiff's trust and co-operation and demonstrating that the defendant or insurer is not going to fight 'tooth and nail' to trial. If, however, the ultimate intention is to structure, care must be taken not to pay so much by way of interim payments that the balance is insufficient to make a structure worthwhile.

8.7   Provisional damages. Another area where the lump sum method has been modified, this time by statute, is provisional damages. The Court can award provisional damages if it can be shown that there is a chance that at some time in the future the plaintiff will develop some serious disease or suffer some serious deterioration in his physical or mental condition. (Supreme Court Act 1981, s 32A.)

8.8   An American perspective. The development of structured settlements can be seen as part of an ever increasing move to improve on the methods by which damages may be provided. The pattern in North America has been one of increasing sophistication. It is highly probable that this pattern will be followed here, and perhaps an early indication of that is to be seen from the case of *W.B.* where a conventional award of £85,000 was structured to provide residential nursing home fees for a 78-year-old plaintiff (see Chapter 2, para 25).

Another development in North America concerns the way in which structured settlements are put together. Rather than evaluate quantum on a conventional basis, agree a discount and then structure ('top down') it is becoming more commonplace to ascertain the plaintiff's needs and then move straight to a structure ('bottom up'). Taking the analogy of learning a foreign language, perhaps this is similar to moving from translating every word to thinking in the foreign language.

8.9   Rehabilitation. In recent times insurers have increasingly been involved in rehabilitation. This development has been in parallel with the growth in the use of structured settlements.

What is rehabilitation? It was defined in the Mair Report ('Medical Rehabilitation: the pattern for the future', Scottish Home Health Department, HMSO 1972) as follows:

'Rehabilitation is not simply treatment by physical therapy. It is a process which involves a whole panoply of services for clinical management of disability and handicap.'

For several years the Association of British Insurers has been sponsoring research into rehabilitation at Edinburgh University. It is likely that the results of this research will be taken into account by the Law Commission in its review of damages. Some insurers are already pushing on down the rehabilitation road. Frank Copley, manager, General Accident, stated in a lecture on this subject:

'I think it is right to say that in the UK Insurance Market there has been a gradual acceptance that rehabilitation advice and treatment rendered at the right time can help the injured party, if not to recover his full faculties, at least to enjoy a better quality of life than if no treatment at all is given. In some instances that enables the plaintiff to get back to some wage or fee earning work and lead an independent life. At worse it relieves his physical and mental pain and enables him to enjoy a better quality of life.'

Other common law jurisdictions are well advanced in this field. The insurance industry in Canada have proposed guidelines for rehabilitation of motor accident claimants in conjunction with a no-fault compensation scheme. These guidelines provide for injured people to receive the maximum care in the shortest time. Bob Gunn, President of Royal Insurance Canada, is quoted in Canadian Insurance/Agent and Broker, July 1992, as follows:

'. . . initiation of the rehab. process as quickly as possible is to the advantage of both parties involved, claimant and company. It creates a positive attitude and quicker recovery for claimants, and it leads to lower costs for the company.'

Gunn goes on to explain that one of the implications of this initiative is the need to move away from the traditional and largely adversarial claims handling system. The techniques used involved telephone or more direct contact with the claimant (or a relative, if necessary) within 72 hours of the accident.

Is any of this relevant to structured settlements? Yes:

— a seriously injured plaintiff is likely to be a candidate for rehabilitation and a structured settlement;
— both rehabilitation and structured settlements require a proactive and non-adversarial approach (per Gunn: 'The earlier after an injury we take a proactive approach, the less that case costs us');
— working out a rehabilitation plan and ascertaining the plaintiff's present and future needs for a structured settlement go hand in hand;
— the rehabilitation package can be funded by interim payments, and this will be very much in the interests of the defendant/insurer in a case where rehabilitation may reduce the overall value of the claim *and* bring forward the time when the plaintiff's condition has stabilised, and thus the time when it is possible to conclude the case by a structured settlement.

8.10   The challenge. The new environment offers a challenge to every one dealing with personal injury claims. Pioneering work has been done by the Association of British Insurers, by individual insurance companies and by some lawyers and specialist intermediaries. Will others take up the challenge? If so will they merely trail in the wake of their opposite numbers in North America?

5 A View from the Exchequer

Neil C Harris

1 INTRODUCTION

1.1 Breaking the mould. PLAINTIFF'S BARRISTER: 'Will you structure this settlement?'
DEFENDANT INSURER: 'I am sorry, my Company doesn't do structures.'
PLAINTIFF'S BARRISTER: 'Yes it does . . . it did one for me last week!'
This exchange ushered-in one Company's second structured settlement. More insurance personal injury (PI) structured settlements, several headline-making, have been concluded since the first Court-approved case (*Kelly*) in 1989. Structured settlements are here to stay. Against this background, defendant insurers need to become masters of structuring personal injury claims.

1.1 Feeling the way. Yet this cameo of development in the law remains apposite. Most senior, experienced, insurance claims practitioners have still to conclude their first structured settlement. Structured settlements have been a plaintiff's end-game, not the defendant's opening gambit. The rules diminish options rather than encourage enterprise . . . the techniques are as yet unsophisticated, the skills unpolished . . . the way ahead beckons, mistily.

1.3 Providing for needs. Structures are a relatively new and, as yet, underexploited option to achieve a satisfactory claim settlement. The legal basis for such settlements is not specifically established. Structures move the basis of compensation towards 'provision for future need'. Further developments in the law may be expected. Extension of demand for, usage of and scope of structured settlements may influence such developments. This view of compensation, geared specifically towards provision for future care and quality of life, dovetails naturally with rehabilitative assessment and treatment at a very early stage.

1.4 The challenge. The aim of the defendant insurer will be to dispose of the insured's liability at the lowest overall cost. Given liability under the policy, the insurer will investigate and evaluate both the defendant's liability and the quantum of the plaintiff's claim. The insurer will defend—through the Pleadings, Interrogatories and Exchange—and will negotiate to the ultimate deadline of trial, in order to agree a settlement which is acceptable to him, bearing in mind the further costs and risks of failure to agree. This process is well practised and understood, but it is widely regarded as unsatisfactory and uncertain because:

- settlement can take years to achieve;
- valuations increase over time;
- costs on both sides assume substantial proportions;
- defendants feel 'ripped off', plaintiffs fear the future and inflation; and
- important early initiatives on rehabilitation and occupational therapy are neglected.

Is there a better way—a way of unjamming the settlement process and of delivering a better result?

1.5   Claims handling strategy. My approach to PI claims handling— my overall strategy—is governed by four key factors:

(a)   escalating levels of damages awards;
(b)   the costs of settlement, incurred by both sides;
(c)   the time taken to settle; and
(d)   the problems of achieving the 'best' compensation.

See figure 5A.

1.6   Escalation in damages. Plaintiffs' solicitors regularly argue that damages awards provide inadequate compensation and do not keep pace with victims' needs in a changing world. Defendants do not see it this way. Special damages in particular have escalated faster than inflation. For example, one study tracked 14% inflation in levels of settlements of major claims (£100,000—£500,000) between 1991 and 1992, at a time when annual inflation of retail prices was running at less than 4% (of pay—less than 6%). Schedules of special damages have become increasingly sophisticated. The leading plaintiffs' solicitors particularise and exploit every conceivable loss or expense. Currently the husband who mowed the lawn and fitted the shelves is awarded more than the father who walked the dog and read bedtime stories to the kids—but not for long, one suspects. This demands of defendant solicitors far greater planning, initiative and expertise than the conventional, reactive 'attack on the Schedule'. Defendants must explore all the options for compensation, including rehabilitation, alternative employment and

FIGURE 5A

INSURER'S CLAIMS STRATEGY
PERSONAL INJURY CLAIMS

Objective:

Lowest economic cost of settlement, commensurate with meeting
(i) full policy entitlement of insured
(ii) reasonable compensation at law for victim's needs consequent upon injury/loss

Approach:

Active, positive, focused claim plan and control
• 'day one' initiatives
• plan to settlement

Innovative, personalised case approach
• mitigation & compensation
• realism & commitment

Specialised handling
• skilled investigators/negotiators
• select advisers

Tight control of costs
• minimum buy-in/early settlement
• clear terms of reference
• hands-on management of solicitors

THE INSURER PAYS, SO HE SHOULD CALL THE SHOTS

structured settlements. They must be skilled in analysing and challenging the Schedule, the individual Heads of Claim and the claim 'in the round'. A positive, pragmatic focus on defining, minimising and meeting legitimate needs—including, but not exclusively through, lump sum damages—is essential if defendant insurers are to regain the initiative.

1.7 Costs. The Civil Justice Review drew attention to the costs of contested actions. In particular, for every £1 recovered by way of damages in the High Court, the total costs of plaintiff and defendant amounted to £0.50 outside London and £0.71 at the Royal Courts of Justice. It further commented that:

(a) a substantial proportion of costs related to 'preparation for trial';
(b) whilst the primary aim is pursuit of high quality justice, another aim is to limit the incidence of delay and cost to the parties;
(c) the PI litigation process should be opened up and accelerated; and
(d) it should be possible to improve the basis of knowledge on which settlements (without trial) are made and to encourage earlier and cheaper settlement of cases which (now) go to the door of the Court or even to the first day of trial.

It did not paint the full picture. Most actions do not reach trial, but considerable costs are none the less incurred. One recent study noted that legal expenses amounted to 13% of damages agreed or awarded on major PI claims, not including the insurers' direct handling costs (which for some insurers include in-house lawyers' costs).

The adversarial system exacerbates this effect. In the USA the contingent fee also fuels this effect: a 1991 study of auto injury claims in Hawaii by the Insurance Research Council reported that medical treatment of a typical neck strain from whiplash cost about $1,300 if handled without a lawyer, on a no-fault basis; the cost to deal with the same injury if part of a tort claim was about $8,000.

The total cost to society of making reparation to the innocent victim is enormous, and is borne largely through insurance premiums. Some remedies are in the hands of practitioners themselves. Avoidance of unnecessary dispute; positive and realistic initiatives to settle; sensible management of costs; and proper concern for the victim . . . all contribute to settlement *at lower cost.*

1.8   Time to settle. PI claims do not improve with keeping, unless the plaintiff is about to die. In part this is because of the escalation in damages and accumulation of costs referred to above. It is also because positions become entrenched, attitudes are adversarial, side issues dominant proceedings . . . and all these features cost money. See Figure 5B.

It is surprising how quickly many claims are, or ought to be, ready for settlement. This process is accelerated when a proper rehabilitation regime is put in place from the outset, with the whole focus upon the victim's long-term well-being. This is because rehabilitation both informs the plaintiff's legal advisers and also inclines them to settlement. So often the obstacle to settlement is the unwillingness of plaintiff's lawyers to conclude matters . . . or their unreadiness so to do. Therefore, key elements of the insurer's case plan must include:

(a)   getting one's own case ready as quickly as possible; and
(b)   promoting early assessment and presentation by the plaintiff of his case, by agreement and co-operation where appropriate.

To be able to do this, the insurer must be well prepared. Strategy must be clearly defined; resources must be available; advisers must be to hand, deployable surely and consistently. A prime responsibility of defendants' solicitors is to facilitate early settlement . . . not just by procedural pressure upon the other side but also by suggestion and assistance wherever possible.

1.9   Money well spent. A fourth factor—less evidently self-serving—is the arrangement of a compensation package which will meet the long-term needs of the victim, and insurers accept that any plaintiff with just cause is a victim. The usual shortcomings are rehearsed elsewhere, in particular in Chapter 3. The most substantial are firstly that there is insufficient up-front funding of accident after-care to maximise recovery and future potential, and secondly that the effects of inflation, taxation, poorly managed expenditure and investment, and life beyond expectancy mean that the lump sum award fails to ensure adequate provision for needs in later life.

The net effect, in the absence of more suitable arrangements for compensation awards, is constant pressure to increase the range of Heads of Damage, to increase the levels of damages and to dispute medical evidence and multipliers. This adds considerably to the social cost without properly addressing the real problem. Over time the levels and

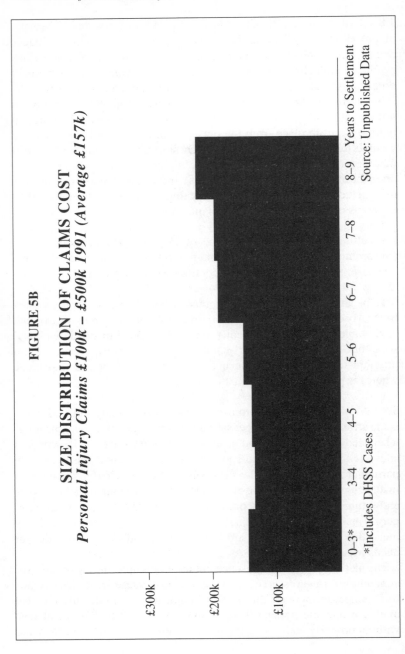

FIGURE 5B

SIZE DISTRIBUTION OF CLAIMS COST
Personal Injury Claims £100k – £500k 1991 (Average £157k)

*Includes DHSS Cases

Years to Settlement

Source: Unpublished Data

methods of compensation will move slowly towards better provision for the victim at the lowest possible cost to society. Disregard of the plaintiff's genuine needs and circumstances will inevitably force up the costs of settlement. The insurer's strategy for PI claims ignores this at his peril.

2   THE CLAIMS HANDLING PROCESS

2.1   Where structuring slots in. Handling PI claims comes down to dealing effectively with a number of key stages in the settlement process, (see Figure 5C). The process is controlled by the insurer, but external advisers and experts fulfil key functions at certain stages. It is important to understand when and how consideration of a structured settlement arises in this process.

2.2   Notification. Notification is the first advice to the insurer of a possible claim. The handler's job at this stage is to obtain as much information as possible to facilitate preliminary consideration of policy liability, legal liability and claim issues and to take effective control of the claims handling process.

It is important to ascertain, as far as possible at this stage, the severity of the injuries, and in particular to identify any potential for permanent disablement or loss of future income. This knowledge will pin-point a possible opportunity or need to explore rehabilitation; and it is the first sign that a structured settlement will be an issue in the settlement of the claim. Many motor claims are advised initially on the basis of damage to the vehicle and injury aspects are ignored or glossed over by the policyholder: it is imperative that specific and pressing enquiries are made to the point where potential injury claims are confirmed and can be followed up (or the handler can be satisfied that there is no PI element).

2.3   Cover. From the information available, it may be possible to determine straightaway whether or not policy cover applies. If there is any doubt, the position under the policy should be reserved and further enquiries should be initiated as a matter of urgency. Non-disclosure, policy coverage and policy conditions issues should all be carefully considered.

FIGURE 5C

CLAIMS HANDLING PROCESS: PERSONAL INJURY CLAIMS

The Aim: 'In discharging our obligations to our Policyholders, we seek to avoid *unnecessary* litigation through *early* and *diligent* investigation, *sensible* evaluation and *positive* interaction with our opponents. When litigation ensues, we require high quality legal representation for our Policyholders which focuses on achieving the *earliest economic* resolution of the claim, including costs and expenses.'

The Process:

Notification	Cover	Response	Investigation	Evaluation	Negotiation/Settlement	Recoveries
Obtain accident details	Check cover applies	Brief insured and contact victim	Instruct in-house and expert investigators	Realistic, informed assessment	Early, skilled approach	Ensure all opportunities taken

'Strucutres' in the Process:

Notification	Cover	Response	Investigation	Evaluation	Negotiation/Settlement	Recoveries
Identify serious injury/income potential		Contact T.P.: ascertain care regime and press rehabilitation (fund or offer rehabilitation management if appropriate)	Ascertain ongoing care needs and income losses	Quantify needs as well as conventional claim: obtain budget assessment of structure costs. Revisit medical position if necessary	Utilise structure option: concentrate on design of package and benefits of structure	Liaise with reinsurers if costs of structure are to become a factor

There will be cases where motor policy cover does not apply, but the insurer will have to deal with the claim under the Road Traffic Act 1988 or as Domestic Agreement insurer. In such cases, it is important to press on with the usual initial actions and enquiries, to minimise the ultimate outlay.

2.4   Response. The handler must now take control of the claim. He must map out his immediate case plan, and then explain to the policyholder what will happen (ie describe the claims process), what he is required to do (eg provision of information, access for inspection, onward transmission of claims correspondence), and tell him what he must not do (eg admit liability, destroy evidence, provide statements to the other side).

In practice, these first three stages are frequently rolled into one in the process of dealing with the first advice of a possible claim.

The other side of the insurer's response (to notice of an accidental injury and a possible claim) is contact with the prospective plaintiff. Traditionally one awaits the claim and then requests details of the allegations and of quantum. This is not a 'head in the sand' reaction: it is the adversarial system at work. The plaintiff's advisers assume little or no responsibility for mitigation, eg post-accident assessment and rehabilitation. Nor do they assume responsibility for post-settlement planning and provision. Their responsibilities are to stabilise the medical condition and to obtain the greatest lump sum compensation. This puts the plaintiff on collision course with the defendant or his insurers.

2.5   Alternative scenarios. The situation is different in the USA, where Workers Compensation legislation requires employers to intervene, allowing insurers to take the initiative on recovery programmes. It is different in Canada, where 'no fault' legislation requires insurers to provide rehabilitation support. Planned provision of a rehabilitation programme, linked to compensation geared towards future needs, are then key elements of the defendant's obligations and approach, driving co-operation between insurers and the plaintiff's advisers (medical and legal). We examine later how rehabilitation works, and the case for reform of the law in this country. But can this approach be induced within the present framework of the law, to secure a better result and in particular to take advantage of the structured settlement option? The answer is 'Yes . . . to some extent . . . provided insurers act early'.

2.6   An insurer's riposte. Insurers can extract advantage by facing up to the inevitability of a claim settlement, in certain circumstances. If the injuries are severe and the defendant is certain to be wholly or largely liable, a successful rehabilitation and re-employment programme will reduce substantially the future losses. There is no certainty of success, and so the plaintiff cannot be required to undertake such a programme in mitigation of his claim. However, the insurer can offer to fund such a programme, without admission of liability if appropriate, without prejudice to the level of damages which the plaintiff may become entitled to. The insurer should set out the potential benefits, offer to arrange the programme and· undertake to fund it. The programme should not be open-ended: the commitment should be fixed, starting with a professional rehabilitation assessment, and kept under review. The plaintiff should be told that if he does not take up the offer, this will be referred to in Court and the Defence will plead failure to mitigate in respect of any damages claimed for.

2.7   Rehabilitation—timing. It is important to put in place such a programme as soon as practical after the medical and surgical conditions have stabilised. Early consideration of the option, followed up by contact with the plaintiff's representatives, is therefore vital. Such an overture is unconventional and will be regarded with suspicion: much persistence and some ingenuity is required to establish a dialogue at this early stage. It is often more readily accomplished with workplace accidents, when the employer can facilitate contact and intervention (and may well be able to provide suitable future employment following rehabilitation). Enlisting the assistance of the employer is therefore an important early action.

2.8   The challenge of workplace accident after-care. Some, if not all, Trade Union solicitors are also very conscious of a wider obligation to the welfare of their clients and may be more familiar with pro-active co-operation in this way. Over time, it is to be hoped that employers, in conjunction with their employer's liability insurers, will 'market' workplace accident aftercare as part of the employment package. This would certainly reduce the costs—to business, individuals and society— of industrial accidents.

2.9 Investigation. Investigations can, and often do, cover policy liability, legal liability and quantum. Our interest lies in cases where a claim will be met under the policy, i.e. there is policy liability, at least a measure of legal liability and a demonstrative entitlement to compensation. It is sensible to instruct your legal advisers at this stage. Solicitors should be given a specific brief—a clearly defined role and responsibilities, with agreed performance standards and targets. This principle applies at every stage of the claim. Managing the claim involves close management of advisers, by:

— establishing common purpose and team approach;
— agreeing plan, including timescales;
— clearly dividing responsibilities; and
— hands-on management and control.

At this stage, the key actions are to:

— identify the issues;
— gather evidence;
— instruct or retain experts and Counsel; and
— consider tactics.

Legal liability investigations should be commissioned straightaway: if the trail goes cold the chances of pleading successfully contribution, let alone no legal liability, reduce.

2.10 Pro-active investigation—the reciprocal advantages. There is also a more subtle aspect to early investigation. Where there is significant contribution, financial compensation will undoubtedly be inadequate over the full term and the incentive to reduce that shortfall by recovery and re-employment is greatest. This should provide incentives to the plaintiff and his advisers to pursue mitigation of losses through rehabilitation; and to pursue provision for long-term compensation through structured settlements. The enterprising insurer who is prepared to advance interims and fund fully initial rehabilitation programmes can, with the co-operation of the plaintiff, both improve the plaintiff's prospects and reduce his own ultimate outlay.

2.11 Investigation—what/how? The full medical picture, and its implications for damages, will take some time to unfold. However, certain initial enquiries are important. In particular, it is helpful to get hold of previous medical records as early as possible, to identify the possibility of pre-existing complaints and overlays which could become factors in the damages assessment. Again, such features are tantamount to a shortfall in compensation which becomes an incentive to mitigate. They are also a powerful pointer in future medical assessments and in settlement negotiations . Further, it is important at this time to line up the right medical consultants, whose services will be available when you need them, and this could involve putting a rehabilitation team on standby.

2.12   Evaluation. Evaluation is the process of assessing what the claim is worth and identifying the negotiable issues which may affect the ultimate valuation. The claims handler will need to evaluate both liability and quantum.

2.13   Evaluation—liability. Evaluation of liability should be based upon the facts of the accident. A test of contribution is whether or not it can be pleaded positively. Contributory negligence can make a major difference to the damages payable and the investigator will spare no effort to demonstrate any contribution. However, Courts are not sympathetic to issues which are not clear-cut and it is sensible to be realistic: an unrealistic appraisal of the possible contribution will only prolong settlement, without necessarily securing a greater contribution in the long run. In particular, if the liability of the defendant is clear-cut the best course is to concede liability straightaway and to focus on the issue of quantum.

2.14   Evaluation—quantum. Evaluation of quantum is based upon the facts, in so far as injuries and the losses arising therefrom are concerned, and the precedents in terms of levels of award. On the conventional basis, damages as claimed are usually optimistic and highly debatable. The Rules of Court provide for speedy service of the Schedule but there are tried and tested means of deferring service, negotiation and trial if it suits the plaintiff.

This can make the task of evaluation particularly difficult for the defendant but it is a necessary precursor to negotiation and settlement. If a payment-in is contemplated, to bring matters to a close, the defendant will have to draw up his own Schedule or Counter-Schedule to value correctly his offer. An alternative process is to assess the likely future financial needs, for care and income, and to evaluate the cost of funding these through a structured settlement. This approach can be explored by the defendant in pursuit of his interests in settlement but, legitimately, it might be invoked by the plaintiff.

2.15 Evaluation—the team. Evaluation should involve the whole team of advisers and experts. The objective should be a realistic assessment, taking into account costs issues. It is an opportunity to review the evidence and to identify the key issues for resolution.

2.16 The drive for accuracy in evaluation. Unrealistic evaluation by defendants, which becomes their expectation of settlement, only serves to precipitate dispute and to protract settlement negotiations. This adds to costs; leads to run-off deficits; does not reduce the true value of the claim and frequently serves to inflate the ultimate settlement figure. It is wholly counter-productive.

2.17 Negotiation and settlement. Negotiation is the process of agreeing, or attempting to agree, settlement between the parties. Whether negotiations are conducted by insurer, solicitor, barrister—or all three— the imperative is to establish contact to resolve the issues in dispute. The insurer should take an active part in initiating and conducting negotiations, managing the contribution of his advisers also. The route to a satisfactory settlement is to avoid avoidable disputes and to find an effective way to resolve the unavoidable ones. Defendants should devote their energies to conducting the speediest resolution of disputes.

Dealings proceed against the backdrop of trial, which will follow a breakdown of negotiations and which will harm one side, benefiting the other. Surprisingly little has been written about the mysteries of claims negotiations, the smoke-filled rooms and darkened corridors. It is a process familiar to all practitioners—claims handlers and lawyers. There are marked differences in approach, technique and expertise and, in the judgement of many, psychology still holds sway over science.

2.18 Negotiation in the context of structures. Our purpose is to explore negotiations in the context of structured settlements. Closing a sale requires a willing buyer who becomes convinced that he is accepting the right deal. This distils down to a plaintiff who now believes he has been offered at least as much as he would obtain with certainty at trial. The plaintiff sees his choice as to accept or try. How much better if he could have a further choice: accept a structured settlement (or a package involving a structured settlement). A choice which goes further than the *possibility* of funding future needs, by *ensuring* funding in the future. Closing the sale, reaching a mutually acceptable settlement, becomes a more achievable goal.

2.19   Structures in negotiation. Structuring a settlement can offer advantage to both parties in several distinct ways. A structured settlement can:

(a)   make more effective use of the damages available;
(b)   provide specifically for the needs of the future; and
(c)   facilitate agreement where there is dispute about the lump sum entitlement.

2.20   A helping hand from the taxman. Where there is agreement on the lump sum recoverable, a structured settlement may confer considerable advantage to the plaintiff, essentially through the tax-efficiency and the benefits of spread of risk and management of the fund. The defendant cannot be required to structure, and it costs him so to do. Therefore he must insist on a realistic discount. The arrangement of the structure package and the balancing of plaintiff benefits and defendant discount will be the nub of the settlement negotiation.

2.21   Future security. In some cases, the essential requirement of the plaintiff is to secure provision for foreseeable, open-ended, future needs. A structured settlement will do this. The evaluation process will focus on this 'bottom up', needs-based assessment. The negotiation will establish to what extent, at what cost, the defendant will fund this.

2.22   Bridging the gap. Dispute about the compensation entitlement is not infrequent and is invariably unsatisfactory to both sides. It is frequently rooted in strongly held beliefs on both sides. There may be disagreement on multipliers, heads and levels of damages and contributory negligence. Judgment may result in both lower damages than are on offer and the penalty of costs to the plaintiff. Structuring of the offer may be the optimum bet for the plaintiff. Elimination of the risks and costs of trial may be just as attractive to the defendant. Therein lies the substance of the negotiation.

2.23 Examples of structuring against a backdrop of imponderables.
In a typical case nasty injuries resulted in loss of employment, slight intellectual impairment and the suggestion of some psychological disturbance. Liability was not in dispute, but future prospects and pre-existing behavioural problems were. The plaintiff's initial Schedule totalled £1.3m. Insurers valued the claim at around £200,000, asserting that diminution of future earnings and the degree of psychological disturbance due to the accident were grossly over valued in the claim. Future care and life expectancy were not issues. Preliminary negotiations resulted in a revised Schedule of £630,000 and an assessment by insurers of £250,000–300,000. Failure to agree led, ultimately, to a payment-in of £300,000. Finally, a pre-trial meeting was convened in an attempt to reach agreement.

The plaintiff, who had made a good recovery, was by now earning reasonable money from contracts in his former line of work. But he had not secured a permanent job, nor did he enjoy his former job security or level of income. He was an embittered and difficult man, who had remarked that 'insurers will pay to keep me for the rest of my life'. Insurer's medical evidence was beginning to look doubtful on the issue of pre-existing disturbance. They reflected that their payment-in might not stand up in the corridor or at trial. A structure was suggested. As the plaintiff was now self-employed and earning money, a structure would be highly tax-advantageous. It also provided the guaranteed income stream he wanted. The structure was finally agreed based on an annuity purchased for £150,000 and £150,000 lump sum. Insurers considered that this represented a substantial saving on their probable outlay had the case proceeded to trial.

2.24 Recovery. It is fairly unusual that there are recovery opportunities with PI claims but the possibility must never be overlooked. Apart from the obvious, being (i) other parties in contract or tort, (ii) the defendant when 'insurer concerned', (iii) agreement insurers, (iv) co-insurers and Reinsurers, there is the additional task of recovering taxation when settlements are structured.

2.25 Summary of the claims handling process. The foregoing describes a dynamic claims handling process which from Day 1 progresses in a proactive and innovative way towards final settlement, embracing in anticipation settlement options which can be of assistance to the handler at any stage. See Figure 5D. Consideration of structured settlements can

FIGURE 5D

DAY 1	PHASE 1	PHASE 2	PHASE 3
Notification/Cover/ Response	**Investigation**	**Evaluation**	**Negotiation & Settlement**
Severe injuries?	*Liability Investigation* • *gather information and evidence*	*Realistic assessment of liability* • *denial/contribution properly evidenced*	*Establish parameters for co-operation* OR *Initiate measures to enforce progress*
Contact points?			
Cover issues: determine or reserve position			
Liability issues: identify for investigation	*Medical Enquiries* • *identify pro-active possibilities* • *identify long-term needs*	*Obtain and assess Plaintiff's Schedule* • *assess approach, heads & costings*	
Assign in-house handler			
Retain external advisors	*Reserve Claim*	*Prepare Counter-Schedule* • *analyse needs* • *cost structure alternatives*	*Structure proposal* OR *Structure option*
Establish plan	*Opponent's Attitude?*		

arise early and can be revived repeatedly to final settlement, whether or not a structure is ultimately agreed. Future claims should develop in this way, now that structures are a possibility, notwithstanding the fact that the legal, taxation and cultural environments are not yet sufficiently willing or adapted to exploit structured settlements to the full.

There is also the passive role of structured settlements, the role which structures have assumed in most such settlements to date. That is, where settlement has been agreed on a conventional basis, or is in the final stages of being agreed, and the alternative arrangement of structuring the payment is put forward. For many claims which arose before structures became a possibility in 1989, or became widely known in the early 1990s, a structured settlement can only arise in this passive way as a last minute alternative. It is, however, a bona fide alternative, where it provides a better deal for plaintiff and defendant.

3   REASONS TO STRUCTURE

3.1   Benefits for the insurer. The prime reason for defendant insurers to consider and promote structured settlements is the opportunity to achieve a settlement at a lower cost. Direct reductions in cost arise primarily because of the possibility of sharing the tax benefit which accrues to the plaintiff through the structure. Structured settlements are highly tax-efficient (Figure 5E): the mechanism is explained in Chapter 1. The benefits cannot be secured without the agreement of the insurer: the levels of discount, from a conventional settlement, are illustrated in Chapter 2. The parties take advantage of the tax efficiency to add value to, whilst reducing the cost of, the settlement. This has been described quite properly as a 'win-win' scenario. There are more specific and tangible financial benefits to the defendant insurer. Court of Protection fees are somewhat lower when the settlement is structured. If the insurer arranges the annuity, he will receive the commission payable (typically 2% to 3% of the purchase price). If the annuity is purchased from an associated company, an additional benefit is retained within the group.

3.2   Containing the settlements. A financial benefit arises also because the structured settlement approach—whereby the income never runs out—is a cost-effective mechanism for assuming the future risks faced by the plaintiff. Risks such as mortality, morbidity, investment, inflation,

FIGURE 5E

TAX SAVINGS BENEFITS

GROSS INCOME Required	Before TAX	To Provide NET INCOME	
£	£	£	
25,435	5,435	20,000	pa
41,711	11,711	30,000	pa
58,378	18,378	40,000	pa

Assuming: single person allowance £3,295

20% on £2,000 Taxable Income

Income tax at 23% on £21,700 Taxable Income

40% thereafter

insolvency . . . all of which have to be faced and which incline plaintiffs and Judges to settle at a higher figure. The law of large numbers comes into play through the annuity basis of funding the structure, the spread of risk eliminating the element of uncertainty. The offer of a structure can also promote an earlier and easier settlement, pre-empting inflation of damages and costs. Structuring involves a different approach to damages, ie thinking about needs from the plaintiff's perspective. This helps address the concerns of the plaintiff and his family about the post-settlement period. Realistic proposals and a less stressful settlement process help deliver a better result all round.

3.3 Example. By way of an example, a net discount of $12^{1}/_{2}\%$ to the insurer would contribute £500,000 per annum directly to profit, if a company settles 80 claims per year in the range £100,000 to £500,000, with an average claim size of £200,000, and structures half of these claims for an average of half of the value of those claims which are structured (ie 40 claims are structured and the average amount structured in those claims is £100,000). If the insurer arranged the annuity, a further £120,000 contribution would be generated by commission. This would be an overall 4% reduction in the total claims spend. Profit is by definition a marginal effect: in the world of competitive underwriting 4% is a very substantial and hard-earned margin. Much larger claims might be fewer in number but are more often suited to a structured settlement, in far higher amounts, generating even greater margins.

3.4 Insurers' image. Insurers must be conscious also of the public image of the 'Defence industry'. Settlements which evidently address future needs of victims, alleviating real uncertainty and concerns, are perceived favourably as proper compensation. Settlements achieved in a co-operative rather than in a competitive way generate approval. There is much greater satisfaction attaching to money well spent than to money doubtfully spent. Over time, socio-political factors determine damages levels: proper compensation is the most effective route to damages limitation.

3.5 Disadvantages for the insurer. There are a number of disadvantages for defendant insurers which have to be set against the benefits which may arise from structured settlements:

(a) *Firstly*, there are the costs and inconvenience of arranging the annuity, administering the payments and reclaiming tax. Moreover, there is loss of interest arising from the delay in recovering tax. The amount of interest lost is determined by the time taken to recover the tax from the Inland Revenue, which can quite easily exceed nine months. Based on current rates of tax and a nine-month delay, it has been estimated as the equivalent of $1\frac{1}{2}$–4% of the annuity purchase price. Some commentators suggest that as deferred tax recoveries are a normal feature of business operations, this effect can be ignored. However, the delay is real and it is particular to structured settlements, so the effect should be included in any assessment of the financial attractiveness of the structure option.

(b) *Secondly*, if reinsurers are meeting the claims payments, any reduction in settlement cost resulting from a structure will accrue directly to the reinsurer. The ceding office is obliged to minimise the reinsurer's outlay, but not at the expense of assuming additional liabilities on its own account (eg loss of interest, administration charges). Where reinsurance is involved, the ceding office should agree in advance a basis upon which it will be compensated from the savings on settlement to the reinsurer.

(c) *Thirdly,* sometimes the view is expressed that the publicity attaching to structured settlements, in particular calculations of their possible ultimate worth, inflates the expectations of plaintiffs and helps to drive levels of damages upwards. (There is no evidence of this: it is rather more likely that the uncertainty of providing for long-term needs through lump sum damages does most to inflate settlement levels.)

(d) *Fourthly,* the key to the financial benefits of structured settlements is the tax saving. Where tax cannot be recovered, for example by mutual insurance companies or by overseas insurance companies, this financial benefit does not arise.

(e) *Fifthly,* the most frequently encountered problem facing defendant insurers is the plaintiff's reluctance to consider—and the plaintiff's solicitor's reluctance to recommend—an alternative to the lump sum. In the United States, structured settlements are still insurer-driven. Despite the benefits to the plaintiff, the structure proposal is usually propounded by the Defence. In the UK, there is much less familiarity with the structured settlement alternative. All the more important, then, for the insurer to sell to the plaintiff the benefits of a structure.

3.6 Benefits for the plaintiff. Firstly, the damages will never run out. There will be an income stream for life and normally the level of benefits will increase over time. The tax efficiency of the structured settlement means that this can be achieved and there is no problem of the lump sum eroding to nothing. See Figure 5F.

3.7 Post-settlement financing. Structured settlement arrangements can be more flexible than the simple investment of a lump sum. Special needs, such as education, transport, medical care, etc, can be anticipated and programmed into the structure. The structured settlement provides sound money management, reliably and at no cost to the claimant. The planned income stream is provided with certainty. There is evidence of considerable concern amongst claimants about how to invest and realise their damages and about how well their investments perform. It has also been estimated that the services of financial advisers cost in the order of £2,000 to £3,000 per annum for managing the investment (of damages sums in the range, say, £100,000 to £500,000). The structuring of settlements provides the plaintiff's solicitor with an opportunity to integrate tax, financial, medical and estate planning into the settlement plan. Thus the lawyer is taking into account, consciously, the post-settlement needs of his client, which extend beyond the delivery of a large amount of damages in settlement.

3.8 Guarding against the Chancellor. A particular example is provided by consideration of rates of income tax. Most experts consider that the prevailing rates of personal taxation are as low as we are likely to see for many years. The effect of an increase in levels of personal tax upon the recipient of the conventional lump sum is the accelerated erosion of that lump sum upon which he relies for provision of future needs. Structuring the settlement now safeguards against increases in taxation later.

3.9 Plaintiffs' objections. What are the problems which plaintiffs, or their advisers, see with structured settlements and how can these be resolved?

(a) *Firstly,* there are objections of principle. The victim should have a sum of money to dispose of as he wishes. Structuring 'makes a little money appear to go a long way'. The defendant should not benefit from a discount off the victim's damages.

FIGURE 5Fa
PAYMENTS FOR LIFE
(*Dale example*)

Years from settlement	Annual annuity £	Monthly payment £	Cumulative damages £
1	15,190	1,266	15,190
5	18,464	1,539	83,934
10	23,565	1,964	191,058
15	30,075	2,506	327,778
		The above payments are guaranteed	
20	38,384	3,199	502,272
25	48,989	4,082	724,975
30	62,524	5,210	1,000,206
35	79,798	6,650	1,371,965
40	101,845	8,847	1,834,949

(1) Payments guaranteed for life. (2) Minimum payment period 15 years. (3) Payments indexed – 5% pa compound. (4) Minimum sums payable under the structured settlement: £327,778. (5) No need to include receipts on Income Tax Return as tax-free. (6) If Mr Dale actually lives for 40 more years then total is: £1,834,949. (7) Cost of structure is £250,000.

FIGURE 5Fb
EROSION OF THE LUMP SUM
(*Kelly example*)

Years from settlement	Lump sum at start of year £	Net annual interest (9.5% gross) £	Professional costs £	Net income generated £	Annual income required £	Balance of damages fund at year-end £
0	300,000	21,037	1,500	19,537	22,390	**297,147**
5	270,738	19,369	1,914	17,455	28,576	**259,617**
10	191,220	14,276	2,443	11,832	36,471	**166,582**
15	27,250	2,589	3,118	(530)	46,547	**(19,827)**

The issue, it seems to many, is a simple one: does the structured settlement proposal meet better the real needs of the claimant? The goal of a tort remedy is to make a plaintiff whole. It is difficult to make a plaintiff economically whole through a lump sum. Medical advances which extend life expectancy and inflation in the cost of care render the lump sum remedy unreliable. 'The single recovery rule is often both capricious and inflexible in its operation so that damages in accident cases . . . often fail to do the job they should if accident law is to perform the function of administering accident losses efficiently in the public interest' (Harper and James, *2 The Law of Torts* 1956).

An insurer may well agree to a structure which is tailored to meet properly the future needs of the plaintiff. The purchase of the annuity must be at a discount from his lump sum obligation, to cover his costs and to incentivise the process. The limit at which such a discount, if calculated, becomes inappropriate is simply one where the discount exceeds the tax benefits available to the plaintiff (ie the *acid test* is whether the net benefits receivable by the plaintiff from an annuity purchased with the conventional lump sum would exceed the benefits received under the structured settlement).

(b) *Secondly,* there are other more tangible arguments. For example, a structured settlement may leave no residual benefit to the estate. Normally there is a Guarantee Period, during which payments will be maintained, and a contingency sum is retained alongside the structured element of the settlement.

(c) *Thirdly,* accepting a promise of future payments can be considered as less secure than cash in hand. In fact the agreement with the insurer is a protected contract with an inherently high level of security (see 8.7 below, this chapter).

(d) *Fourthly,* a structured settlement cannot be changed once it is put in place. Therefore there can be less liquidity and less flexibility in dealing with the claimant's financial affairs (depending on how the lump sum is invested). But there is no reason why a claimant cannot accrue savings from the regular payments, and indeed finance borrowings on the basis of those payments. Careful arrangement of the structure, for example to provide specifically against anticipated one-off expenditures or an increase in level of needs, combined with appropriate contingency fund provision, create much greater liquidity and flexibility than the claimant would have enjoyed before the accident.

(e) *Fifthly,* whilst annuities provide a good and reliable rate of return, this may not always meet the claimant's needs or represent his most effective investment. For example, although the structure will provide increasing benefits to counter the effects of inflation, it cannot respond totally to a massive hike in inflation in the future. This is a problem also with the lump sum settlement, but there is some relief if interest rates rise with inflation. At times of low interest rates, as for example in the USA in the early 1990s, annuity rates of return are depressed.

None the less, the return (net of tax) on any secure investment by the claimant is most unlikely to exceed that received via a structured settlement (see Figure 5G). It is widely held also that individuals are unlikely to secure annuity terms on impaired lives as advantageous as those offered to insurers who arrange regularly structured settlements.

(f) *Sixthly,* a reservation sometimes expressed is that the plaintiff is less informed about the annuity market than the Defence. This seems to be founded more on unfamiliarity and, perhaps, on suspicion of the co-operation implicit in concluding a structure than on substance: the plaintiff and his advisers will have before them a specific proposal which they can accept or reject on its merits.

(g) A practical problem which is a genuine concern of plaintiffs' solicitors is that immunity from income tax is subject to the approval of the Inland Revenue. This approval is to all intents and purposes assured provided a settlement is concluded in accordance with the Model Agreement and is set up to extinguish the debt (in damages) owed by the defendant to the plaintiff (see below). However, annuity quotes are guaranteed for only a very short time and have to be accepted within that period. The Revenue may not approve arrangements within that timescale and therefore the agreement has to be entered into upon the assumption of Inland Revenue approval. The Revenue has set out guidelines and demonstrated by precedent the basis of Agreements which command approval. In practice, therefore, this is more a theoretical than a real problem for the plaintiff. However, it would be in the interests of both sides if the position was made more specific and certain by legislation.

3.10   Win–Win. The bottom line is that in many cases there are significant advantages to both sides from considering and concluding a structured settlement. Firstly, consideration of a structure requires and

FIGURE 5G

COMPARISON BETWEEN ANNUITY AND INVESTMENT RETURNS

		Investment with building society 90 day 8.6%	Annuity purchased by plaintiff	Annuity purchased by insurance co on behalf of plaintiff
Initial Capital		£400,000	£400,000	£400,000 invested by defendant
Annual Income	Capital	£—	£10,048	£34,936
	Interest	£34,400	£24,888	
Single Person's Allowance		£3,295	£3,295	N/A
Tax	20%	£400	£400	N/A
	25%	£5,425	£4,898	N/A
	40%	£2,962	N/A	N/A
Total Tax Liability		£8,787	£5,298	N/A
Plaintiff's Net Income Per Annum		£25,613	£29,638	£34,936

therefore encourages co-operation between the parties in arriving at a settlement which meets the future, post-settlement needs of the claimant. Secondly, the taxation benefits are considerable and present an opportunity to conclude a settlement more favourable to both sides. Thirdly, provision of a predictable stream of benefits on an open-ended basis eliminates a major concern which can all too often lead to trial: structuring the settlement is a powerful means of bridging the inevitable gap, by adding value acceptable to the plaintiff at a cost acceptable to the defendant.

This enables us to take a view of the circumstances in which a structured settlement is most appropriate.

3.11   When to structure. The following circumstances in particular lend themselves to a structured settlement:

(a) Future pecuniary loss/costs of care: need for lifetime payments. This first category includes any victim with uncertain life expectancy. It includes victims who suffer from very serious injuries to the head or the spinal chord, serious burns, loss of limbs or sight, multiple fractures or death. In summary, claims for victims who are severely disabled or impaired.

(b) Financial circumstances of claimant. This second category would embrace claims for persons with poor financial skills; those with no immediate need of money (for example, people who already have capital); minors and people whose post-settlement income will be in the higher tax brackets.

(c) High damages. There has been much debate about the practical threshold for structuring a settlement. In the USA there have been a few examples of structuring very low levels of benefits. However, normally the tax benefit would need both to add value to and reduce the cost of the settlement and to cover the administrative costs. This suggests that the minimum size of a structure, that is the purchase price of the annuity, would be in the order of £100,000. Certainly it is worth exploring the possible benefits of structuring if the residual damages after a contingency provision will exceed this sum.

3.12   The public policy dimension. There is also the matter of public policy. Proper life-long provision for the victim is a moral and social imperative from which defendants cannot and should not escape: but society, through the law, must regulate this provision within reasonable bounds. Greater flexibility in the compensation system increases the chances of reconciling these goals. Public policy can arise also in individual situations. Notwithstanding considerations of the freedom of the individual, it is generally felt that where the settlement would be grossly misapplied then the plaintiff should be assisted in the management of his needs by regulating the receipt and therefore the disposal of his moneys. This category embraces people with the potential to dissipate moneys (for example because of family or peer pressure or addictions). The usual example is the simple-minded imbiber who with his mates proceeds to drain the proceeds in an orgy of dissolution. An unusual example was where the victim lived in an IRA stronghold and would not have held on to his entitlement for any time before it was refreshing the arsenal of local terrorists.

The Law Commission commented: 'The state can also be said to have an additional and valid interest in courts being able to make compensatory awards in a form which may prevent plaintiffs becoming a burden on social security and hence on the taxpayer' (Consultation Paper No 125 'Structured Settlements and Interim Provisional Damages' para 3.73). However, at present neither the Defence nor the Court can impose a structured settlement: it has to be agreed to by the plaintiff.

4 HOW DO STRUCTURES OPERATE?

4.1 The annuity market. The key to providing a structured settlement is, at the moment, finding a Life Assurance underwriter who will provide an annuity quotation for the life in question. It is a restricted, specialist market and premiums vary widely. This reflects the uncertainty about life expectancy in the majority of PI cases.

4.2 Seeking quotations—when? It has been the practice to seek quotations when the medical evidence has been virtually exhausted, even if life expectancy is still disputed between the experts. This is because the decision is required on the option to structure at the conclusion of settlement negotiations. However, in the American market, where structured settlements have been commonplace for many years, claims handlers start to cost structures at a much earlier stage, in much the same way as we take a preliminary view of the settlement value of a claim before negotiations have even started. In effect, dual bases of evaluation operate in the USA environment and this will develop in the UK.

4.3   The role of the annuity underwriter. Annuity underwriters turn round quotations very very quickly, on the basis of all of the medical reports which are to hand. An indication of the benefits to be bought for a given sum can normally be extrapolated on a pro rata basis, so the Negotiator can assess the implications of settling at a different level of benefits.

If the Negotiator is prepared to take a view upon life expectancy from the medical evidence, he can even estimate quotations from the Annuity Tables of the life offices with whom his company deals. We may be some way off this at the present time but it will surely come.

The problems facing the annuity underwriter are very much those facing the Judge: from the medical evidence, how closely can you judge the future expectation of life? The answer, as the following table shows, is 'Not very well'. This table shows the views of six Chief Medical Officers all of whom examined the medical records of seven different victims and advised their underwriters of the basis on which to quote. See Figure 5H.

If the medics cannot agree, what chance does a Judge have?

With the present UK damages system there will always be winners and losers and no-one comes out 'alright'.

4.4   The fail-safe dimension of life assurance. The life assurance solution, of annuity payments in a structured settlement, ensures that everyone emerges 'alright'. The underwriter may make a profit or a loss on an individual case but will make a fair return over his whole portfolio. Every victim will receive his appropriate level of income for life; none will go short. Society will not bear the cost of over compensation nor the stain of under compensation.

4.5   The insurer's check-list for the structure package. The stages to conclude a structured settlement are few and simple. They are:

(a) design annuity package;
(b) obtain annuity quotation;
(c) obtain, if necessary, Accountant's Report setting out the appropriateness and benefits of the proposed structure, eg to provide a comparison of the accumulated value of the structure payments over time with the income and value over time generated by a corresponding lump sum settlement;
(d) prepare and sign the Model Agreement;

FIGURE 5H
WEIGHING THE EVIDENCE – LIFE EXPECTANCY

	CMO 1	CMO 2	CMO 3	CMO 4	CMO 5	CMO 6
PLAINTIFF 1	20	12	20	12	25	25
PLAINTIFF 2	5	8	15	15	15	15
PLAINTIFF 3	20	25	35	—	35	25
PLAINTIFF 4	5	15	25	30	25	15
PLAINTIFF 5	30	35	35	35	50	35
PLAINTIFF 6	15	20	25	20	20	15
PLAINTIFF 7	10	10	20	15	15	15

Table showing the views of six Chief Medical Officers on the appropriate number of 'added years' for Annuity quotation purposes on each of seven different injured parties.

(e) obtain Inland Revenue approval for the Agreement;
(f) complete proposal form for and pay premium for the annuity;
(g) make arrangements to pay both the annuity receipts and tax rebate to claimant;
(h) make arrangements to reclaim tax deduction from Inland Revenue.

These steps require routine procedures and, in some circumstances, routine support from an accountant.

4.6   Structure advisers—remuneration. There are companies and accountants who specialise in arranging structured settlements. They are usually remunerated through the commission on the annuity purchased and possibly by a fee. This can be a substantial reward in return for relatively little expert contribution. It may be significantly less expensive for the insurer to carry out the work and to pay an accountant on a time basis for such specific professional support services as are required. The insurer will then benefit through receipt of the annuity commission. Again, this is the way in which the market has developed in the USA. Some insurers have in-house broking specialists who place their annuity business for structured settlements. The tasks described above are simply supplementary tasks in connection with delivering a *structured* settlement.

5   DESIGN ANNUITY PACKAGE

5.1   Purpose of structure. The purpose of structuring the settlement is to guarantee, as far as possible, that the plaintiff will receive an income-stream for the rest of his life sufficient to meet his foreseeable needs. Indeed, the Inland Revenue have indicated that for the purposes of approving an Agreement the income-stream must bear a recognisable relationship to the losses as suffered. To meet these objectives, the structured package should be carefully designed to generate the appropriate income in a cost-effective way.

5.2   Protection against inflation. Normally the plaintiff will require some insurance against inflation. This can take the form of fixed indexation (eg benefits increasing at 5% per annum) or indexation tied to the Retail Prices Index.

5.3 Specific requirements. It may be necessary to take into account anticipated one-off needs (eg purchase of a new motor car or provision of school fees) or changes in care requirements (eg when parents become too elderly to assist or when the plaintiff may need more constant attention or institutional care).

5.4 Immediate and future needs. Immediate needs will be taken care of by a contingency sum, which will include interims already paid. Future needs are best assessed through a rehabilitation report, but consideration of the medical reports and the family background should enable both parties to take a view.

5.5 Court of Protection. The proposal must also take account of the requirements of the Court of Protection, which is especially sensitive to the need for reserves for emergencies.

5.6 Future care, aids and equipment. Conventionally the costs of future care are based upon providing professional support for activities or functions which the claimant cannot perform independently as a result of the accident. Specialised equipment and housing/vehicle adaptations should be claimed for on the basis that they will reduce dependence on others or will restore a degree of personal comfort and convenience. When assessing future income requirements, it is more appropriate to predict what money will be spent rather than speculate upon what might be done and what it could possibly cost.

The results of recent research carried out by the University of Edinburgh Rehabilitation Studies Unit suggest that the Schedules beloved by plaintiff's solicitors may not predict either the services and aids which will be called upon or the actual costs incurred.

Key findings, from a large group of seriously disabled victims who received substantial compensation and were assessed on average ten years after accidental injury, throw a totally different light upon actual needs catered for. For example:

(a) the main change in personal circumstances is an upgrade of housing;
(b) apart from housing expenditure, the general pattern is that of a settled existence with household and other expenditure partly or wholly covered by non-means-tested benefit income;

(c) care is typically provided by family members, with less than one-fifth of continuing care provided partly or wholly by non-family nursing or care-assistance staff;

(d) except for medical services, few claimants are in contact with professional services;

(e) services used tend to be those which are free of charge;

(f) where payments are made for services, the majority is spent on practical help (eg cleaning, gardening, decorating) rather than professional help;

(g) the vast majority of such practical help is provided free of charge by carers or others.

'Hellyer' lists of equipment/adaptations may be relevant only to persons with very severe incapacity or behavioural disturbance. Most housing adaptations funded in the early stages of recovery are abandoned, eg when claimants move to more up-market housing after settlement.

5.7   Realistic assessment of expenditure necessary for care and comfort. The adversarial approach fosters mistrust and exaggeration. Plaintiffs frequently feel compelled to catalogue a battery of expenses: and defendants see fit to resist every one. Michael Davis J inter alia said in *Moser v Enfield & Haringay* (1982):

'Again, terrifying figures were put forward by Mr. Hellyer, a consultant to the Special Injuries Association . . . For example, at one stage he was advocating what could almost be described as a fleet of wheelchairs . . .'

and concluding

'The total under item four, accordingly, is £10,978. As a matter of comment, the figure as calculated by the accountant . . . seems to have been £85,198!'

With the compliance of both Counsel 'reason once more prevailed in the end' in this case. But coercion and intelligent speculation are no substitutes for informed and practical analysis. There is a growing fund of knowledge about how disabled people manage their lives and adjust to disability. Services are available to assist them in doing this. Specialist professionals can assess properly what support they will need, and what they will not need. Judges, solicitors, Counsel and insurers should absorb these insights—encouraging both sides to work together to assess and provide for real needs, properly. That assessment is critical to the design of the structure.

5.8 Continuing rehabilitation. An unfulfilled need is for readier access to a full range of advice on services, benefits and opportunities—medical, personal, social and financial—which would provide greater security and comfort for accident victims and their carers. A continuing rehabilitation service would be a valued adjunct to the claim settlement, whether provided by insurers or funded through the structure.

5.9 Guarantee period. Annuity payments are normally made monthly and a Guarantee Period can be arranged to ensure a minimum payout in the event of the early death of the claimant (eg monthly payments will continue for five or ten years).

5.10 Tenor of payment. It is normal to arrange for payments during the plaintiff's lifetime, assuming he has no dependants. But in a fatal case, or where there may be dependency beyond the lifetime of the claimant, it is possible to arrange for annuities based upon life of another or joint lives (eg of the plaintiff and spouse) or for a set period (eg to provide for the plaintiff's needs until receipt of normal pension or to provide for the needs of children up to a certain age).

5.11 Who negotiates with the plaintiff? It is the claims negotiator who needs to agree the appropriate basis for the structure with the plaintiff's advisers. This is a specialist role. Large sums in settlement are at stake. A detailed knowledge of the conventional basis of settlement as well as of the annuity market possibilities is required. A thorough understanding of the future needs and life patterns of disabled people, and the care and support arrangements which can be made, is essential. A negotiator must also be able to sustain goodwill throughout the negotiation process. In short, this is a job for specialist, top-level negotiators. It is an area of claims handling where insurers must develop in-house expertise to safeguard their interests.

In the sense that they act as mediators in the settlement process, this may be so. The Law Society cautions solicitors that the plaintiff requires independent advice in connection with a structured settlement. The parties therefore have to decide for themselves the role, if any, of accountants in designing and negotiating the annuity package, taking into account overall costs and the need to broke and obtain approval for the settlement.

6   OBTAIN ANNUITY QUOTATION

6.1   The four versions of permitted annuities. The Inland Revenue approve four types of annuity within the terms of the Model Agreement. These are:

(a) Basic Terms—these provide for a series of payments of pre-stated amounts to be made for a fixed period. The payments may be specified to increase at a fixed percentage rate during the period.

(b) Indexed Terms—these provide a series of payments for a fixed period, commencing at a pre-set amount and varying thereafter in line with the Retail Price Index.

(c) Terms for Life—the pre-set payments will continue until the death of the life assured. If required, payments can increase at a fixed percentage rate. It is also possible to specify that payments will continue for a minimum period, to ensure a minimum payment in the event of the early death of the life assured.

(d) Indexed Terms for Life—again, the benefits are linked to the Retail Price Index.

These annuity products are standard Life Assurance products but specialised underwriting is required for impaired lives. If life expectancy has been reduced, the annuity benefits may be greater than normal. The Underwriter has to assess this variation based upon the medical evidence when he provides his quotation.

6.2   Young lives. The ability of life offices to index payments of this kind is based upon the availability of index-linked Government security stock. Government stock maturing to the year 2030 is now available. However, in the case of some very young lives, where life expectancy is around or beyond 2030, life offices may qualify the indexation beyond that date. Agreement has been obtained by the Inland Revenue, the Court of Protection and a High Court Judge to a form of Agreement wording which addresses this point, subject of course to the agreement of the plaintiff and of the life office. The ABI has provided details of the arrangement to member companies.

6.3 Broking the arrangement. Obtaining the best annuity quotation, or suite of quotations, is a straightforward insurance broking function. The key action is to determine the basis of the annuity or annuities which provide the required package of income benefits over time. Annuity payments can commence immediately or they can be deferred; they can run for a set period or until death; the Life Assured may be the claimant or another (eg spouse); payments may be monthly or may be separated by much longer periods (eg five years); the payment amounts may be fixed, indexed at a set annual percentage rate or at RPI; a minimum number of payments may be guaranteed. Sometimes a combination of a variety of different types of annuity in different amounts will be necessary to generate the required income-stream. In this case, it is important to remember that some life offices will only quote for certain types of annuity: the broker needs to know what type and size of annuity an office will quote for as well as the relative competitiveness of offices on price.

6.4 To do or not to do? The process of delivering the structure is essentially down to the defendant: it is after all the defendant who pays for it. It is, as set out above, a routine task, once understood. It is the defendant's prerogative to do the work himself; to use his normal solicitor or accountant; or to engage a specialist structured settlement practice. In terms of managing their costs and overall outlay, insurers are well advised to contract out to specialist professionals only those tasks which insurers are unable to carry out for themselves.

6.5 Competing views. One major UK composite insurer which set out to arrange structured settlements is now on record as preferring to involve a specialist intermediary, preferably engaged by the plaintiff. They make the point that the plaintiff requires professional advice upon future needs and the suitability of the structure package. The alternative view is that provided the insurer's negotiators have sufficient experience to assess the plaintiff's requirements and the insurer has suitable arrangements to obtain annuity quotations, he can act properly in his own interest in this specialist field. However, where only small numbers of cases will be handled, it is prudent and practical to engage a specialist intermediary.

6.6   Once a structure always a structure. All parties must remember that once arranged the structured settlement cannot be varied: the payments will be made precisely to plan. Great care is therefore necessary to ensure that the structured settlement will be adequate compensation: it must not be defeated in its purpose by subsequent financial hardship. A key part of the package is to ensure the optimum balance between any up-front or contingency lump sum and the residual structure.

7   FORMALISING THE SETTLEMENT

7.1   The accountant's role: Introduction. The professional accountant frequently has a key role to play in the handling of PI claims. Both sides may engage cccountants: the plaintiff to set out and support the Schedule and the defendant to analyse the Schedule or prepare a Counter-Schedule.

7.2   Court approval/the Court of Protection. In Court of Protection cases the evidence of an accountant in support of an agreed settlement is essential, and this must be provided on behalf of the plaintiff. Court approval is required very quickly to ensure that annuity quotations which form the basis of the proposed settlement can be taken up within the short time available. A Practice Note (Appendix) has been drawn up to facilitate this.

7.3   Contrasting structured offers with lump sums. When presenting to the plaintiff a schedule of benefits under a proposed structured settlement, the insurer is bound to be asked how these benefits compare with the income available from a conventional lump sum settlement. The insurer's accountant—or indeed the claims department if it develops an appropriate PC spreadsheet programme—can readily display this. Comparisons can be based upon net income from annuities purchased or can be based upon standard rates of interest. The latter will show how speedily the lump sum is eroded to nothing. (See Figure 5E (b)). For the purpose of negotiations, these analyses can be prepared for a range of lump sums, possibly between the plaintiff's claim and the annuity purchase price anticipated by the defendant. They can also be based on a range of assumptions, including interest rates, tax rates, management costs, etc.

7.4 The model agreement. The agreement must be drawn up in the correct format, detailing the schedule of payments and the debt which will be extinguished, and it must be signed. The antecedent debt which is satisfied by the schedule of payments must be shown in the Agreement. (There is not always formal agreement on the amount of damages due. However, such a figure must be stated and the Inland Revenue are insisting that if there is a Guarantee Period then the antecedent debt must exceed the sums payable in that period.)

7.5 Revenue approval. It has been mentioned that in normal practice the Revenue are sometimes unable to approve proposed settlements sufficiently quickly in advance to enable take-up of the annuity quotation. If there are any unusual features in the proposed settlement, it may be possible to obtain an informal view in advance. However, in the absence of a proper basis at law the rule is to stick absolutely to the Model Agreement and to a simple, explicable benefit stream. The annuities must be of the appropriate types described above. The annuity purchased by the insurer must tally with the damages paid by instalments to the plaintiff. The Revenue will not permit an arrangement which generates surplus moneys to the insurer in the event of the death of the Life Assured. The Agreement cannot be entered into after judgment has been entered. (In the *Everett* case the Judge had to adjourn the Hearing for three months, to allow exploration of the possibility of achieving a structured settlement, failing which judgment would have been entered at a figure agreed between the parties.)

The Revenue set out its view on the tax aspects of structured settlements in an article published in 'Litigation Letter' (Vol 7, No 10, February 1989).

7.6 Purchasing the annuity. Speed is of the essence in taking up an annuity quotation. The Agreement must be concluded before the annuity is purchased and the annuity must be purchased within the limited period for which the quotation is guaranteed, or a quote will have to be obtained.

7.7 Making payments. The insurer must remain liable to the claimant for the settlement instalments to secure the Income Tax relief for the annuity payments. Therefore it is not technically possible for the life office to issue an annuity payable directly to the claimant. However, administratively the defendant insurer may wish to arrange for the life office to act as his 'paying agent'. To ensure that the Revenue does not claim such an arrangement is in effect the issue of an annuity direct to the claimant, a document in the form of a letter or statement of agreed procedure between the defendant insurer and the life office should be prepared. The insurer may also seek to forward the tax rebates via the life office. In this case, care is needed to ensure proper administration of the total payment to the claimant by the life office. Alternatively, the insurer will make the settlement payments to the claimant direct and receive the annuity payments from the life office and the tax recovery from the Inland Revenue.

7.8   Tax refund. The life office will prepare a statement of the tax deductions which have been made and the insurer should make the appropriate application for exemption from income tax to the Inland Revenue. The rebate is, of course, subject to approval of the underlying Agreement. The insurer assumes the defendant's liability, in the terms of the Agreement. The Inland Revenue accept this for tax purposes. Payments by the insurer are treated as payments of debt by way of damages, ie they are not taxable in the hands of the claimant. The annuity income of the insurer is taxable, the settlement instalments are tax-deductible, and these net out as tax-neutral. The insurer has to obtain the tax deduction for the annuity purchase as he would normally for a claim payment. The Inland Revenue propose various treatments of the purchase and the ABI has issued a paper detailing its Structured Settlement Panel's view of the tax treatment. Of the various Revenue proposals, the preferred approach seems to be to treat the purchase of the annuity as a form of reinsurance purchase, so that the premium is accepted as tax-deductible. In practice, the payment is charged against the claim to secure the integrity of reported claims figures and equal asset and liability entries are retained in the balance sheet. The insurer must involve his tax and financial officials and auditors to ensure the correct treatment of these transactions in the accounts of the company.

8   PROBLEMS WITH AND BARRIERS TO STRUCTURED SETTLEMENTS

8.1   Unfamiliarity and unwillingness. Many insurance claims managers and handlers and many solicitors, both for defendants and plaintiffs, are as yet unfamiliar with the potential for and the processes attaching to structured settlements. Unfamiliarity is a powerful disincentive to taking action: suspicion can lead to rejection. One is more inclined to respond to reasons not to proceed than to seek reasons to proceed. This will change with greater understanding of the opportunities, increasing credibility of the benefits. Those insurers who have forced themselves and their advisers to pursue and promote structured settlements at every sensible opportunity are increasingly confident that they have stolen a march on their more conservative competitors.

8.2 Limited scope. The limited scope of the Revenue-approved Model Agreement both restricts and inhibits structured settlements. Mutual insurers and overseas insurers are unable to reclaim the tax deducted and therefore cannot obtain financial advantage. In one case, a mutual insurance company was able to arrange for the periodic payments to be made by the defendant Local Authority. This device will not always be available and it does not conform strictly with the terms of the Model Agreement, so that any such arrangement would need to be separately negotiated with the Inland Revenue. The position of these insurers in relation to structured settlements is one of agreeing to structure without the benefit of the tax relief on an annuity. Such an arrangement has been concluded in a structured settlement entered into by a Regional Health Authority in a medical accident case. In the case of Sian Boyd O'Toole, the major part of the award was in the form of a series of future payments of unknown amount and duration. The Health Authority are to pay regular sums starting at £20,000 per annum together with lump sums every five years based on a figure of £5,000 and all payments are guaranteed to be index-linked and to be paid for as long as Sian is alive. Sian is not liable to tax. The settlement is highly advantageous to Sian and the cash-flow and investment implications for the NHS would seem to be beneficial. The arrangements for reclaim of tax at Lloyd's are off-putting.

8.3 Revenue approval. Technically, Inland Revenue approval is required for each individual Agreement and this may not in practice be obtained within the very limited lifetime of annuity quotations. In practice, therefore, the decision to proceed may be taken against the possibility that Inland Revenue approval of the tax recovery may not be forthcoming. This is not a real risk for simple structures readily defined within the Model Agreement, but it is an increasing risk when sophisticated payment schedules are required. Indeed, the Inland Revenue may not approve proposals which involve additional periodic lump sums; a death benefit; stepped annuity payments, etc. There is a growing perception that a simple, inflation-protected annuity with a Guaranteed Period is the appropriate basis for most structured settlements. Plaintiffs can save and invest from these payments against future planned expenditure and, indeed, can raise capital against them.

8.4   Absence of a basis at law. Whilst structured settlements have now been recognised by the law and, indeed, parameters for approval have been set out, there are many outstanding issues. Amongst these, uncertain attitudes to discounts—indeed the concept of a discount as definable or relevant—can give rise to difficulty. It was not technically possible for the defendant to protect himself against future costs by paying-in on a structured basis. (It has been suggested that an equivalent approach is to make an open offer on a Calderbank basis but there are practical difficulties of application in the final analysis)..

8.5   Administration costs. The insurer is responsible for the maintenance of payments to the claimant. He must arrange for direct payment of the tax deducted and must arrange to recover that tax. He has to deal with any queries or problems which arise with annuity payments. These could be chores as simple as notifying change of address or bank account to problems as serious as recovering overpayments or dealing with non-payment by the life office. The basic task is simple and undemanding but it is one which has to be done and it is a long-term commitment. Indeed, if the settlement obligation could be transferred to the life office this would simplify accounting requirements for the defendant insurer and it would bring all considerations of insurer insolvency within the ambit of the Policyholders Protection Act. Whilst there is no immediate prospect of such reform in the tax laws, lobbying has commenced.

8.6   Interest loss. Example calculations are set out elsewhere but there is a loss of interest to the insurer for the period during which he has paid out to the claimant tax deducted and not yet recovered it from the Inland Revenue.

8.7   Security. The position of both the defendant insurer and the structured settlement beneficiary is substantially protected in the event of the failure of the life office providing the underlying annuity. This is because s 10 of the Policyholders Protection Act requires the Policyholders Protection Board 'to secure that a sum equal to 90% of the amount of any liability of the company in liquidation towards any policyholder under the terms of long-term policy which was a United Kingdom policy at the beginning of the liquidation is paid to the policyholder as soon as reasonably practicable after the beginning of the liquidation'. In the event of the failure of the defendant insurer, the Policyholders Protection Board has advised that sums owed by the insurer to a third party, pursuant to s 151 of the Road Traffic Act and a structured settlement conforming to the ABI Model Agreement, would be expected to qualify for protection under s 7 of the Policyholders Protection Act (provided that all applicable eligibility criteria contained in the latter Act were met). This protection does require that a consent order is obtained to the settlement. In the case of Lloyd's Syndicates, the cessation of a syndicate would be covered by the normal transfer of liability to the next syndicate. In the event of a valid claim not being met, then Lloyd's Central Fund would ultimately be available.

A plaintiff who entrusted his lump sum in the care of the Bank of Credit and Commerce International (BCCI)—and, let us face it, some will have done so—felt pretty sick on 5 July 1991, when the demise of the Bank shocked the country. The invalid whose investments were in shares or Unit Trusts in October 1987 now faces a bleak future. These collapses remind us that nothing is totally secure: no investment, job, marriage, health nor life itself. On balance, even the astute investor is unlikely to secure a future income as certain as a structured settlement.

9   MOVES AFOOT

9.1   Law Commission. As long ago as 1978, the Pearson Commission made a majority recommendation that compensation for future pecuniary loss caused by death or serious or lasting injury should be by way of periodic payments; and that an obligation be placed on the Court to make such an order unless it were satisfied, on the application of the plaintiff, that a lump sum award would be more appropriate. Also, the plaintiff's legal adviser should bear a duty to point out the benefits of periodic payments to his client. These recommendations were not progressed but the Law Commission is currently reviewing the law relating to PI compensation. It is widely expected to encourage a move towards structured settlements by proposing some powers for Courts to make awards on this basis and generally to facilitate the agreement of a structured basis in appropriate circumstances. Unless the tax rules are amended to make it possible for insurance companies to manage their own funds on the same basis of taxation as Life Funds, this may not be entirely appropriate. For example, if a competitive annuity quotation could not be obtained to support a structure award, the defendant insurer would be left to provide for and make payments of instalment damages for an unspecified period during which he would be paying tax on investment income.

9.2   Use of damages. As part of its Review, the Law Commission has enlisted the assistance of the major insurers in an exercise to ascertain how previously awarded damages have been utilised. It is generally expected that this survey will demonstrate that the vast majority of sums agreed or awarded: (i) will have been used within a relatively short time after settlement, (ii) will not have been used at all in the way anticipated in the Schedule of damages, and (iii) the claimants now face a very uncertain financial future.

The Rehabilitation Studies Unit of the University of Edinburgh Medical Faculty has already undertaken a major study of this subject. Their findings are just becoming public. This study found very little evidence of profligacy or financial hardship. It found that the pattern and level of actual expenditure bore little resemblance to that as anticipated by the Schedules upon which damages had been assessed. The vast majority of claimants retained a substantial residue of their awards long after settlement. Generally this was saved or invested against future contingencies. There is evidence of a simplistic and anxious approach to management of capital, with insufficient access to independent financial advice.

These findings may endorse two views which are increasingly widely held in insurance circles. Firstly, the conventional basis on which plaintiffs' advisers present and Courts evaluate damages bears little or no relationship to post-settlement lifestyle. It has had the damaging social effect of increasing levels of damages whilst failing to address the fundamental concern and need of the claimant. Secondly, the prime concern of victims is long-term financial security, sufficient to cater for their needs as time goes on. Coping with disability and disadvantage is one thing; coping with fear and uncertainty is quite another.

The Law Commission observed that 'there is an inconsistency in a plaintiff arguing that a particular need exists, such as for an adapted house, and then using the money for something completely different . . . If the money is not to be spent on the need, then the need cannot be real' (see The Law Commission Consultation Paper No 125, para 3.73.)

9.3 Obligation on the plaintiff's solicitor. As well as facilitating periodic payments of compensation, the Law Commission may well import a specific obligation upon plaintiffs' legal advisers to positively consider and encourage rehabilitation, recovery and future employment. As the focus shifts from maximising the lump sum to securing the provision of appropriate payments in the future, it is entirely appropriate that the focus should shift to future quality of life. The solicitor who neglects the one becomes as culpable as the solicitor who neglects the other.

9.4 ABI. The Association of British insurers has been closely involved in the development of structured settlements from the start. It was the ABI which agreed the Model Agreement with the Inland Revenue, to establish the basis for structured settlements in this country. Insurers are impatient for a proper basis in law for structured settlements and the ABI is likely to propose specific law reforms in advance of the Law Commission Review. In particular, the desire to achieve rapid or automatic approval for a wider range of Agreements, the ability to assign the Agreement to the life office and clearance for gross payments direct from life office to beneficiary are high on the agenda.

9.5 Rehabilitation. 'Rehabilitation implies the restoration of patients to their fullest physical, psychological and social capability' (MIAR Report, 1972). It is a medio-social approach to accident aftercare. The key to effective rehabilitation is accurate assessment. What are the patient's problems and what action is to be taken to reduce them?

According to Professor Cairns Aitken of the Univeristy of Edinburgh:

'Of greatest importance is prevention of possible complications, both medical and psychological. The aim is to reduce functional loss. Efforts to minimise physical dependency and maximise mobility are worthwhile. Efforts to minimise emotional dependence and to maximise motivation/morale are also worthwhile. These efforts are included in a variety of treatments.

Of equal importance is action to reduce social disadvantage. It is more likely to involve casework. The aim should be to minimise boredom and avoid poverty. Access to buildings for wheelchairs is being improved to encourage integration. The freedom of choice through equality of opportunities is important. Equipment to assist independence should be prescribed, and assistance available for personal care if necessary. Assistance to encourage useful employment should always be considered.

The purpose of the assessment is to obtain for the patient appropriately whatever services are both required and available, no more and no less. Assessment is as much to determine capabilities as disabilities, and so what the patient does not require is as important as what he does. Assessment must not encourage demands for excessive help, but rather encourage self-care and independence.'

Several professions can be involved in providing rehabilitation services, including physio-therapy, occupational therapy and clinical psychology.

9.6   After-care services and rehabilitation. There are now organised, multi-professional disability teams in the private sector and in complex cases a rehabilitation co-ordinator may be engaged to assist continuity of clinical management. Although these services are available in NHS Hospitals, many areas are poorly provided for. There is increasing emphasis on provision of aftercare services in the community by voluntary services and by informal care such as relatives.

9.7   Rehabilitation—the extent of 'take-up'. Studies at the University of Edinburgh Rehabilitation Studies Unit showed that there was very little take-up of rehabilitation/re-settlement services amongst a large sample of accident victims. Less than 5% had any involvement with occupational/industrial therapy, employment rehabilitation or involvement with the DoE's training services, despite many claimants having some difficulty in return to employment. Patients seemed not to be referred to available services more on account of lack of awareness of the potential value than because of their unavailability.

9.8   Rehabilitation and structured settlements? Where is the link between rehabilitation and structured settlements? Rehabilitation is required as soon as possible after the injuries and the structured settlement is required to fund continuing future commitments. In combination they realise the best possible future prospects. The one best defines future needs: the other delivers the funding programme to address them.

9.9 A formal link—Canada. The link is formalised in Canadian Motor Insurance Rules. Accident victims are entitled to a wide range of goods and services, whether medical or non-medical in nature, which the injured person requires because of the accident. This includes rehabilitation, life skills training and occupational counselling and training.

According to Bob Gunn, CEO of Royal Insurance Canada, an insurance company's participation in rehabilitation is motivated by two principles:

— The automobile policy contains specific rehabilitation benefits to which every qualified policyholder is entitled.
— Initiation of the rehabilitation process as quickly as possible is to the advantage of both parties involved, claimant and company. It creates a positive attitude and quick recovery for claimants and it leads to lower loss costs for the company.

In his view:

'In order to move away from the traditional and largely adversarial claims handling system and develop claims management expertise, a team approach is required. This team would include the rehabilitation case Manager from the insurance company, the health care professional and the individual's family, employers, and any other person who can assist in the overall process.'

According to Gunn:

'The widely accepted rule of thumb in the rehab. business is that for every dollar spent on rehab., there is an estimated saving of $7 on the ultimate loss-cost of a claim. Whether or not this number is accurate is difficult to say. What is clear, however, is that early rehabilitation is cost-effective, is an injured policyholder's right under our policy, and is a path we must take as an Industry if we are to survive.'

Gunn's guidelines for establishing an effective rehabilitation policy are as follows:

— We will react quickly because it is in our own best interests. The general rule is that if a patient is taken into a rehabilitation centre within three to six months of their injury, around 85% will return to work. After six months, there is a very sharp drop-off, and when a year goes by, only a tiny percentage of disabled people ever return to work.

— Injured policyholders are entitled to rehabilitation services at once, not as a last resort.

— Paperwork and process must never take precedence over people.

— Rehabilitation cannot be restricted to medical and vocational assistance only. The psychological trauma of an accident can require specialised treatment that goes far beyond the bounds of these conventional approaches. To restrict treatment to a narrow range of options is unprofessional and unfair.

9.10   The USA perspective. In the USA, Workers Compensation Legislation allows defendants to become involved in mitigating damages as they occur. Defendants can become involved in managing the consequences of accidents. Some insurers even have rehabilitation nurses—licensed nurses—in their Workers Compensation Claims Units. They assess and advise on the rehabilitation programme and evaluate if employment is possible, although they do not normally directly provide treatment or job placement. This in-house expertise allows defendant insurers to assess the plaintiff's approach to rehabilitation in other actions where they may be at arm's length, and this is an important negotiation tactic.

9.11   A UK dimension? Should this intervention be necessary in the UK? A partner in Lawrence Graham wrote in the Law Society Gazette in July 1989:

'It should be a matter of concern to the profession's indemnity insurers that many of those handling personal injury claims remain totally unaware of the concept (of structured settlements), and of the advantages it may offer their client.'

Should that observation not be extended to rehabilitation? Rehabilitation is about doing the best for the client's future life. It is also about mitigating his possible claim. The defendant who puts an early, positive, supportive proposal to the plaintiff's advisers must hope that the offer is taken up: but should not shrink from citing, and pleading, failure to mitigate if it is not.

10   SUMMARY AND CONCLUSION

10.1   Future prospects? The number of structured settlements, from small beginnings, is sky-rocketing. Industry estimates suggest that nearly 150 settlements were structured in 1992, involving annuity purchases of around £30m. Another company analysis concluded that as structures 'catch on' and as its people catch on to structures the company might expect to structure ten times as many settlements in four to five years time. This could mean a market of 1,500 settlements and £300m annuity purchases per annum before the end of the century—provided plaintiffs and defendants succeed in realising the mutual advantage.

10.2   Pressure to change. Most PI claims are far too small to structure. By no means all large PI claims will structure. But the emerging obligation to consider positively the structure option, in many cases—and with it the pressure to assess objectively future needs and to act to improve prospects—will transform the tenor of PI litigation. Structured settlements—more particularly the approach to structuring a settlement—presage an altogether more constructive and pro-active approach to arriving at proper compensation. An approach in tune with the social and economic imperatives of the day. An approach which brings the parties together to agree, rather than keeping them apart to dispute. To agree on compensation targeted effectively at real need; achieved swiftly, efficiently and at relatively low cost.

10.3   The insurer's interest. The tangible benefits, as we have seen, are discounts off conventional settlements. Benefits less easy to track are the reductions in overall cost from early, agreed settlements. Intangible benefits flow from the basis of settlement which relieves post-settlement stress and is perceived as being fair.

But perhaps the most significant benefit to the insurer is that he—the Exchequer—will regain the initiative in the settlement process. Taking a positive, enterprising, firm and constructive approach to claims handling—to which the plaintiff and his advisers must respond in similar vein—will in my view contribute much in the long run to 'administering accident losses efficiently in the public interest'. The special opportunities afforded by structured settlements confer focus and power on hitherto impotent initiatives to unjam the settlement process.

10.4   Only the best will do.   PI litigation and structured settlements demand of insurers specialist expertise, committed case management, sound strategy and professional advisers in tune with their principal's requirements. Some insurers are now becoming familiar with structuring settlements; planning ahead to structure claims and building up expertise in the process. If the American experience is anything to go by, they will benefit through achieving better settlements all round. Other insurers will follow. Success depends on change in attitudes, of insurance practitioners and legal advisors; on enlisting professional experts in the rehabilitation field; on preparations to arrange the annuity package and administer payments and tax, and perhaps above all on the deployment of top-class evaluation and negotiation skills in an exciting new environment.

6 Accountancy and Taxation Issues

Brian W Taylor and Linda Cheung

1 GENERAL

1.1 Introduction

For a number of years professional accountants have played an important role in assisting those dealing with personal injury compensation claims. For this reason many accountancy firms now offer 'forensic accountancy'. It sounds impressive, but what does it actually mean?

1.2 Forensic accountancy

Forensic accountancy can be described as 'the application of accountancy skills to legal matters'. These matters often necessitate financial investigations and potentially or actually involve litigation. Furthermore, they may require a professional with extensive experience of forensic matters—the forensic accountant.

1.3 The forensic accountant

The nature of a forensic accountant's work calls for particular attributes and specialist skills, and includes:

— speedy identification of the major financial issues in a case, which are then put into the appropriate legal context;
— assimilation of large quantities of information, having regard to the necessity for attention to detail;
— investigation into the circumstances, facts and evidence to quantify and analyse the amounts involved;
— assisting counsel and those instructing us to develop the financial argument;
— preparation of reports which are intelligible to the non-accountant, fully substantiated by evidence and of direct relevance to the case;
— with the benefit of clear and impartial advice on quantum, the parties may be able to settle matters more readily. Alternatively, the forensic accountant can assist by giving evidence at trial.

The level of assistance provided by the forensic accountant will depend on many factors, including the size and complexity of the issues involved and the experience of other professionals in the 'team'. Likewise, whether acting for the plaintiff or defendant, the forensic accountant's approach must be flexible and designed to bring out matters relevant to the case.

Having looked briefly at the general nature of a forensic accountant's work, it is now appropriate to consider his role in the alternative method of settling personal injury and fatal accident cases—the structured settlement.

2 THE FORENSIC ACCOUNTANT'S ROLE IN STRUCTURED SETTLEMENTS

2.1 Introduction

It is often said that structured settlements are a panacea when quantum cannot be resolved on a conventional basis; they are not and should only rarely be regarded as such. Similarly, the forensic accountant's involvement is not a panacea and should be considered with particular reference to the case in question. This will necessarily involve having regard to the skills and experience of other members of the 'team', including:

—   instructing solicitors;
—   general insurer;
—   counsel; and
—   the plaintiff/plaintiff's representative.

In our experience the forensic accountant's involvement in structured settlements mirrors his role in any other assignment and aims to provide a valuable input in the litigation process. We have already considered, in paragraph 1 above, the particular attributes and specialist skills which the forensic accountant may bring to the 'team'. It is important for the accountant to appreciate that he is part of a team, when determining the level of professional support required from him.

2.1.1 *Kelly and Another v Dawes*

During 1989 the case of Catherine Kelly received widespread publicity as the first Court-approved structured settlement in the UK, for a UK resident to receive damages by instalments.

The facts of this case have already been included in Chapter 2, hence it is not necessary to reiterate them here. It is relevant, however, to look at the approval of the case by the High Court and in particular the judgment of Mr Justice Potter on 14 July 1989. This judgment has been used as a reference to assist practitioners and the judiciary implement and approve structured settlements. Furthermore, the judgment sets out what information it was thought appropriate to place before the court for cases where the structure requires approval.

This information is contained in six paragraphs within Mr Justice Potter's judgment. It is, however, the second paragraph which recognises the contribution of the forensic accountant:

'(2) A report by accountants or other financial experts as to the fiscal and investment advantages to the plaintiff of the structured settlement proposed, with particular regard to the life expectancy and the likely future costs of car'.

In addition to the above, it is likely that the forensic accountant's role will include assistance with the following:

'(3) A draft of the form of agreement proposed, together with confirmation that the Inland Revenue regard such an agreement as within the scope of any revenue provisions or practice on which the value of the structured settlement depends.

(4) Where appropriate, confirmation of the approved terms of the agreement by the Court of Protection conditional upon the approval of the settlement by the Court.

(5) Material to satisfy the court that there are sufficient funds available outside the structured provisions to meet any foreseeable capital needs of the plaintiff, whether by means of a "lump sum" element in the settlement or by reason of other resources available to the plaintiff.'

As the judgment explicitly states, the settlement must be in the overall interests of the disabled plaintiff. In certain circumstances therefore, provision of the information contained in Mr Justice Potter's judgment may not suffice and further queries may arise. Only when all the concerns of the Court are satisfied will approval of the settlement be granted. Depending on the nature of the queries, the forensic accountant's input may be valuable.

2.2   Life after the *Kelly* case

It is nearly four years since the case of *Kelly and Another v Dawes* made legal history and from this time there has been significant growth in the number of cases where a structured settlement has been considered. Practitioners have grasped the opportunity they offer with enthusiasm and consequently the market has expanded its activities in some interesting and innovative ways.

Notable dates include:

31 October 1991   Mr Justice Phillips approves the terms of the settlement in the case of Rebecca Field against Herefordshire Health Authority.

A new legal precedent was created as this was the first medical negligence case in the country where a structured settlement was implemented.

This settlement opened the way for any case involving the Crown, or a statutory authority, to be structured.

12 February 1992   A practice note is issued regarding the settlement of personal injury and fatal accident claims where approval of the Court is required and which include a structured settlement.

The practice note is appropriate whether or not the Court of Protection is involved. In cases where the plaintiff is under a mental disability then the consent of the Court of Protection is required and the practice note sets out the additional steps which must be followed.

A copy of this practice note is reproduced as appendix II.

30 March 1992 Master Keith Topley's practice note comes into effect, following its issue on 12 February 1992.

14 August 1992 The Lord Chancellor's department issues a press notice with reference to the new rules for Court of Protection fees in structured settlement cases.

21 August 1992 The case of Sian Boyd O'Toole is settled between the girl's family and Merseyside Regional Health Authority.

This medical accident case represents the first in the country to be settled by means of a self-funded structure.

The settlement is to be funded by the Department of Health, rather than from an annuity purchased by the defendants from a life assurance company.

The result is that there are substantial cash savings for the NHS and the ability to retain significant amounts of cash within its funding.

24 August 1992 The Court of Protection (Amendment) Rules 1992 come into force. These rules determine how to treat payments of damages under structured settlements in calculating a patient's clear annual income for the purposes of calculating Court of Protection fees.

The rules provide that half of any annuity payments received by a plaintiff under a structure are to be treated as income for this purpose.

The first payment made under a structured settlement, usually a lump sum, will be ignored. Likewise, any interim payments made prior to a structured settlement are ignored.

3   THE FORENSIC ACCOUNTANT'S REPORT

3.1   Introduction

We have already looked at paragraph (2) of the judgment in the Catherine Kelly case, which refers to 'a report by accountants or other financial experts'. Similarly, paragraphs (3) to (5) of the judgment refer to matters which the forensic accountant may incorporate into his report or where he may be of assistance.

Turning to Master Topley's practice note, appendix II, it is interesting to note that, subject to minor amendments, all the information referred to above is included at paragraph 6 thereof. Paragraph 6 (iii) includes specific reference to a report of forensic accountants, in place of 'accountants or other financial experts'. Likewise the reference to ' . . . fiscal and investment advantages to the plaintiff . . . ' has been replaced by ' . . . the advantages and disadvantages, if any . . . '.

Whether our instructions are received from solicitors or insurers, we recognise that the timely preparation of the forensic accountant's report may be of crucial importance to the progress of a case. Although we believe that the best results are often achieved when forensic accountants are instructed at the earliest opportunity, on many occasions reports have been produced within a short timescale with very satisfactory results.

Although we refer in this section to 'report' in the singular, we stress that the forensic accountant's approach to each case must be flexible. It is likely in some cases that two reports are required, particularly where no final conclusions have been reached regarding the implementation of a structure.

It is perhaps appropriate at this stage to consider some of the issues which the forensic accountant may address in his report:

— the advantages and disadvantages of a structured settlement;
— determining the structure;
— annuity quotations from Life Offices;
— structured settlement or traditional lump sum;
— the plaintiff's capital situation;
— the plaintiff's income situation.

A closer examination of the issues raised above now follows in the ensuing paragraphs.

3.2 The advantages and disadvantages of a structured settlement

The mechanics of structuring, together with the advantages and disadvantages thereof to both plaintiffs and defendants, have already been illustrated in earlier chapters. It is not therefore the purpose of this section to repeat the detailed arguments already given. What we intend to do is to look briefly at the forensic accountant's role when these issues are considered in practice.

It is essential that both parties have expert financial advice on the advantages and disadvantages of a structured settlement. Furthermore, this advice should be given at an early stage in the litigation process so that all matters can be fully explored and any concerns or scepticism can be extinguished. By doing this a 'team spirit' can be established, together with the necessary co-operation of both parties before any negotiations commence.

The forensic accountant may provide the advice referred to above at a preliminary meeting with either the plaintiff and his advisers or the defendant's advisers. In our experience, the extent of the forensic accountant's role is determined by the experience of the solicitors, insurer and Counsel involved. It may also be of assistance if the forensic accountant regularly acts both for plaintiffs and defendants independently.

In all cases, maximum benefit to the plaintiff and the defendant—the 'win–win' situation—can only accrue if the advice given is impartial and relates specifically to the circumstances of the individual case. By a careful assessment of the plaintiff's needs, taking into account the medical condition and life expectancy, it is likely that a clear indication will emerge as to whether any form of 'structuring' is advisable or likely to be beneficial.

Having established the potential advantages of 'structuring' in an individual case, with the defendant's co-operation, it is necessary to consider exactly what is to be structured.

3.3 Determining the structure

Quite clearly it is the plaintiff's damages which are to be structured, but is it all the damages? As we have already seen from earlier chapters, this is unlikely to be the case. Neither is it the case that structuring merely involves the purchase of an annuity by the defendant's insurer.

In assessing the amount of damages available to purchase the annuity it may be necessary for the forensic accountant, in conjunction with the plaintiff's advisers, to consider the following:

— interim payments;
— the plaintiff's immediate requirements;
— contingency fund;
— insurer's discount.

Information regarding the first three items can be deduced from a thorough examination of the plaintiff's present financial position and future likely or desired requirements. This may involve consideration of the financial circumstances of the plaintiff's family and responsibility for dependants.

This examination must cover all aspects of the plaintiff's life, including care, transport, accommodation, other equipment and therapy requirements. Furthermore, the examination must have regard to the plaintiff's medical assessments and life expectancy, together with the requirement for income and capital. If any moneys from previous interim payments remain available, they can be utilised to fund part of the plaintiff's immediate requirements or the contingency fund.

3.4   The contingency fund

What exactly is the contingency fund? The contingency or emergency fund is an amount which is paid by the defendant's insurer in the traditional 'lump sum manner'. This sum can be invested by the plaintiff or his receiver independently, or if appropriate by the Court of Protection. The concept is that such funds will be available for emergencies and additional non-recurring expenditure not covered by the regular income from the annuity. Clearly, it is important that adequate consideration is given to the determination of that proportion of the plaintiff's damages which will form the contingency fund.

The plaintiff's contingency fund overcomes one of the problems of the purchased annuity, 'flexibility', and allows for a change in circumstances. It is essential therefore that the plaintiff, together with his advisers, takes appropriate advice regarding the possible investment options for the lump sum. This should include an explanation of the risk involved and taxation consequences thereof.

3.5 The insurer's discount

The insurer's discount—how much? This is undoubtedly a 'hot topic' amongst both plaintiff and defendant advisers. It may be said that just as the concept of structuring has 'caught on' so has the insurer's discount. A useful guide to a reasonable level of discount for the insurer may be given by an examination of the taxation benefits to be obtained by the plaintiff from the annuity instalments. One school of thought suggests that the present value of the taxation benefits to the plaintiff over the period of his life expectancy should be divided equally between the parties. Clearly, these calculations involve estimates of future tax rates, amongst other matters, but at least they form a basis for negotiation.

In other cases the insurer's discount has been a figure, seemingly plucked from the air, which is then converted into percentage terms. This itself is not without complications because it can lead to widespread confusion as to what the discount is a percentage of—the lump sum that would otherwise be payable in a conventional settlement, or the sum required to purchase the annuity?

It is only by negotiation and discussion between the parties that an appropriate discount for every individual case will be derived. This discount is not just a figure to be incorporated into your next structured settlement; it is a vital component which results from an adequate consideration of the circumstances in each case. Nevertheless, some discount is appropriate, not merely to reflect the time saving to the plaintiff but also the future transactions to be processed by the defendant insurer and the loss of cash flow to the insurer due to the delay in recovering the time deducted by the life assurer.

3.6 Putting the elements together

Once sufficient information regarding the four items above has been gathered, they can be valued individually and deducted from the total award of damages. The resultant figure represents the amount available to purchase the annuity, as shown by the example in Table 6A below.

It may be that once annuity quotations are obtained the values of certain component parts of the structure have to be reconsidered. If the case requires consent from the Court of Protection, it is beneficial for the forensic accountant to be aware, at an early stage, if the Master has any specific requirements, eg a certain size of contingency fund. Liaison between the plaintiff's advisers and the Court of Protection is therefore essential to ensure that adequate time is available to consider the Master's concerns and rectify the structure as appropriate.

TABLE 6A: Elements of a structure

	£	£
Damages awarded on conventional lump sum basis		700,000
less:		
Interim payments already expended	162,000	
Immediate requirements*	33,000	
Contingency fund	70,000	
		265,000
		435,000
Insurer's discount		35,000
Moneys available to purchase an annuity		400,000

*   These would be funded by a further lump sum payment of £30,000 from the insurer, together with moneys available from previous interim payments.

Whilst the example above is based on establishing the total lump sum damages on the conventional basis and then valuing the component parts for a structured settlement, this is not essential. We are increasingly becoming involved in cases at an early stage, where the intention is to agree the component parts of the structure for their individual value rather than as an allocation of the value of the total sum of damages.

At this point in the process of structuring, the forensic accountant or independent intermediary is likely to survey the market for competitive annuity quotations. This is necessary because ultimately the defendant's insurer will probably purchase an annuity from a Life Assurance Company (Life Office), to place it in funds to pay the plaintiff the agreed series of payments under the structure.

4 THE ANNUITY

4.1 Introduction

One of the attractions of a structured settlement is that the financial package is designed to meet the plaintiff's needs by way of periodic payments guaranteed for life. This contrasts with the conventional lump sum which may be extinguished whilst the plaintiff is still alive. Alternatively some of the damages may be left over, which could mean that the plaintiff has 'gone without'.

It follows from the above that annuities are therefore a useful tool in the structuring process. Although they can be purchased on different bases, the most popular form is the annuity written on an individual's life. This is payable for the life of the individual, however long that may be, and payments would normally cease on death.

4.2 Guarantees

It is possible that payments can continue for a minimum period regardless of when the individual's death occurs. This period is often referred to as the 'guarantee period' and is useful for the following reasons:

— it removes the risk of losing a large amount of capital, if the plaintiff were to die shortly after the annuity was purchased;
— if the plaintiff has dependants, whether it be a spouse or children, the annuity payment will still be made during the guarantee period and form part of the plaintiff's estate.

4.3 Varieties of annuities

It should be remembered, however, that the annuity represents deferred payments of damages to the plaintiff and is not intended to be for the benefit of the plaintiff's estate.

In general terms an annuity can be regarded as a lump sum investment offered by Life Offices. As a result of a contract between the purchaser, which will be the defendant's insurer, and a Life Office, an annuity provides a series of future payments. In the context of structured settlements, these future payments:

— duration   can be for a specified term, ie 5, 10 or 15 years
<u>or</u>
for life;

— escalation   may escalate by reference to the Retail Price Index (RPI), ie index-linked
<u>or</u>
at a fixed compound rate, eg 5%;

— commencement   may commence as soon as the annuity is purchased ie immediate
<u>or</u>
commence at a specified date in the future, ie deferred
<u>or</u>
commence immediately but increase in amount at a specified date in the future, ie stepped;

— frequency   can be made at varying intervals, ie monthly, quarterly, half-yearly, annually, or at even longer intervals such as five-yearly.
The above payments can usually be made in advance or arrears.

4.4   Surveying the market

As an annuity is generally a fixed-interest investment, the return is calculated by reference to current and anticipated rates of interest, taking into account the life expectancy of the individual. Other factors which can affect the return on an annuity are:

— If the annuity is index-linked there is no certainty as to what future payments will escalate to. Life Offices are able to offer these because there are securities that can be purchased in the market which are linked to the rate of inflation, ie British Government index-linked stock.

    A potential problem arises in 2029, from which date indexation increases will be subject to the continuing availability of suitable British Government Securities. Most Life Offices in the structured settlement market have overcome this, however, by offering a fixed percentage rate of escalation in the year 2030 and thereafter, eg 5% or 7%, should suitable stocks no longer exist.

The details set out in Table 6B illustrate, for three Life Offices, how the initial return on an index-linked annuity compares to the return on an annuity escalating at a fixed 5% per annum. As annuity rates are not static, the returns for each of these annuities can vary quite significantly within a short period of time.

— Any terms which make the annuity more attractive for the individual, eg a guarantee period, are likely to make the initial return for a given lump sum investment smaller. Exceptions can occur when the individual is young, or if a particular Life Office is chosen.

The effect of a ten year guarantee period on various annuity quotations is shown at Table 6C.

TABLE 6B: Comparable structured settlement annuity quotations

Investment   £400,000
Female   age 36¹/₂ years
Life expectancy   normal

	Annuity receivable in first year		
	Quote 1	Quote 2	Quote 3
	£	£	£
Index-linked annuity no guarantee period	19,630	22,442	19,184
Ten-year guarantee period	19,585	22,372	19,184
Annuity escalating at 5% per annum compound no guarantee period	17,871	21,760	19,870
Ten-year guarantee period	17,838	21,686	19,821

It will be seen from the above that index-linked annuities can start at a higher amount than for ones escalating at 5% per annum. The rating of an index-linked annuity will vary dependant on the perception of future inflation. Thus during 1991 index-linked annuities were significantly more expensive than ones escalating at 5%, but this reversed for much of 1992.

6.4.5   The effect of reduced life expectancy

In personal injury cases the life expectancy of the plaintiff may be reduced due to the injuries suffered. If the life expectancy is likely to be less than that of a normal person, of the same age and sex, then a higher level of return may be agreed. This is because an annuity guarantees future payments for the life of the individual and in these cases the Life Office anticipates that the payments will continue for a lesser period than normal.

In Table 6C we demonstrate the effect of a significant reduction in anticipated life expectancy on annuity returns. For a comparable lump sum investment, the boy aged 11 years can receive a higher annuity return than the lady aged 36½ years. This is because the quotation for the 11-year-old boy is based on an adjusted age following the assessment of his life expectancy at a further 25 years, rather than normal.

TABLE 6C: The effect of life expectancy on annuity quotations

	(A)	(B)
Investment	£400,000	£400,000
Sex	male	female
Age	11 years	36½ years
Life expectancy	25 years	normal
Guarantee period	NIL	NIL
	£	£
Annuity receivable in first year		
Index-linked	26,353	19,630
Escalation at 5% per annum	25,459	17,871

The rating of impaired lives for annuity purposes can lead to a higher return for the individual, unlike ordinary life insurance where impaired lives are rated such that the benefits are more expensive. There is clearly a case to ensure that assessments are based on extensive medical opinions, from both the plaintiff's and defendant's experts. Up-to-date medical reports are therefore essential for a Life Office to cost an annuity.

4.6 Obtaining the quotations

The information required by a Life Office includes:

— the date of birth and sex of the plaintiff;
— the escalation rate for payments;
— the frequency of periodic payments;
— the size and incidence of any future regular lump sum payments;
— whether the payments are to be made immediately or at a later date in the future;
— either the size of the periodic payments or the lump sum available to purchase the annuity or annuities; and
— medical reports prepared on behalf of the plaintiff and the defendant.

Given the variables involved, it is important to determine the most suitable form of annuity payments for each individual case. It may be that a structure consists of several annuities, where at least one is stepped or deferred, to take account of the plaintiff's changing needs in the future. Some of the structures implemented to date have also included a series of regular lump sums which may be utilised for capital purchases, for example equipment or a motor vehicle.

One important point to remember is that a structure should be a tailored financial package which reflects the plaintiff's needs, within the constraints of the moneys available to the individual. For this reason each case is likely to require more than one set of quotations particularly as the negotiations proceed and the plaintiff's needs are 'fine tuned'. The parties often find themselves performing what can best be described as a cost benefit analysis until the final structure emerges. This is essential because once the structure is established it cannot be varied.

Each set of annuity quotations, or illustration, is only valid for a limited period, usually in the order of 14 days. As annuity rates may change in line with movements in interest rates generally, it is important to obtain new quotations (re-quotes) as appropriate.

When selecting a Life Office for the purchase of an annuity, it is normal to look for an office with an established reputation and consistent investment performance. The market for structured settlement annuities is in a state of flux, with some Life Offices entering and others retiring. A few Life Offices have remained active throughout, often utilising the experience of their overseas counterparts.

5   STRUCTURED SETTLEMENT OR TRADITIONAL LUMP SUM

5.1   General

Why should any plaintiff accept a proportion of their damages in the form of an annuity rather than as the traditional lump sum?

The problems associated with the traditional lump sum are well known:

— uncertainty of the return which can be obtained on investment;
— the burden of managing the investment.

In return for these 'problems' the plaintiff may receive a degree of freedom and responsibility for his future, which few individuals get during their life-time. Even if sensibly invested, however, experience suggests that it is difficult to provide for the plaintiff's increasing needs. The lump sum investment is subject to the ravages of many factors, not least:

— future inflation;
— future changes in taxation rates;
— an uncertain stock market; and
— the plaintiff living beyond the life expectancy anticipated in the assessment of damages.

As the income yielded from the investment is subject to tax, experience suggests that plaintiffs increasingly need to have recourse to their capital. Consequently, the lump sum may be prematurely exhausted during the plaintiff's life.

As we have already seen from earlier chapters, structured settlements offer an alternative:

— the defendant's insurer makes payments to the plaintiff for his life, or a guaranteed minimum period should this be longer;

— these payments are usually increasing and secured by the purchase of an annuity from a Life Office;

— providing the settlement is structured within the Model Agreement (a matter which we shall examine more closely in the next section), the plaintiff will not pay any tax on the annuity payments even though they may be index-linked; and

— there is no requirement to refer to the annuity payments on the plaintiff's income tax return.

Once the plaintiff's optimum financial package has been determined and preliminary annuity quotations obtained, the forensic accountant is able to prepare detailed calculations to compare and contrast investment of the lump sum in the traditional manner with the purchase of the annuity under the structured settlement. An important point to note is that for the calculations which reflect investment in the traditional manner, the lump sum must consist of both the equivalent amount used to purchase the annuity and the insurer's discount.

These calculations are often presented in the format of computer-produced schedules and included in the forensic accountant's report. They serve to illustrate the benefits to the plaintiff of structuring in a number of different ways, which may include:

— schedules to demonstrate the timescale within which the traditional lump sum may be exhausted during the plaintiff's life; and

— schedules to show the equivalent lump sum which must be invested in the traditional manner, to produce the same annual net income for the balance of the plaintiff's life expectancy as may be enjoyed from the structure.

5.2   The plaintiff's capital situation

Where approval of a structured settlement by the Court is required, it is necessary to satisfy the Court that the foreseeable capital requirements of the plaintiff can be met by means outside the structure. The current practice note, Appendix II, also makes reference to evidence of other assets available to the plaintiff beyond the damages award under consideration.

It is possible that this matter can be encompassed in the forensic accountant's report, as he is likely to be aware of the plaintiff's financial circumstances from his earlier involvement in the determination of the structure.

The contents of this section of the report will clearly vary from case to case, but consideration should be given to:

— the balance of any interim payments made by the defendant which are not required to meet immediate purchases;
— any further lump sum due from the defendant;
— any savings or investments the plaintiff has outside the amount of the damages award; and
— the plaintiff's future accommodation, transport and equipment needs and how these are to be funded. It may be that at least one of these requirements will already have been incorporated into the structure. Reference should be made to this fact as appropriate.

It is important to note that any income generated from investment of moneys outside the annuity and the balance of any annuity payments can be accumulated with the plaintiff's existing capital. This will have the effect of enhancing the value of the plaintiff's contingency fund and thus afford greater flexibility in the event of unforeseen changes in the future.

5.3   The plaintiff's income situation

Having looked at the plaintiff's capital situation, the forensic accountant should conclude his report by considering the plaintiff's overall level of income. This will incorporate not only the income from the annuity or annuities but the plaintiff's income from all sources.

In our experience, it is usually preferable to illustrate our comments by a schedule to show the plaintiff's annual income position, taking into account the structured settlement. This may include particular reference to:

— the annual amount receivable from the annuity, or annuities;
— an estimate of the investment income receivable from the contingency fund, less tax as appropriate;
— investment income from any additional sources outside the structure, less tax as appropriate;
— any DSS benefits which the plaintiff may continue to receive once the damages are awarded;
— any earned income or pension benefits, net of tax as appropriate.

The forensic accountant will then be in a position to demonstrate how the annual income can be utilised to satisfy the plaintiff's requirements. These requirements will differ depending on the circumstances of each case but may include expenditure on:

— care;
— transportation;
— therapies;
— daily living and household expenses;
— holidays and other leisure activities;
— professional fees; and
— Court of Protection fees as appropriate.

5.4   Miscellaneous matters

In this section we have examined various issues which the forensic accountant may address in his report, or reports. A common theme to all the issues is 'relevance'. The accountant's comments and calculations must be relevant to the circumstances of the case in question and not expressed in general terms. Furthermore, they must be based on evidence, whether it be in the form of factual information or verbal explanations.

We are conscious that we have not examined in detail all the issues to which the forensic accountant may refer and where he may provide valuable assistance. One specific example is where the consent of the Court of Protection is required.

This chapter would not be complete, however, if we failed to recognise the importance of the tax treatment of structured settlements and the Inland Revenue's Model Agreement.

6   TAXATION ISSUES

6.1   Introduction

At the cornerstone of every structured settlement is the issue of tax, whether it is to maintain the tax-free status of payments to the plaintiff or the tax deductibility of the claim for the insurer.

In the following sections we will therefore look at the tax position of the plaintiff and the insurer in more detail.

6.2   The plaintiff's tax position

Why are the periodic annuity payments tax-free in the plaintiff's hands?

It is perhaps a useful starting point to consider the plaintiff's position on receipt of a lump sum award in the conventional manner and then compare this to the position under a structured settlement.

6.2.1   *Conventional award*

— The lump sum is not liable to income tax or capital gains tax.
— However, any interest received from investment of the lump sum for the benefit of the plaintiff is liable to income tax.
— Capital gains realised on investments purchased with the lump sum would be chargeable to capital gains tax.
— On death any remaining capital sum would form part of the plaintiff's estate, liable to inheritance tax.
— Professional fees for investment advice and tax compliance work may be significant.

6.2.2 *Structured settlement*

— If the settlement is in the agreed form, payments to the plaintiff are treated as instalments of capital. Consequently, these payments are not taxable in the plaintiff's hands.

— The fact that the payments increase periodically, for example by linking them to the retail price index, does not affect their capital nature. This merely protects the capital value of the repayments against inflation.

— On death, inheritance tax would be charged on assets in the deceased's estate. This would include the present value of any guaranteed payments which may continue after the life of the plaintiff.

— The tax position of the contingency fund and any additional lump sums would be as described above for the conventional award.

— The burden of professional fees for any tax compliance and investment advice should be significantly lighter.

So far we have considered the tax status of the plaintiff and the nature of the annuity payments under a structured settlement. At this point it is therefore appropriate to consider who is actually making the settlement.

The initial claim by the plaintiff is likely to be against an insured individual and not an insurance company. However, by virtue of the Model Agreement, there is a provision for the insurer to stand in the place of the insured. By doing so the plaintiff drops his claim against the defendant in return for entering the structured settlement with the insurer.

6.3 The insurer's tax position

We understand that there is more than one way in which the insurer can deal with the receipt of the annuity from the Life Office and the payment of the capital instalments to the plaintiff under a structure. The solution put forward by the Inland Revenue is perhaps the most constructive. The purchase of the annuity is treated as a form of reinsurance by the insurer and the lump sum expended is tax deductible. This treatment has the approval of both the Association of British Insurers (ABI) and the Department of Trade and Industry (DTI).

The annuity payments from the Life Office are liable to tax in the hands of the general insurer. However, the insurer is able to deduct from its corporation tax profit an amount equal to the cost of the instalment payments to the plaintiff. These payments will be 'grossed up' to include the tax element so that the plaintiff receives 'tax free' instalments. Whilst the whole arrangement is fiscally neutral from the insurer's position, there is a timing difference in respect of the period during which the general insurer has to fund the tax deducted at source by the Life Office. In practice this time lag may be in the order of 9 to 21 months.

6.4 The position of the Life Office

The purchase of the annuity by the general insurer will form part of the Life Office's general business. Each annuity payment made by the Life Office to the general insurer consists of two elements—capital and income. It is necessary for the Life Office to deduct tax at the basic rate from the income element only of the annuity when making payments to the general insurer.

It is interesting to note that if the plaintiff chose to purchase an annuity himself from a Life Office, then he would still benefit from a guaranteed income for life. However, as the income element of the annuity is taxable, the plaintiff in these circumstances would receive the annuity payments net of tax from the Life Office direct. This compares to the 'grossed up' payments receivable under the structured settlement.

6.5 The Model Agreement

6.5.1 *Background*

In practice the most important feature of the tax treatment of structured settlements is undoubtedly the agreement of the Inland Revenue to treat the payments made to the plaintiff as capital in their entirety.

The approach of the Inland Revenue to the taxation of these payments was set out in a letter from their Specialist Division and placed before the Court in the case of *Kelly*. The gist of this letter is that payments by the insurer, of sums equivalent to those received under the annuity it had taken out, would be treated as the discharge of instalment payments of a capital debt.

The authority for the treatment of these payments as capital is to be found in three cases:

— *Commissioners of Inland Revenue v Ramsay*
— *Dott v Brown* [1936] 1 ALL ER 543
— *Commissioners of Inland Revenue v Church Commissioners for England*

Each case referred to above is authority for a different principle. All three principles, however, have a relevance and can be applied to structured settlements.

Commissioners of Inland Revenuev Ramsay	The settlement figure creates **an antecedent debt** of an agreed sum which is **certain**.
Commissioners of Inland Revenue v Church Comissioners for England	However, once there is an antecedent debt for an agreed sum, that sum can be satisfied by
Dott v Brown	**payments for life** and each instalment will be **capital in nature**.

The circumstances in which the Inland Revenue is prepared to allow this treatment are set out in detail in the Model Agreement.

6.6   The 'Agreement'

In July 1987 a form of structured settlement agreement was approved, following discussions for some time between the ABI and Inland Revenue—the Model Agreement.

The terms of the agreement are such that payments made under the agreement as drafted should be free of income tax, ie treated as capital, in the plaintiff's hands.

If there is any deviation from the wording of the Model Agreement then it does not automatically signify 'failure' as far as the tax position is concerned. The tax consequences, however, will depend upon the Inland Revenue's interpretation of the agreement as drafted.

Careful adherence to the Model Agreement ensures that the contractual relationship between the parties is maintained. There must not be any reference in the agreement to the purchase of an annuity by the defendant's insurer, this is an entirely separate contract between the insurance company and the Life Office.

The Model Agreement, an example of which is included as Appendix III, allows for four different types of structured settlement which are reflected in four alternative schedules. These are as follows:

Basic terms   This is the simplest form of settlement, where the payments are made for a pre-set period and are of pre-set amounts.

This form may be used in cases where the plaintiff wishes the periodic payments to cease at a certain future date.

Indexed terms   This form is comparable to that above, however the payments are index-linked ie they increase in proportion to any rise in the index of retail prices over the period in question.

Terms for Life   This form provides for the plaintiff to receive pre-set amounts which continue until the date of death.

There is an option to pre-set the minimum number of payments, which would continue and be payable to the plaintiff's estate in the event of his premature death.

Indexed Terms for Life   This form is comparable to Terms for Life, except that the payments are index-linked.

It is likely that this form will be popular amongst plaintiff's and their advisors, subject to cost considerations should the rate of inflation escalate again.

Whilst the supporting schedule to the structured settlement agreement can be amended to reflect the various settlement terms, the agreement itsel, is comparatively straightforward and provides:

— that the insurer is substituted for the insured;
— a statement of the level of settlement, ie the debt;
— a statement that the debt will be satisfied by payments made in accordance with the schedule;
— a statement that proceedings against both the insured and the insurer by the claimant shall be discontinued; and

— a schedule showing the pattern of payments which comprises the settlement. The four alternative forms of this schedule have been examined earlier.

6.7 The antecedent debt

In accordance with the Model Agreement there is a requirement to state an amount which constitutes the settlement figure. As we have already seen from the case of *Commissioners of Inland Revenue v Ramsay*, this settlement figure creates an antecedent debt of an agreed sum.

But what does the antecedent debt comprise in the context of the structured settlement agreement? In practice we understand that the Inland Revenue recommend that this figure is the total of, at least, all guaranteed payments under the contract, to include:

— any interim payments already made to the plaintiff *and*
— any further lump sum payments already made or to be made *and*
— the total payments that will arise under the annuity during the guarantee period.

This ensures that the Inland Revenue are satisfied that the aim of the agreement is the discharge of the original debt, which will result in the taxation advantages we have already outlined.

If the payments are index-linked, then a reasonable rate of inflation must be assumed for determining the total payments during the guaranteed period.

7 FURTHER PRACTICAL CONSIDERATIONS

7.1 Introduction

As the structured settlement market develops it is inevitable that practical problems will arise as cases are considered for structuring. The current 'fear' amongst practitioners, that there might be grounds for a negligence case against them in the future if they do not inform their clients of the possibility of structuring the settlement, may be expected to increase their popularity.

In this final section we take the opportunity to identify some areas of the structuring process where potential problems exist and consider how they may be overcome.

7.2   Inland Revenue approval

As the wording of the structured settlement agreement should conform to the Model Agreement, care has to be taken in drafting. What seems like a seemingly innocent provision may not be within the terms of the Model Agreement. We recommend that *before* any agreement is put into place the Inland Revenue's approval is sought and advance clearance obtained. In our experience this may take some time, which should be incorporated into the timescale for implementation of the structure.

If Inland Revenue approval has not been received by the time of the application to approve the structured settlement, the arrangements should include a contingency against any refusal by the Inland Revenue to recognise the agreement as falling within the scope of the Model Agreement.

7.3   Court approval

For structured settlement cases where approval of the Court is required, guidance can be obtained from the current Practice Note, Appendix II. One of the aims of the practice note is to overcome the difficulties caused by the short period of time over which the annuity quotations from Life Offices remain valid.

This practice note is appropriate whether or not the Court of Protection is involved. However, if the plaintiff is under a mental disability additional steps should be taken as set out at paragraph 6(viii) and 8 of the practice note.

7.4   Security

The general insurer may purchase an annuity from a Life Office to fund the instalment payments to the plaintiff under a structured settlement. This does not, however, transfer the original liability from the general insurer and the instalment payments remain its responsibility.

If the Life Office providing the annuity became insolvent this would not extinguish the general insurer's liability to the plaintiff, as there are two entirely separate relationships; between the Life Office and general insurer and, between the general insurer and the plaintiff.

Of more concern to the plaintiff is the solvency of the general insurer, some protection may be afforded by the Policyholder's Protection Act or, if a Lloyds syndicate is involved, the Lloyds Trust Fund.

7.5 Health authorities

Following the *Rebecca Field* case in October 1991, and the *Victoria Lovell* case in November 1992, the Treasury and the Department of Health have now permitted health authorities to implement structured settlements in medical negligence actions. As health authorities and NHS trusts are tax-exempt they have to recover the tax element of the annuity payments by submitting a claim to the Inland Revenue.

One question, however, which remains un-answered is whether the health authority should meet its liabilities under a structured settlement by purchasing an annuity from a Life Office or whether it should 'self-finance' the instalments. In both the above cases the settlement was funded by the Department of Health rather than via a purchased annuity. These cases clearly pave the way for further self-funded structured settlements.

As defendant health authorities may merge, change or simply cease to exist over the long period of a structure, it is necessary to obtain an undertaking from the Department of Health that any annuity would continue despite the demise of the authority.

Before any award against a health authority is structured it is necessary to undertake a 'value-for-money' investigation on its behalf, to contrast the financial implications of a conventional award and a structured settlement.

7.6 2029

What is the relevance of 2029? At present the latest index-linked government stock in issue has a redemption date in the year 2029. This is particularly relevant as such stock forms the basis of the Life Office's investment fund for RPI- or index-linked annuities.

We understand that should further index-linked stocks become available with maturity dates beyond 2029, then index linking backed by government stock can continue.

In the event that this is not possible, it is in the insurer's interest to ensure that a pre-determined percentage increase is built into the annuity contract for the period beyond 2029.

The percentage escalation rate provided by the Life Office to the general insurer should be incorporated into the schedule to the Model Agreement between the insurer and the plaintiff. This will prevent the possibility of the insurer losing out if different rates are incorporated into each agreement, and ensures the arrangements are 'back to back'.

7.7   The tabloid press

We have referred earlier to the settlement figure included in the Model Agreement—the antecedent debt—and the approach used to calculate this sum. It follows that the resultant figure is likely to bear no relation to the value of the plaintiff's award on the conventional basis and furthermore be substantially greater than this latter sum.

This clearly encourages misleading press and media coverage of structured settlements, particularly by the tabloids who emphasise the extraordinary figures in a sensational way.

Despite reference to any figures in the settlement, a recent trend is for the press to produce their own calculations based on a figure for annual payments to the plaintiff and an assumed normal life expectancy.

Be aware of this and do not encourage it.

7.8   The future

The future of structured settlements is to a large extent in the hands of the Inland Revenue and the professionals:

— solicitors
— insurers, including re-insurers
— counsel
— accountants.

Considerable expertise has been gained since the case of *Kelly & Another v Dawes*. It is therefore essential now to capitalise on our experience and consider how to further develop the concept, perhaps even in terms of specific tax legislation.

This will of course involve time and effort, but what better way to start than to spend some time understanding the experience that has been developed in the United States.

7 A Case Study

Alastair Graham

This is an adaptation of a paper delivered at a conference in 1991. It should be noted that there have been changes in the law since the events which are described here took place.

Our younger daughter, Olivia, had a fall on the fourth of June 1979, when she was six-and-a-half years old. She was referred to the casualty department of the hospital that serves Heathrow Airport and the M4. The medical negligence that was admitted, six-and-a-half years later, occurred both in casualty and after readmission later that evening. To protect her future we took legal advice, served writs on the area health authority and, perforce also, the casualty officer. A date was set for the Court hearing in early 1986, with liability and causation being disputed all the way by the defendants. Three weeks before the case was due to be heard, our leading counsel abandoned the case, advising us that it likely clashed with another he was involved in—two months after his clerk was aware of his unavailability for us. We had to apply for—and pay for—the date to be set aside. The next date possible for all concerned was 16 March 1987—nearly eight years after the accident. Nearly five-and-a-half years after the writs were served, the defendants admitted liability—while still disputing the non-point of causation—and in due course paid half a million pounds into Court as their offer of settlement. During the three working hours before the hearing was due to start negotiation between leading counsel for the defendants and the plaintiffs increased this sum by 10% for special damages. In Court the judge, identified two working days beforehand, announced his own calculations and confirmed the award which we had agreed in advance; he also decreed costs against the defendants and approved the Trustee scheme which formed an integral part of the settlement. The lump sum was invested—four months before the Stock Market crash; there is still no taxation of the costs, ten months after we were awarded them. After all this we might feel little reason for doubting the force of Bernard Shaw's dictum: 'All professions are conspiracies against the laity.'

To summarise the timetable: it took all but eight years to bring the case to Court. When the defendants eventually admitted liability, our daughter had been severely disabled for seven-and-a-half years—more than half her life till then. Ten months later the lump sum remains untouched, thanks to her age and parental circumstances. The £50,000 special damages awarded have been swallowed up in preferential costs. The total costs remain in dispute within the system and, as usual, will never be recovered in full. I cannot over-emphasise how exceptionally lucky we were in finding a firm of solicitors whose senior partner was prepared to undertake a case knowing how many years it could drag on for and willing to forgo any cash payments whatsoever on the way until was settled. His knight-errantry and faith in Olivia's cause have been as essential to us as his sage advice and exemplary activity.

Our saga of stress and striving, cost and complexity, delays and disputation is clearly typical of cases where liability is contested by the defendants until the last possible stage. The Royal Commission on Civil Liability and Compensation for Personal Injury reported that 86% of all personal injury claims are settled without writ; only 1% reach the courts—but as long ago as 1973 this represented 2,500 cases annually. It is of only marginal help and comfort to the 13% of plaintiffs a decade ago that their cases were settled at the eleventh hour. Clearly it is the claims for major scales of compensation which continue to be pursued at this stage; and Julian Radcliffe is recently on record as stating that 'there are about one thousand cases a year of compensation awards over £100,000.' Further, William Pitt advises that 'structured compensation only becomes worthwhile once the amount exceeds £50,000'. My family's case should therefore count as a significant exemplar of what we are all seeking to change: the need to prove fault and the method of financing claims—the major defects in the law relating to compensation for personal injury.

It is encouraging that the Bench is not oblivious to these: at the end of the case when an award of seven figures was made for the first time, Mr Justice Hirst deplored the 'once for all basis' on which the Court was obliged to compensate a plaintiff. 'Under the present law there is no scope for a continuous assessment either of need or of loss of earnings, to be decided from time to time as his future unfolds . . . This case highlights once again the crying need for a review of this branch of the law, which judges have so frequently urged but which only Parliament can undertake.' My wife and I have written to 40 MPs of our acquaintance, from the Prime Minister downwards, about this—and about the dangerous inadequacy of the BMA's proposals for a 'No fault' compensation scheme. The Parliamentary Under-Secretary of State for Health's response referred to the 1978 Pearson Report and admitted 'a notable increase in the number of cases coming before the courts'; she did not mention the fact that there was a majority recommendation in the Pearson Report in favour of periodic payments being available in cases of death or serious and permanent disablement—let alone that this has yet to be implemented.

One of the major reasons in favour of periodic payments is, of course, that the victim of personal injury can relatively improve or deteriorate after a 'once for all' award—indeed our daughter's condition has substantially worsened in the last few months. It is a mercy that she does not, for a few years, have to support herself from the interest on her award-capital.

I was interested to read the other day the reported statement by Dr John Wall, deputy secretary of the Medical Defence Union: 'We've been offering annuities for years but plaintiffs won't accept them.' During the seven years of litigation on behalf of our daughter, including the four months between the admission of liability and the settlement agreed under legal duress, this alternative possibility was at *no* stage mentioned to us by the defendants. He also said, as quoted in the same report: 'It's the dependants of the plaintiffs who insist on going to court.' In this case, the plaintiff had no dependants.

Our experience lines us up behind the opinion of our solicitor, an experienced expert in medical negligence who has very often acted for defendants and knows all about 'playing games' within the limits of the system. He wrote to me about a case similar to Olivia's:

> 'The mother of the child made it clear that in her view the most sickening part of the whole performance was the delay on the part of the defendants to admit liability, with the needless anxiety that caused. To my mind, throughout the whole of Olivia's case, and I suspect in many comparable cases, the unforgivable factor is the refusal of the Health Authority and the doctor's insurers to admit the most obvious liability immediately, or at an extremely early stage. In her case it was patently obvious by the time the writ was issued in September 1981 that there was no defence to the claim as would have been evident if it had been properly investigated at the Health Authority's end.'

It was not just our confirmed conviction of this seven years ago that impelled us to go to Court; there was absolutely no alternative means of securing our daughter's financial future. It is important to understand that at the age of six she had a reading age of eleven; she now has scant prospects of GCSE certification and none of employment and normal companionship over the next sixty years or so.

It would, however, be wrong to suggest that, when we started preparing Olivia's case or served the writs, we were adequately aware of the trauma we would undergo in addition to her personal injury: the escalation of urgent paper work, the meetings and consultations and costs apparently required us to meet in advance the defendants' legal moves within the adversarial system; the protection of our family from the stresses these caused; the iniquitous catch-22 situation we were placed in by the defendants' payment into court of a substantial but arguably quite inadequate sum; the crucial impact on the decision whether or not to settle out of court made by the identification of the judge only two working days before the hearing; and the media-attention provoked by the award having to be ratified in court before a full press-gallery—we were understandably ignorant of these aspects of the 'once for all' award scheme.

We survived all this, just. As experience made us more aware of realities over the last three years of the case, our extra sense of dismay has focused on the burden on the Health Service's budget. The average cost of litigation (ie of the consequences of defendants contesting liability) is 85p for every pound awarded as compensation. Society should not accept this—and surely would not if it were more generally known.

Incidentally I cannot accept at face value the fears, as reported by William Pitt, that moneys awarded are frequently 'being frittered away'. The figures published from the Canadian insurance industry showing that 'payments of over £50,000 were spent in the first year by no less than 50% of recipients' may well indicate the inordinate expense of rehabilitation and the need to fund unrecovered legal costs rather than profligacy or mismanagement of unfamiliar capital.

I do, however, take the point that indexed annuity-payments, made by a third party and linked to expert advice about financial management and rehabilitation for both the victim and the family, would remove the risk of delay, dereliction and distress. There is a good deal more to be said in detail about the nature of such payments and the reviews on which their repetition would depend. First, long-term support at an appropriate level *must* be built in unequivocally to cases of long-term disablement and loss of earnings; how otherwise, for example, would a victim of personal injury have any prospect of obtaining—or sustaining—a mortgage.

Secondly, the reviews must be set up and conducted with the benefit of the victim principally in mind. I have sadly to say from experience that this does not seem to be the case at present, e g with local authority reviews of mobility allowances and many specialists used by defendants in contested cases: ignorance of the basic facts readily available in the reports, and insensitivity towards the dignity of an already damaged person seem to be the norm. The process of review must revolve around the victim's GP *and* if necessary involve home visits rather than summonses at professional convenience to offices where the victim is likely to feel insecure, where the context is foreign to the way of life being assessed, and where vital, simple things like parking and access are dauntingly difficult.

Thirdly, how can the victim be sufficiently protected from unreasonable dispute by the compensating party at every review? The defendants can afford considerable sums to keep the succeeding payments down; the victim cannot match this muscle. Where will the interest of the third party lie?

We have been fortunate in that the award made at least underpins Olivia's financial security. It was achieved by the expertise, industry and determination of our solicitor, and adequately by the Counsel put our way by the Chairman of the Bar Council. They are well aware of what Dr Wall appears totally to overlook: the strains imposed on plaintiffs by the UK adversarial system of law, and the other casualties almost inevitable among the families of victims; he seems to charge them with being wilfully litigious. It is stressful enough to have the anxieties of uncertain recovery, of helping a child to come to terms with disablement, the demands of the rehabilitative process, and the schedule of medical consultations and treatment on top of the practical disadvantages of impaired mobility. Has he no understanding of the additional consultation, inquisitions and responses demanded by the adversarial nature of litigation? And all these are doubled and redoubled when there is more than one defendant, each with the right—applied by their insurers—to claim their own separate medical experts for each aspect of the case.

My wife and I have a positive suggestion to make about this practice; it was not taken up when we put it earlier, but perhaps experts can make a note of it for serious consideration in appropriate circles. When a writ has been served can it not be made either mandatory or standard practice for the senior medical assessor on each side to get together and appoint an agreed panel of medical specialists for the case? It cannot be right that Olivia, for example, had to undergo during one term a dozen medical inquisitions simply for the purpose of litigation: these had nothing to do with treatment or rehabilitation. This is one of several aspects of the law arising from the procedural distinction between medical negligence cases and other forms of personal injury; disclosure of medical reports by defendants is another.

In the case of *Wilsher v Essex Health Authority*, in which judgment was handed down on 24 July 1986, Sir Nicholas Browne-Wilkinson had this to say:

' ... the procedures adopted before trial were such as to make the trial quite unnecessarily difficult to conduct, and to create a real risk of injustice ... All this could have been avoided if there had been adequate clarification of the issues before the trial ... I believe that practitioners do their clients and the interests of justice no service by continuing to pursue this policy of concealment. Certainly ... there can be problems in making a defendant disclose his experts' reports. Nevertheless, these and similar problems are faced and solved all the time in cases before the Commercial Court and the Official Referees, where it is now axiomatic on technical issues that all the cards must be on the table before the trial begins. Those cases are concerned with money. Here, there are also human issues of great importance. To me it seems wrong that in this area of the law, more than in any other, this kind of forensic blind man's buff should continue to be the norm.'

The same defect in the English system of trial of medical negligence cases has recently led to it being described in even more drastic terms— by an American lawyer in the talk given to the Lawyers Support Group of Action for the Victims of Medical Accidents: he calls it simply 'trial by ambush'!

Having digressed this far let's go further away from structured compensation in order to return more positively to it. One can never, under the present system, expect the appropriate level of compensation to be agreed by the advisers of the plaintiffs and the defendants, until the arbitration of the court is imminent. They might surely get closer together in their figures if the court were empowered to exercise arbitration on quantum in the Japanese mode: opting for the higher *or* the lower figure. This amendment would consign to history the pernicious and inequitable effects of the payment into court system which was designed to protect the plaintiff but which is now likely, or even possible intended, to lose him the costs of both sides.

'A disabled child means a disabled family': we know the truth of this remark made to us by a consultant. My wife has borne the burden of Olivia's case in both senses, since 4 June 1979 while remaining fully committed as a teacher, examiner, headmaster's wife, hostess and mother to both our children. Her health has been drastically undermined. Our other child Annabelle, is only 22 months older than Olivia; they used to be each other's best friend and playmate. Inevitably she was constantly runner up for our attention between the crucial (and unrepeatable) years of 7 to 16; it was no doubt equally inevitable that she succumbed to an anorexia nervosa at the age of 14. If I needed a further reason for writing this, it would be to salute her publicly for dragging herself back up to success and health out of that pit.

I say nothing of myself, except that my job obliges us to live in a borough which mercifully agreed to fund Olivia's special education at the Lord Mayor Treloar College—which has been marvellous for her and where she is as happy as she can be, among a variety of disabled children, many of them in a worse case than she. There is no way in which we could have afforded her place there ourselves, the fees being about twice as high as Eton's; again one must doubt whether another borough or county would have undertaken to support her at Treloar if I had been offered advancement elsewhere. My wife and I are aware that our professional positions, including the education and the secretariat, as well as the articulacy and range of acquaintance and general 'know-how' that go with them, have given us the capacity to fight a just case effectively; and we are therefore conscious of the obligation to help others who have similarly suffered personal injury but who do not have such advantages. My wife has become a trustee of AVMA and my contribution to this book is another effort in the same direction.

It is time that I return to the heart of the matter. What *is* the plaintiff's position in so far as this 'next friend' of a plaintiff can speak to the question of structured compensation? In a phrase, reasonably optimistic, very determined—and far from convinced.

As I understand the scheme for Structured Compensation, it cannot apply where liability is seriously in dispute; and the grounds for this are as likely to lie in the scale of financial consequences as in moral liability. The Scheme's purposes and suggested practices *should* apply to cases where liability *is* initially disputed. If structured compensation can indeed lead to very early settlement of the 14% of cases where liability is still contested, vast unhappiness and effort can be saved.

What I urge is the removal of the need for victims of personal injury to become plaintiffs at law in any but the most exceptional cases. The key to that happening is the realisation on the part of insurance companies that structured compensation represents a better deal for them—financially and in terms of their public image—than their practice of disputing liability to the door of the court.

The role taken by insurance companies lets me feel initial optimism, but what about the health authorities? As I understand it, they—unlike individual medical practitioners and private citizens—do not take out insurance cover: they regard the premiums as too heavy to carry in their budgets. The Prime Minister's PPS confirmed to me our supposition that a health authority faced with a substantial claim will always on principle make it as difficult as possible for as long as possible for the claim to be pursued. This policy represents both a breach of consumer rights and professional morality; in the case of medical accidents there is a special need for openness at an early stage: unlike in ordinary personal injury, there is a moral duty on the defendant to compensate the victim who has placed him or herself in the care of the health professionals. In addition, one has to wonder about the practical efficacy of the policy. How regularly are comparisons made between the total of compensation paid in any given area and period (plus 85% legal costs *and* the time taken away from their proper functions by medical experts called in to examine cases, compile reports and attend court) and the total of premiums that might have been paid out in advance to cover them? And has the insurance industry been making a regular and researched case to present cover by insurance in a better light than compensation by litigation? At least a health authority, like a householder, could budget for regular premiums, whereas the coincidence of several large awards must come like subsidence and dry rot together for the rest of us.

It is a fair tribute to our solicitor if I give him one of the last words on this; I quote again from a letter:

'What is really needed now is for the Minister to issue instructions to the health authorities to stop playing games, once they have made the most frightful medical mistakes. It would be a quite simple matter which would not require any changes in the law whatsoever.

It would certainly remove from both the plaintiffs' and the defendants' solicitors a very large amount of costs which are needlessly being thrown away: but I, for one would relish dealing with more of these matters quickly and at little cost, particularly bearing in mind that many of the potential plaintiffs cannot afford to get their cases off the ground. This should not be necessary when such mistakes have been made.'

Julian Radcliffe has been a prime mover in the ABI making structured compensation a workable prospect and a preferable alternative to the 'once for all' lump-sum award system whose trauma my family can speak only too much about. He makes the positive advantages clear; I need not dwell on them having chosen to spell out the disadvantages of the present system. The achievement in negotiating the tax-free status of indexed annuity payments made by third parties is clearly crucial; so is the acceptance of the plaintiff's rights to serve a protective writ and to subject the insurer's proposals to his or her legal advisers.

It must also be important to the Lord Chancellor's office that the proposed scheme matches the limited purposes of the Civil Justice Review and requires no change in the law. Most sides stand to gain: the insurers, the insured, the victims of personal injuries and their families, court administrators, solicitors and the Bench. Julian Radcliffe is reported as envisaging Structured Compensation Limited 'building bridges between the parties'. I wonder if he is aware of the personal motto which George Thomas chose for himself on his retirement from being Speaker in the lower house and his elevation to the upper? It is: 'bydd pen, bydd pont' (if you wish to be a leader you must be a bridge).

8 The American Experience

David R Gross and Cynthia Maner Campbell

1   STRUCTURED SETTLEMENTS IN THE UNITED STATES

1.1   Defining structured settlements

The Canadian thalidomide baby cases introduced structured settlements in North America in the late 1960s. Structured settlements first became popular in the United States in the late 1970s. Since the birth of the concept, the use of structured settlements, or periodic future payments in lieu of an immediate lump sum award, has been most common in cases with large damages such as medical malpractice and wrongful death cases. However, the use of structured settlements is by no means relegated to catastrophic injury cases solely, but are even used today in environmental litigation and in cases drawing smaller settlement values, such as workers' compensation and discrimination in employment litigation. And recently, structured settlements have been used in the marital dissolution context.

There has been a meteoric rise in the popularity of structured settlements since their introduction in the United States. The law involving structured settlements has evolved over the years to meet the demands of their popularity. Structured settlements have proved to be more cost effective for defendants or their insurers; and, whether deservingly or not, plaintiffs see the structured settlement arrangement as a boon.

Simply defined, a structured settlement is an arrangement whereby the defendant or its insurer agrees to make periodic payments to the plaintiff. Once the parties agree upon this arrangement, it is typical for the defendant or its insurer to sell the obligation to an independent third party assignee, commonly a life insurance company.

Structured settlements often combine an initial payment sufficient to cover immediate expenses, liens, and attorneys' fees and an annuity that provides payments made periodically over the lifetime of a claimant. The periodic payments are frequently guaranteed for 20 to 25 years. Should the claimant live for a shorter period of time, the payments will continue to be paid to his or her estate or named beneficiary until the end of the guarantee period. Where the structured settlement does not include a guarantee, payments will cease upon the death of the claimant, leaving any unpaid portion of the settlement lost to the claimant's estate or heirs.

Structured settlement payments are usually designed to meet the individual needs of the plaintiff. Tailored payout arrangements often include an initial cash payment, periodic and regular payments that can replace or supplement income, specific payments for medical expenses or college tuition, and periodic lump sums. The payment period does not have to be stated in specific calendar time, but can also be stated in terms of specific events. Any of these payments can be incident-driven or driven by a single specified date, such as a date for the establishment of a retirement fund. There may be periodic increases in the monthly payment to hedge against inflation or to pay for anticipated medical expenses. Payments may even decrease over time.

The attorney who best serves his plaintiff client is also aware that the structured settlement is not a liquid investment. Cognizance of this fact is critical because no changes can be made to the arrangement once it is established. If the plaintiff has unanticipated expenses, such as unforeseen medical needs, the plaintiff will not be able to get additional funds to meet the new demand. Thus, it is very important for plaintiff's counsel to consider very carefully the assumptions that are being made in calculating the future payments to the plaintiff.

Many casualty companies assign the obligation to make the future payments to a third party who is in the business of assuming such obligations. The assignment is most often made to a top-rated life insurance company through the insurer's purchase of an annuity offered through the assignee's program. This assignment method is virtually risk-free for the plaintiff, as life insurance companies are some of the most economically stable companies in the United States. Indeed, most insurers do assign the obligation to a third party. Without the assignment method, an insurer may be reluctant to offer a structured settlement.

According to two commentators, this reluctance may be attributable to two factors. Firstly, transferring the obligation allows the insurer to close out its file completely on a particular case. Secondly, and perhaps more importantly, are the tax consequences of *not* making an assignment.

Before 1984, insurance companies could deduct the entire premium cost of the annuity in the year in which it was purchased. However, under the Deficit Reduction Act of 1984, insurance companies were prohibited from making deductions until 'economic performance' occurred (Internal Revenue Code, section 461(h)(2)(C)). After the Deficit Reduction Act, the cost of a structured settlement had to be amortised over the life of the annuity. Therefore, deductions could only be taken in the year in which a scheduled payment was made. However, even after the 1984 Deficit Reduction Act, if an insurer assigns to a third party its obligation to make the future payments, the entire cost of the structured settlement is still fully deductible in the year in which the structured settlement deal is made (Richard G. McMillan and Carolyn Yamasaki, 'Misconceptions Concerning Structured Settlements', 20 Hawaii Bar Journal 137–144 (1987)).

1.2 Structured settlements v lump sum awards — inherent benefits

There are both economic and non-economic benefits to accepting a structured settlement. The most important benefit to the recipient is the economic benefit. Under current tax laws, should a plaintiff decide to take a lump sum settlement and purchase his own annuity policy, the interest accumulating on the principal is taxable upon receipt. With a structured settlement, however, both the principal and the interest, whenever paid, are tax-free if the settlement was made pursuant to the rules of the Internal Revenue Code Section 130 (26 U.S.C., s 130 (1988)).

A major non-economic benefit to accepting a structured settlement rather than a lump sum award is the intangible benefit of peace of mind. Statistics have shown that almost 100% of all recipients of lump sum awards completely exhaust their funds within five years of their receipt. Since many of the largest awards are given to personal injury plaintiffs who have suffered catastrophic, disabling injuries, the personal injury plaintiffs who mismanage their award will no longer have the funds to pay for the extraordinary critical care that the award was calculated to cover. Many recipients, therefore, end up being wards of the State.

Not only personal injury plaintiffs risk ending up on the dole. Often the survivors of a wrongfully killed decedent squander their settlement and are no longer able to maintain the life style previously provided by the decedent's income. The minor who receives a lump sum that has been held in escrow until he or she reaches the age of majority, and then suddenly receives thousands or even millions of dollars, is a candidate for public assistance later in life. Instead of receiving and mismanaging the vulnerable lump sum award, any recipient of the structured settlement is guaranteed payments calculated in the amount and planned for the time that is most beneficial to the recipient. Because the payments under the structured settlement arrangement cannot be changed, the recipient can rest assured that adequate funds will be available for the guarantee period or for his lifetime, whichever is longer.

Structured settlements also benefit defendants. The cost to the defendant can be significantly reduced when he, she or its insurer offers a structured settlement rather than a lump sum payment. Also, because the plan will be designed to meet the plaintiff's needs, more accurate information about the plaintiff, such as precise medical and financial needs, is on the table. Negotiations, therefore, can be more collaborative and less adversarial.

There may be a disadvantage to insurers, though. Potentially, the total payout over the lifetime of the plaintiff or the plan, whichever is longer, can be significantly greater than the actual cost of the plan. The reported value of the award, ie what the annuity will pay out over the projected life of the claimant, is inflated way beyond the present value of the settlement. Therefore, what is reported as a multi-million dollar award may be misleading as it is likely to be much more than the insurer actually paid. This misperception may serve to increase the number of lawsuits filed, and potentially more payouts by the insurer, and help to create an even more litigious society.

1.3   Inherent disadvantages

Structured settlements are not a garden of roses in the view of everyone. There are some attorneys in the United States who rarely recommend a structured settlement as a plaintiff's best option. One reason for the resistance is the belief that the plaintiff will almost always get less in a structured settlement than if given a lump sum.

Some commentators discuss the opinion that inherent in structured settlement arrangements is a potential for a conflict of interest among the plaintiff, the plaintiff's lawyer, the insurance company and the courts. The plaintiff's lawyer *may* get a higher fee under a structured settlement than he would receive based on a lump sum award. Courts are always eager to resolve a matter expeditiously, and would rather see it settled before time is invested in a trial. Any of these parties may be more interested in seeking a structured settlement than a plaintiff may be in receiving one.

At least one American attorney never advises that his client choose a structured settlement over a lump sum. He would urge that a written acknowledgment always be received from a client accepting a structured settlement. The acknowledgment should state that at least the following items have been disclosed and discussed with the client:

1   the present value of the award;

2   that the terms of the settlement arrangement are fixed and cannot be changed to accommodate future needs;

3   that payments to the client are tax-exempt given current laws, but that the tax status could change with a change in the tax laws;

4   that unless there is a written guarantee upon the recipient's death, any future payments will not be made to the recipient's estate or heirs;

5   that the client can choose a lump sum instead that he can invest in any way he chooses;

6   that if the client invests the settlement proceeds himself, such interest income received is normally taxable unless invested in tax-exempt vehicles or unless medical expenses are so great that the income is virtually exempted from taxation; and

7   that the state guarantee fund only protects the annuity payments up to a certain sum.

(Abraham Fuchsberg, 'Pitfalls in Structured Settlements', Trial Lawyer's Quarterly, Volume 20, No 2, Fall, 1989.)

Some attorneys warn that some aspects of the typical structured settlement agreement are merely sweeteners and bear no true benefit to the plaintiff. Such an inducement is the typical 20-year guarantee. The additional cost of the guarantee only nominally increases what the cost of the annuity would otherwise be to the defendant. Similarly, the typical 3% increase in the amount of periodic payments is claimed to be a hedge against inflation. However, the plaintiff can easily invest his or her money in a manner that will yield far in excess of 3% on the investments.

Also, lump sum payments may offer the same tax advantage as extended payments where the victim is catastrophically injured. Medical expenses are likely to be extremely high when there has been a catastrophic injury. Medical expenses in the United States over a percentage of income are tax-deductible. Where the cost is enormous, particularly when incurred continuously over the lifetime of an injured person, the deductibility of this cost will absorb most, if not all, of any taxable investment income earned on a lump sum award.

Finally, although the payor of the obligation may offer a guarantee of a set minimum number of payments, the payor itself is not guaranteed against its own insolvency.

1.4   Inherent risks

A structured settlement is not without its risks. Claimants and their attorneys are not so concerned with the annuity itself, as with the insurer issuing the annuity. Thus, it is important for the claimant's attorney to investigate the financial stability of the insurer or assignee, even though the life insurance industry has exhibited overall financial strength, particularly as compared to other depository institutions and insurers.

The owner of the annuity, ie, the defendant or its insurer, might enter bankruptcy or be liquidated. In evaluating the settlement offer, this risk must be taken into consideration. Previously, when a plaintiff accepted a structured settlement from a defendant, the plaintiff became a general creditor of the defendant. Should the defendant then default, the plaintiff would have had no greater rights to the annuity than did any other unsecured creditor. The bankruptcy courts frequently treated the annuity as just another asset of the defendant to be distributed.

In November 1988, Congress amended the Internal Revenue Code to protect the recipient of structured future payments from the risk of their debtors' insolvency. An amendment to section 130 stated that recipients under a structured settlement arrangement are to be treated as secured creditors, rather than as general creditors.

If the provider of the annuity, ie the life insurance company, enters bankruptcy or liquidation, the plaintiff may not be harmed. The obligation to make the periodic payments remains with the defendant, if so specified, assuming no assignment has been made. The defendant would simply have to make other financial arrangements in order to meet its obligation to the plaintiff.

2   SPECIAL ISSUES RELATED TO STRUCTURED SETTLEMENTS

2.1   Legal malpractice — calculating attorneys' fees: cost v value

An increased risk of legal malpractice claims has come along with the increase in complex structured settlements. Typical areas of exposure can be easily avoided by the practitioner, once he or she has learned to recognise them.

Disputes over how the attorneys' fees were calculated is a common problem area because many contingency fee agreements do not anticipate the structured settlement arrangement. To avoid this pitfall, it is advisable that the contingency agreement stipulate whether, in the case of a structured settlement, the attorney will take his fee in a lump sum up front or in periodic payments over time. It is also advisable that the agreement specify that the attorneys' fee will be based upon the agreed proportional relationship to the value of the settlement, whether or not it is structured, and what proportion the attorneys' fee in dollars will bear to the actual cost to the defendant of the structure.

2.2 The structured settlement broker

The services of a structured settlement broker are available to explain the 'value' of the structured settlement, something which might be elusive to many plaintiffs and attorneys as well. In fact, a plaintiff's attorney might be very prudent never to finalise a structured settlement deal without the service of one.

Although it is more common for a broker to assist the defendant, there are those who may be willing to work with a plaintiff in evaluating whether the deal offered is in the best interest of the plaintiff, both long-term and short-term. The broker may be able to assist in explaining to the plaintiff — often less sophisticated in financial planning matters — the advantages of periodic payments, guaranteed over time and tax-free, as compared to self-investing. More importantly, the broker can help design a package tailored to the plaintiff's needs. This package may be the basis of the plaintiff's negotiations.

Commonly having access to various life insurance companies, the broker assisting the plaintiff can assure plaintiff's counsel that the defendant is getting the best possible price in the marketplace. Naturally, the better the price, the more funds available to benefit the plaintiff. Many people, including some attorneys, do not have a full understanding of annuities and the time-value of money, making the assistance of the professional structured settlement broker even more beneficial.

2.3 Refusal to disclose the cost of the structure

When structured settlements were a burgeoning phenomenon, defendants often attributed their reluctance to disclose the cost by hiding behind a specious and self-serving interpretation of federal tax laws. Defendants argued that it was to a plaintiff's benefit not to know the cost of a deal because knowledge constituted constructive receipt. Constructive receipt negates the tax benefit of future payments.

US Treasury Regulation Section 1.451-2(a) defines 'constructive receipt' as:

> Income, although not actually reduced to a taxpayer's possession is constructively received by him in the taxable year during which it is credited to his account, set apart for him, or otherwise made available so that he may draw upon it at any time, or so that he could have drawn upon it during the taxable year if notice of intention to withdraw had been given. However, income is not constructively received if the taxpayer's control of its receipt is subject to substantial limitations or restrictions.

The IRS corrected this misconception in 1983 with the issuance of its Private Letter Ruling 83-33035. The IRS took the position that 'knowledge is not determinative in deciding a question of constructive receipt, but that unqualified availability is decisive'. Defendants still resistant to disclosing the cost of a structure at least cannot hide behind notions of constructive receipt.

The role of tort litigation is not only to compensate the injured party, but also to obligate the defendant to pay his fair share towards that compensation. Allowing a defendant to escape that obligation by using smoke and mirrors in its presentation of a structured settlement may ultimately be unfair to the injured party and the basis of a legal malpractice claim. To allow a defendant to pay $600,000 today to purchase an annuity that will yield in total periodic payments a guaranteed $2.3 million later may seem inequitable to the plaintiff who, as he sees it, could receive $2.3 million now and wisely invest it to yield $6 million later.

Plaintiff's counsel may consider hiring one's own structured settlement broker when the defendant refuses to reveal the actual cost of the programme. The plaintiff's broker can provide some idea as to how much a structure, such as the one offered, would cost.

2.4 Cost v present value

Some economists caution that the cost of a structured settlement is not to be confused with its 'present value'. The concept of present value is both quite simple and simply misleading when applied to determining the value of a structured settlement. The cost of a structured settlement is just that — the immediate out-of-pocket cost to the defendant or the defendant's insurer. The present value of the annuity purchased is the amount that one must invest today at an assumed interest rate for the plaintiff to receive a specified sum in the future. It is easy to confuse cost with present value, but the two concepts are not interchangeable. The dollar amount attributed to present value may be higher than the dollar amount in actual cost, thereby giving an inflated appearance to the value of the settlement.

There are also software packages available to assist in the evaluation of a structured settlement offer or assist in the development of one's own, such as Shepard's 'Determining Damages: Structured Settlements'. A plaintiff's attorney with his or her own structured settlement plan is in a good bargaining position. A structured settlement software package can calculate the present value of a structured settlement, discounted by various assumed interest rates.

2.5 The wording of the agreement

Another area of caution for the practitioner is the actual wording of the settlement agreement. One of the appealing features of the structured settlement is that periodic payments of principal and interest are received tax-free to the plaintiff. There are standard forms available from life insurance companies that contain the language that will ensure that the periodic payments are tax-free. The National Structured Settlements Trade Association located in Washington, DC, has designed for its members standard forms that can be used as, or serve as the basis for, structured settlement agreements.

To avoid the appearance of constructive receipt, which would void the tax-free status of any future payments, the agreement must be quite specific as to dates that the payments will be issued and the dollar amount of each future payment. The well-designed settlement agreement must also specifically state that the defendant or the insurer is responsible for making the periodic payments. This allocation of responsibility must appear in the agreement even if the defendant assigns its obligation to a third party.

Consider for a moment a situation in which the applicable language does not appear and the necessity for it becomes crystal-clear. A situation might arise where the plaintiff, for any imaginable reason, does not receive one or more scheduled payments. Perhaps this is due to a bookkeeping error, or the insolvency of the assignee. If the settlement agreement states that the defendant is responsible for future payments, the plaintiff need not be concerned with the cause of the defaulted payment and can simply make a claim against the defendant for the missing payment. If that statement of obligation were absent from the agreement, the plaintiff would not have a clear claim against the defendant or the insurer.

It is customary in the industry to use standard forms to accomplish a structured settlement agreement and an assignment. These standard forms meet all Internal Revenue requirements. A sample 'Release and Settlement Agreement' is reproduced at Appendix A to this chapter. A sample 'Uniform Qualified Assignment and Release', recommended when an insurer assigns the obligation of future payments to a third party, is reproduced at Appendix B.

2.6   Beneficiary provisions

Beneficiary provisions can also be a problem. The legal practitioner would be well advised not to think of the structured settlement agreements as a will. What happens if the recipient dies before all of the guaranteed payments are made? The plaintiff's attorney should guarantee that the beneficiary language in the agreement is very clear and precise, not ambiguous. Terms such as 'to the heirs of John' may be too imprecise for an annuity company, which may be liable to suit for breach of contract if it pays the wrong person. Therefore, an assignee may choose not to pay rather than risk paying the wrong person. This is a detriment to the plaintiff's beneficiaries only.

Both parties might agree upon a provision in the agreement that states that upon the death of the recipient, future payments will be made to the person or persons provided on a list issued by the estate of the deceased recipient, and that the assignee will not be liable for any payments made in compliance with this list. Plaintiff's counsel may also seek a provision that allows the recipient to change at any time the name or names of the beneficiary or beneficiaries.

3   HOW ATTORNEYS' FEES ARE PAID THROUGH STRUCTURED SETTLEMENTS

Plaintiffs' attorneys can receive their attorneys' fees either as part of the periodic payments made to their clients or up front, based on the cost of the structured settlement.   Of course, if the plaintiff's award is partly lump sum and partly periodic payments, the attorneys' fees can be likewise structured.

An insurer can make payments to the attorney in two separate ways. The insurer can act as the plaintiff's agent and make payments to the attorney for the plaintiff. In such an instance, the attorney's fees would be subject to the plaintiff's creditors. On the other hand, the insurer can assume the client's obligation to pay the fees. In this instance, the unpaid fees would be free from any claims by the client's creditors.

If an attorney prefers to have his or her fee paid when the case is initially settled, the fee should be computed based upon the cost of the annuity. This would mean getting fewer net dollars than if the attorney chose to receive a percentage of the plaintiff's future payments. By way of example, assume the settlement agreement calls for an immediate cash payment of $1,250,000; periodic payments of $60,000 per year, each subsequent year for 10 years, payable monthly; $75,000 each subsequent year thereafter for 10 years; then $125,000 each year thereafter for life. Further assume that the agreement includes lump sum payments of $250,000, payable once every five years commencing five years hence, and that there is a 20-year guaranty on the entire arrangement. Assume also that the cost of the structured portion of the settlement is $1 million and that the attorney's contingency fee agreement was based on one-third of the settlement.

Given the above assumptions, let's now take a look at two different scenarios. In one, the attorney chooses to receive his or her payments up front. In the other, the attorney prefers to receive one-third of all future payments when they are made to the plaintiff.

In the first instance, where the attorney has chosen to receive the full attorney's fee up front, the attorney would receive one-third of $1,250,000, plus one-third of $1 million —the cost of the structure — for a total fee of $750,000. On the other hand, if the attorney instead chose to take periodic payments of the attorneys' fee, he or she is guaranteed to receive a total of $1,200,00 over 20 years. The attorney would continue to receive payments for the life of the client if the client survives the guarantee period. If the attorney predeceases the expiration of the guarantee period, his or her estate will receive the payments for the remainder of the 20-year period.

Some attorneys have based their fee upon the value of annuity. However, many economists have posited that the actual cost to the defendant to purchase the annuity is the most appropriate basis upon which to calculate the attorneys' fees, especially when the attorney is receiving his or her fee as a lump sum payment up front. This approach, however, is made difficult by the common defence tactic of refusing to disclose the actual cost. However, not knowing the cost of the package muddies the waters for the plaintiff who is trying to evaluate the actual worth of the structured settlement offer. This may lead to a plaintiff unwittingly settling a case for less than its value. In all cases, the writer advises all attorneys *not* to accept a structure unless the full cost of the structure is made known to you and your client.

There may be several reasons influencing an attorney's decision whether to take up front compensation or payment over a period of years. An attorney might expect future tax increases or might prefer to invest his money himself. Taking future payments, though, may guarantee the attorney income at a time when he may be approaching retirement years or may otherwise wish to scale back his practice.

The Internal Revenue Service appears to be looking unfavorably upon arrangements that provide for future payment of attorney fees. On 7 May 1991, the IRS issued Technical Advice Memorandum 9134004 (TAM9134004). A Technical Advice Memorandum is not binding precedent; however, in TAM9134004 the IRS ruled that an annuity purchased pursuant to a structured settlement to pay attorneys' fees was taxable to the attorney in the year the annuity was purchased.

In the case that gave rise to the memorandum, the personal injury plaintiffs entered into a contingency agreement with their attorney whereby the attorney was entitled to a certain percentage of their settlement as a fee for his services. The agreement specified that a portion of each payment made to the plaintiff was to be paid to the attorney. The agreement also specified that the insurer would delegate to a third party insurance company its obligation to make payments. The insurer provided the third party with the premium necessary to obtain an annuity contract that would make payments to the attorney. The insurance company was the owner of the policy; however, the attorney was the sole annuitant and payee. The attorney's estate was the beneficiary. The attorney had no control over the payments, which could not be accelerated, deferred, increased or decreased. The attorney could neither assign nor encumber his rights, nor could he forfeit payments.

Under these facts, the IRS considered whether the attorney would be immediately taxed in the year in which the structured fee arrangement was made or whether he would be taxed on the amount of the fee when he received each annuity payment. The IRS answered the question by ruling that the annuity's fair market value would be taxable in the year the annuity was purchased and, therefore, must be included in the attorney's gross income amount for that year.

To reach this conclusion, the IRS relied upon section 83 of the Internal Revenue Code, which addresses property transferred in connection with the performance of services. Section 83 of the Code provides that a person who receives property in exchange for services will be taxed upon receipt of the property when the property is transferable and not subject to a substantial risk of forfeiture. The Code states that, by definition, a substantial risk of forfeiture exists when a person's rights to full enjoyment of such property are conditioned upon the future performance of substantial services by that individual. The Code continues by stating that the property is considered transferable only if the rights in such property of any transferee are not subject to a substantial risk of forfeiture.

A cash basis taxpayer must include amounts of gross income when they are actually received by him. Section 83 of the Code then serves to codify a doctrine that controverts this principle — the economic benefit doctrine. The economic benefit doctrine provides that when the right to future payments generates an immediate economic or financial benefit to the taxpayer, then the fund thereby created is to be included in the taxpayer's gross income. In essence, the IRS ruled in its memorandum that an annuity purchased to provide periodic payments of an attorney's fee generates a sufficient economic or financial benefit and that the attorney's ownership and enjoyment of the fund is therefore not so limited as to cause the income to be taxable only upon the future receipt of the periodic payments. The IRS considers the promise to pay income in the future that is funded and secured to be a promise that generates an immediate economic benefit upon the person to be paid (Rev Rul 60-31 1960-61 CB 174; Treas Reg section 1.451-2(a) (as amended in 1978)).

There was a forewarning of TAM 9134004 in the IRS's Announcement 87-3, issued in 1987. (See Announcement 87-3, 1987-2 IRB 40.) Although the Announcement did not specifically identify structured arrangements for attorneys' fees, the IRS did state that agreements deferring the receipt of income to a later year may constitute constructive receipt in the year of the arrangement of the amount so deferred, especially when the recipient's right to receive the income is not subject to substantial limitations or restrictions.

Although TAM9134004 is not binding precedent, it is a substantial authority. To avoid the ramifications of TAM9134004, it is possible that the plaintiff can remain obligated to make payments to the attorney. The plaintiff himself can purchase an annuity payable to the plaintiff, and then upon receipt of payments make payments to the attorney. It seems conceivable that one might successfully argue in this instance that the attorney would be receiving no immediate economic benefit, as the annuity is in the name of the plaintiff and payments are being made to the plaintiff. In such a circumstance, then, the attorney would be taxed only upon actual or constructive receipt of a payment from the plaintiff.

4   RELATIONSHIP OF STRUCTURED SETTLEMENTS TO TAXATION RULES

4.1   Overview

The Internal Revenue Code has been amended to bestow the same tax-free status upon future periodic payments made in compensation for personal injuries as was previously afforded only to lump sum payments. The use of the structured settlement arrangement was further facilitated when Congress amended the Code to exclude from gross income the amount paid to the third party who assumes the ongoing obligation.

Section 104(a)(2) of the Internal Revenue Code of 1986, as amended, provides that recoveries for personal injuries are tax-free to the recipient. The tax-free status applies whether the recovery is the result of an award or a settlement, and regardless of whether the recovery is administered in one lump sum or in periodic payments. A lump sum payment is tax-free in its entirety when it is given. However, the agreement to pay the award in periodic payments may give rise to issues of constructive receipt if the agreement is not carefully worded. It is important that the structured settlement agreement contain language that comports with the Internal Revenue Service Rule that bestowed tax-free status upon both the principal and interest components of the periodic payments.

Also, a plaintiff's attorney should be sure that the cheque that will be used to purchase the annuity does not pass through the plaintiff or the plaintiff's counsel. Likewise, the cheque should not be made out to the annuity company and the plaintiff's counsel. Such practices also give rise to issues of constructive receipt. Further, if a claimant accepts a lump sum settlement and then purchases his own annuity, he must forever pay taxes on the portion of the annuity payments that constitute interest. However, if the parties agree upon a structured settlement whereby the defendant or its insurer assigns the payment to a life insurance company, all parties thereby avail themselves of the provisions of Internal Revenue Ruling 79-220 and section 130 of the Code. Then, all of the future payments to the claimant are tax-free, even that part of the payment that constitutes interest.

4.2 Background

Prior to 1979, the federal tax status of periodic payments was unclear. In July 1979, the IRS issued Revenue Ruling 79-220 to answer the question whether the exclusion from gross income provided by section 104(a)(2) of the Internal Revenue Code applied to the full amount of monthly payments received in settlement of a damage suit or only to the discounted present value of such payments. The IRS held that the exclusion from gross income provided by section 104(a)(2) of the Code applied to the full amount of the monthly payments received by the recipient because the recipient has a right to receive only the monthly payments and does not have the actual or constructive receipt or the economic benefit of the lump sum amount that was invested to yield that monthly payment. The IRS also held that if the recipient were to die before the end of the guaranteed period, the payments remaining paid to the recipient's estate or beneficiary are also excludable under section 104(a)(2).

With the signing of the Periodic Payment Settlement Act by President Ronald Reagan in January 1983, Revenue Ruling 79-220 became law. The Act accomplished two things. Firstly, it laid out clearly the requirements to be fulfilled to ensure that the periodic payments are received free of federal income tax by the recipient. Secondly, the Act established the framework for assigning the defendant's obligation to make periodic payments to a third party. If a structured settlement is properly arranged, the recipient will receive tax-free payments excludable from gross income. The defendant may obtain a current income tax deduction. These aspects of the tax effect of structured settlements will be discussed in more detail later in this section.

As previously stated, recoveries for personal injuries are tax-free to the recipient. To be tax-free, however, the recovery must be for 'damages' received on account of a 'personal injury' or sickness.

Regulations interpreting the term 'damages' define the term to mean amounts received through the prosecution, or settlement in lieu of, a suit or action based in tort or tort-type rights. (See Treas Reg s 1.104-1(c) (as amended in 1970).)

'Personal injury' is another term whose interpretation can affect the tax status of payments. Both the IRS and the courts interpret the term to include injuries received from a battery and other typical torts, such as infliction of emotional distress (*Fono v Comm*, (1982) 79 TC 680); injury to personal reputation (*Church v Comm*, (1983) 80 TC 1104); and libel and slander.

Although the IRS affords favorable tax treatment to damages out of personal injuries, it looks less favourably upon damages received for professional injuries. Reversing a tax court decision (*Roemer*, 79 TC 398) in 1983, the United States Court of Appeals for the Ninth Circuit ruled that a defamatory credit report was a personal injury although the consequences were to have an impact on the taxpayer's business reputation. The Ninth Circuit held that the damages received were not subject to federal income taxes (*Roemer v Commissioner*, 716 F 2d 693 (9th Cir 1983)). However, the IRS announced that it would not follow the 9th Circuit (Rev Ruling 85-143, 1985-2 CB55). For example, in 1984 the IRS determined that damages received from a sex discrimination suit were actually compensating for a professional injury, not a personal injury. (See Priv Ltr Ruling 8437084 (13 June 1984).) However, the IRS takes the position that for damages compensating for pecuniary losses, such as lost wages, the amount received will be taxable.

Some courts have applied the 'origin of the character of the claim approach' to determine whether damages received should be excluded from taxation.

Under this analysis, courts look to the nature of the injuries. If the injuries are of the type that would normally result from a personal injury inflicting tort, the recovery will be tax-free as per Code s 104(a)(2). This is so at least to the extent of the liquidated damages, excluding any amount attributable to lost wages.

4.3 Punitive damages

The Revenue Reconciliation Act of 1989 amended s 104(a) of the Code. Prior to the Act, IRS took the position that punitive damages were fully taxable. (See Rev Rul 84-108, 1984-2 CB32.) Section 7641(a) of the Act resolved the question whether the punitive damages portion of a recovery was excluded from gross income under Code, s 104(a). It excluded from gross income punitive damages received in connection with personal injury and sickness cases. However, punitive damages received in connection with injuries or sickness that are *not* physical in nature are taxable. Thus, under s 104(a), as amended, punitive damages received for non-physical injuries are taxable and those received for physical injuries are tax-free.

4.4 Miscellaneous issues

One commentator suggests that the character of the payments to be received should be specified in the settlement agreement because some recoveries may not be excludable from gross income. The recovery for some injuries alleged in the complaint may be excludable, others may not. The release can specifically state what allegations the recovery is for. That may help substantiate a recipient's claim for favourable tax treatment if the recipient is challenged by the IRS (Mark A Coel, 'Tax Aspects of Personal Injury Awards and Structured Settlements', The Florida Bar Journal, Vol 66, No 5, pp 78–81, 1992).

The same commentator suggests the following examples illustrate the potentially significant difference in tax consequences between lump sum recovery versus periodic payment.

In Example 1, the plaintiff accepts a $1,000,000 lump sum settlement from the defendant in exchange for defendant's full release from liability. If he invests the full recovery in a 20-year taxable instrument yielding 10% annually, the plaintiff, obviously, will earn $100,000 interest after one year. This interest earned is includable in plaintiff's gross income subject to federal income tax. Assuming the recipient will be taxed at 31%, the recipient's after-tax return on his $1,000,000 investment is

$69,000 per year. Over 20 years, the recipient's recovery will total $2,380,000, assuming, of course, he does not reinvest any of his annual interest earned.

In Example 2, defendant pays to plaintiff an annual figure determined by the present value of a stream of payments that at 10% yields $1,000,000 over 20 years. The annual figure is determined as $117,459, received tax-free. If the recipient invests $48,459 each year (the difference between the annual payments in this example and the annual interest earned in Example 1) in tax-exempt zero coupon bonds yielding 6%, maturing in 20 years from settlement date, the plaintiff would earn $1,782,592. Plaintiff's total recovery after 20 years would be $3,162,592 ($782,592 more than the plaintiff in Example 1).

4.5   Deductibility

Under 26 USC, s 162 (1988), payments of civil damages arising out of ordinary business operations are deductible by the defendant as a business or trade expense. However, payments of civil damages made out of a personal obligation are not deductible. Code s 461(h) allows for the deduction of payments only upon 'economic performance', which is defined as occurring only as payments are *made* to the recipient. Therefore, a defendant can deduct individual payments only in the year in which they are made. In the typical structured settlement arrangement, the defendant will purchase an annuity that will provide the income to meet the defendant's obligation.   The defendant cannot deduct the purchase price of the annuity because, in order for the payments to be tax-free to the plaintiff, the plaintiff can have no ownership interest in the annuity. Therefore, the payments from the annuity will be paid to the defendant who will then be taxed on that income. However, when the defendant makes the payment to the recipient, the defendant can deduct the payment when made, provided the payment is being made as a business or trade expense.

4.6   Assignment

It is also typical for a defendant to assign the obligation to make periodic payments. Code s 461(h) allows a defendant to deduct the full amount paid to an assignee where the assignee takes on full responsibility to make payments to the plaintiff and where the assignment satisfies the requirements of Code s 130.

Code s 130 provides that the amounts paid to the third party are not to be included in gross income by the third party if the assignment satisfies all the requirements of Code s 130. Payments received by plaintiffs from third parties are still excludable from income where the assignment satisfies Code s 130. However, this applies only where payments made are for damages resulting from personal injuries or sickness.

Assignments under Code s 130 usually involve (1) assignment by a defendant or its insurer; (2) to a third party, usually another insurance company; (3) of its liability to make periodic payments. To be released from liability to make future payments to the plaintiff, the defendant pays a third party to assume the obligation. The amount paid will not be treated as income to the third party to the extent the amount is used to purchase investment instruments that in turn are used by the third party to meet its obligation to the plaintiff. See 26 USC, s 130(a) (1988). This is called a 'qualified assignment'.

This qualified assignment must satisfy the following criteria under 26 USC s 130:

1   A third party assumes obligation from a party to a lawsuit or a party to a settlement agreement;
2   Periodic payments must be fixed and determinable, or in other words, structured as to time and amount;
3   The recipient cannot have influence or control over the payments, or in other words, the payments cannot be accelerated, deferred, increased or decreased by the recipient;
4   The assignee's obligation on account of personal injury or sickness can be no greater than the assignor's obligation; and,
5   The periodic payments must be excludable from income of the recipient under Code s 104(a)(2).

The assignee must only purchase 'qualified funding assets' to fund its obligation to make payments (26 USC, s 130(a) (1988)). A qualified funding asset is an annuity contract issued by a company licensed to do business as an insurance company under the laws of any state, or any obligation of the United States (treasury bills, treasury notes, etc), provided that:

1   Said annuity contract or obligation is used by the assignee to fund periodic payments under a qualified assignment;
2   The payment periods under the annuity or obligation is reasonably related to the payment schedule under the qualified assignment, *and* the amount of the annuity or obligation payment does not exceed the amount of the periodic payment;
3   Said annuity contract or obligation is designated by the assignee as being taken into account under Code s 130;
4   Said annuity contract or obligation is purchased by assignee *no more* than 60 days *before* the date of the qualified assignment and *not later* than 60 days *after* the date of the assignment   (26 USC s 130(d) (1988)).

Therefore, a properly structured settlement:

1   Allows the defendant to deduct fully the amount paid in exchange for a release of the obligation to make periodic payments;
2   Does not affect the plaintiff's ability to exclude the payments received from gross income;
3   Allows the assignee to exclude from gross income the amounts received for accepting the assignment to the extent the amount does not exceed the total cost of the qualified funding asset (the annuity or US obligation).

It has been suggested that, where the plaintiff feels uncomfortable with the security level or rating of the insurance company that will issue the annuity, perhaps a settlement trust can be established. For a release of liability from the plaintiff, the defendant would assign its obligation to a trust and name an independent third party as the trustee and the plaintiff as beneficiary. The assignment must meet the requirements of a qualified assignment under Code s 130. The defendant would provide a fixed amount to the trust, which would then be used to purchase qualified funding assets, which then would provide the funds to make payments to the plaintiff. The plaintiff cannot be entitled to receive the amounts paid to the trust by the defendant, and cannot have rights to the annuity or the annuity's payments.   The plaintiff can only be entitled to receive payments from the trust. In the opinion of the commentator, this arrangement should result in payments being excludable from gross income (Mark A Coel, 'Tax Aspects of Personal Injury Awards and Structured Settlements', supra).

5 HOW ISSUES RELATED TO STRUCTURED SETTLEMENTS HAVE BEEN TREATED IN US COURTS

As you know, the court system in the United States is both state and federal. Each state interprets its own procedural rules as it sees fit. Therefore, of the various states which have dealt with structured settlements, some have done so in different manners. Most frequently the courts have addressed the basis for calculating the cost of the settlement and the value upon which attorneys' fees will be based. However, courts have also addressed the timing of the payments of attorneys' fees. The issue of whether a structured settlement is a viable option when the plaintiff is an infant has also been addressed, as well as how to calculate the reduction of a judgment rendered against a non-settling tortfeasor to consider the amount recovered from a tortfeasor who has agreed to a structured settlement. Issues related to structured settlements have been addressed by state legislatures as well as courts.

5.1 Attorneys' fees and the cost of the structured settlement

The calculating of attorneys' fees has been addressed by federal courts and state courts. At least two federal courts have held that the basis for calculating an attorney's fee is the present value of the settlement. The present value of a settlement was determined to be synonymous with the cost of the settlement package.

In *Wyatt v United States of America*, 783 F 2d 45 (6th Cir 1986), counsel argued that the present value of a settlement included 'unique' benefits to the plaintiff. These benefits were intangible, asserted plaintiff's counsel, and included beneficial tax consequences and the benefit of having virtually squander-proof payments. The government argued that the attorneys fees should be based upon the cost of the settlement package to the government.

The Sixth Circuit held that plaintiff's counsel failed to show that the present value of the structured settlement was anything other than the cost of the settlement and that the attorney's fee is to be based upon the present value of the total settlement, excluding any speculative or intangible benefits to the plaintiff (ibid at 47, 50). The Sixth Circuit ruled that the proper base amount for determining attorneys' fees in Federal Tort Claims Act suits resulting in structured settlements is the present value of the settlement; absent submission of any contrary evidence, the present value of the structured settlement is the cost of that settlement. (ibid at 48).

The *Wyatt* Court's reasoning was consistent with the rationale of *Donaghy v Napoleon*, 543 F Supp 112 (DNJ 1982), a trial court case out of the District of New Jersey.

In *Donaghy*, plaintiff's counsel set forth three alternative methods of calculating the attorney's fee:

1   one-third of the total payout, pursuant to the retainer agreement;
2   percentage allowable under state law based on total payout; or
3   one-third of the minimum cash guarantees.

The court rejected each of plaintiff's counsel's suggested alternative methods of calculating the fee and held that the fee must be calculated on the cost of the settlement package and by percentages of recovery supplied by New Jersey court rules (ibid at 113).

In 1981, the Superior Court of New Jersey decided *Merendino v FMC Corp*, 438 A 2d 365 (Law Div 1981). In *Merendino*, after settling the case, plaintiff's counsel made the appropriate application under the New Jersey Court Rules for approval of attorneys' fees in excess of the contingent fee provided for in the retainer agreement or allowable pursuant to rule governing attorneys' fees.

Plaintiff's counsel valued the settlement by adding the cash lump payment to the value placed upon the payments to be made to the plaintiff. The valuation of the settlement was based on calculations involving interest rate estimates for the future.

Plaintiff's attorney in his fee application suggested that the value of the settlement rather than the cost of the settlement was the appropriate base from which to calculate attorneys' fees. However, the court held that the actual present value or marketplace cost of the settlement structure is the appropriate basis upon which to calculate attorney's fees (ibid at 368).

In 1982, a New Jersey court again looked at an attorney's fee application involving a structured settlement. In *Tobias v Autore*, 440 A 2d 1171 (Law Div 1982), the maximum attorney's fee permitted under the Rule was 18.84% of the total recovery minus disbursements. In his application, plaintiff's attorney requested an attorney's fee of 25.64% of the net sum recovered.

Relying upon *Merendino*, the Court stated that attorneys' fees are to be calculated on the actual cost to the paying party of the settlement. Also, the court identified the following advantages of structured settlement:

the structured settlement would protect plaintiffs against squandering or loss of their money damages; the annuities and balloon payments capitalised on a prevailing high interest rate, freeing the plaintiff from unnecessary investment risks; and the settlement reduced valuable tax benefits to the plaintiff (ibid at 1174).

As in *Merendino*, the court permitted an attorney's fee greater than that provided by the rule.

The calculation of attorneys' fees in structured settlements was treated differently by New York courts. In *Matter of Estate of Muccini*, 460 NYS 2d 680 (Sur Ct 1983), the structured settlement was evaluated by the attorney's economist by discounting the deferred payments at 8% per annum and projecting tax savings by the plaintiff over her 40 years of life expectancy. The court disagreed with the economist's methods for calculating the value of the settlement package. The court stated instead that the present value of the settlement can only be calculated based on the cost to the defendants or their insurers to provide the settlement package (ibid at 682).

The attorney requested that his fee be based upon the present value of the settlement as calculated by the actual cost of the settlement to the defendants' insurers and be made payable out of the up front portion of the settlements in one lump sum (ibid at 683). Such a distribution would result in the attorney receiving 82.88% of the up front portion of the settlement. The court, however, refused to consent to this distribution of attorneys' fees, reasoning that any calculation of attorneys' fees based upon a percentage of the up-front portion of the settlement would result in the attorney receiving a higher portion of the award than was reasonable.

As the retainer agreement was silent as to any payments to the attorney out of the initial lump sum portion of a structured settlements, the court reasoned that it was patently inequitable for the attorney to have immediate ownership and control over his fees prior to the client receiving future payments. The court held, therefore, that the attorney's fee should be payable to the attorney upon the receipt of each payment by the clients under the terms of the structured settlemen (ibid at 683). In New York, two calculations must be made to determine attorneys' fees (*Ursini v Sussman*, 541 NYS 2d 916 (Sup Ct 1989); see also *Marulli v Pro Security Service, Inc*, 583 NYS 2d 870 (App Div 1992).) The initial calculation is a calculation of the attorneys' fee based on a determination of the present value prior to the deduction of the attorney's fee. The second calculation requires the determination of the future payments to the plaintiff after the deduction of the attorney's fee.

In 1982, the Superior Court of Pennsylvania held in *Johnson v Sears Roebuck & Co*, 436 A 2d 675 (Pa Super Ct 1982), that attorneys are only entitled to contingency percentage of cash payments plus the cost of annuity and not to a contingency fee computed from the total cash payments plus present value of the annuity. The Pennsylvania Court's reasoning was similar to that of other courts which have so held. The court found that it is most equitable to base the attorney's fees on the cost of the annuity. It reasoned that the cost of the annuity takes into consideration a possibility that the plaintiff may or may not live out his anticipated life expectancy. This contingency, the court stated, was accounted for in the price of the annuity (ibid at 678).

A dissenting judge stated that the cost of an annuity is an improper basis upon which to calculate and determine attorneys' fees. He said that it is the value to the recipient of the payments that determines the value of the settlemen, and further that the present value of the benefit has long been determined by actuarial tables (ibid at 679). The majority, however, countered this argument by stating that the use of actuarial tables to determine the present value of a benefit is only an accurate method when the sum so considered is guaranteed to be received (ibid at 678).

5.2 Manner of paying attorneys' fees

Courts have held that unless the attorney–client contingency agreement specifically states that an attorney can receive an up-front fee where a structured settlement is negotiated, the attorney must be compensated only when the client is paid — even if this means that the attorney will be paid over a number of years.

In a 1982 decision, the Supreme Court of Minnesota agreed with a plaintiff who appealed from an Order that directed payment of attorneys' fees in the amount of $39,054.33 plus expenses from a $45,000 up-front payment due the plaintiff under a structured settlement of a personal injury claim (*Cardenas v Ramsey County*, 322 NW 2d 191 (Minn 1982)).

The structured settlement provided an up-front payment of $45,000 plus specified guaranteed payments totaling $110,800 over a ten-year period (ibid at 192). The plaintiff and his attorney entered into a contingency agreement whereby the plaintiff agreed to pay the attorney 'one-third of the total amount recovered, or of a compromised amount upon settlement' (ibid at 192). Plaintiff's counsel had no prior experience with structured settlements. The contingent fee agreement, therefore, was silent on the issue of the basis for determining attorneys' fees.

Plaintiff argued that he was not required to pay his attorney more than one-third of each payment due under the settlement as and when he received the payment. Plaintiff argued that the term 'recovered' in the contingent fee agreement should be interpreted to mean received by him. Plaintiff's counsel argued that 'recovered' should be interpreted as meaning agreed to settle. The issue, therefore, was whether the attorney was entitled to one-third of the present value of the structured settlement or to one-third of the up-front money as well as one-third of each future payment as it is received by counsel's client.

The court held that the unique fiduciary relationship existing between an attorney and the client requires that where the attorney–client contingent fee contract is not explicit as to the time and manner of payment of attorneys' fees, and a structured settlement is negotiated, that as a matter of law the word 'recovered' in the contingency fee contract must be construed to mean 'received'. Consequently, the attorney was entitled to one-third of each payment his client received when it was received by the clien (ibid at 193).

In *Sayble v Feinman*, 142 Cal Rptr 895 (Ct App 1978), the California Court of Appeals determined what interpretation should prevail where the contingent fee agreement between counsel and client is not explicit on the terms of payment of attorneys' fees where a structured settlement has been recovered. The contract at issue provided that 'the attorney(s) shall be paid $28^1/_3\%$ of any money recovered in this matter . . .' (ibid at 897). Neither counsel nor client contemplated a structured settlement. The structured settlement included an initial lump sum settlement of $200,000 plus an annuity which would provide $2,500 per month for the lifetime of the plaintiff. Plaintiff's life expectancy at the time of the settlement was 46.7 years.

Counsel and his client could not agree upon the amount and method of payment of attorneys' fees. The attorney argued that he was entitled to $28^1/_3\%$ of the $200,000 initial payment plus $28^1/_3\%$ of the present cash value of the annuity portion of the settlement. Plaintiff argued that her attorney was entitled to $28^1/_3\%$ of the initial $200,000 lump sum, but $28^1/_3\%$ of the annuity payments only upon her receipt of each payment.

The court's decision rested upon the interpretation of the word 'money' in the contingent fee agreement, which stated that counsel was entitled to $28^1/_3\%$ of 'any money recovered'. The court reasoned that the term 'money' in its ordinary sense implies a circulating medium of exchange, and that the right to be paid money from an annuity does not equate to 'money recovered' (ibid at 898–9). Further, referencing the California Uniform Commercial Code, the court stated that cash proceeds are money, cheques, deposit accounts, and the like, and that all other proceeds are non-cash proceeds (ibid at 899, quoting the California Uniform Commercial Code s 9306).

Further, reasoned the court, the plaintiff does not actually recover money from the annuity until she actually receives it, as any future payment may or may not be paid depending upon the actual life-span of the recipient. Thus, held the court, counsel should not be entitled to attorneys' fees based on $2^{1}/_{3}\%$ of the present value of monthly payments that the client may not in fact ever receive (ibid at 899).

5.3   Judgment against non-settling defendant

In 1984, the California Court of Appeals considered an issue of first impression regarding structured settlements — the proper reduction of a damage award against a non-settling tortfeasor when the plaintiff and other defendants agree to a structured settlement calling for periodic payments.

In *Franck v Polaris E-Z Go*, 204 Cal Rptr 321 (Ct App 1984), the California Court of Appeals considered what was the proper reduction of a damages award against a non-settling tortfeasor under its code of civil procedure when a plaintiff and other defendants agree to a structure settlement calling for future periodic payments (ibid at 323).

Plaintiff settled with one tortfeasor to the extent of tortfeasor's single accident coverage limit or $100,000 (ibid   at 323). Some $25,000 was to be paid to the plaintiff up front. The remaining $75,000 of the policy was to be used to purchase an annuity which would provide $190,000 in future payments. The plaintiff settled with a second defendant in the amount of $2,500 up front. A judgment was rendered after a trial in favour of the plaintiff, and damages were assessed at $300,000.

Section 877 (a) of the California Code of Civil Procedure provided that 'where a release, dismissal with or without prejudice, or a covenant not to sue or not to enforce judgment is given in good faith before verdict or judgment to one or more of a number of tortfeasors claimed to be liable for the same tort . . . [said], release, dismissal or covenant shall reduce the claims against the others in the amount stipulated by the release, the dismissal or the covenant, or in the amount of the consideration paid for it whichever is the greater; . . . ' (ibid at 326).

The remaining defendant contended that the words in the code 'amount stipulated by the release' was to be read literally and the award reduced by the total amount of future payments stipulated in the settlement agreement. The plaintiff argued that the future payment must be discounted to the present cash value to arrive at the amount by which the judgment should be reduced (ibid).

The court reasoned that maximisation of recovery to the plaintiff and encouragement of settlement strongly urged concurrence with plaintiff's conclusion. It held that to ensure that the plaintiff receives the full recovery to which the plaintiff is entitled at the time of judgment, when a plaintiff and one or more co-defendants in a tort action enter into a structured settlement calling for future periodic payments, the amounts by which the judgment award against a non-settling defendant is reduced under the pertinent California Code of Civil Procedure is to be the present cash value of the future payments (ibid at 329).

5.4   Infant settlements

An interesting controversy arose in New York in 1988. A justice sitting on the New York State Supreme Court issued a memorandum dated 1 March, 1988 in which he declared he would not approve structured settlements for infants' cases (New York Law Journal, V 199, N 109, p 3, 8 June 1988). The justice felt that such annuities were risky investment vehicles and that the rate of return on the investment must be deemed secondary to preserving the principal sum. The justice stated that the applicable New York rules and case law specified the types of investment vehicles allowed and did not allow annuities.

In support of his decision, the justice cited New York's Civil Practice Law and Rules, section 1206, which stated in pertinent part that the court may order that money constituting any part of any property to which an infant is entitled be deposited in one or more specified insured banks or trust companies or be invested in one or more accounts in insured savings and loan associations. The court may elect that the money be deposited in a high-interest yield account such as an insured savings certificate or an insured money market account. The court may further elect to invest the money in one or more 'insured or guaranteed United States Treasury or municipal bills, notes or bonds'.

Effective 1 October, 1988 the New York legislature did in fact amend CPLR, s 1206(c) to provide for structured settlement agreements relative to the disposition of proceeds relating to an infants claim. Said section currently reads in pertinent part that 'the court may order that money constituting any part of the property be deposited in one or more specified insured banks or trust companies or be invested in one or more specified accounts in insured savings and loan associations or it may order that a structured settlement agreement be executed, which will include any settlement agreement whose terms contain provisions for the payment of funds on an installment basis, provided that with respect to future installment payments, the court may order that each party liable for such payments shall fund such payments in the amount necessary to insure future payments in the form of an annuity contract executed by a qualified insurer and approved by the superintendent of insurance . . . '

5.5 Legislation and court rules

In New Jersey, the rules governing contingent fees and the calculation of attorneys' fees in structured settlements is defined in Rule 1:21-7(c) of the Rules Governing the Courts of the State of New Jersey. In 1984, by amendment to Rule 1:21-7, New Jersey defined how a contingent fee shall be calculated when the recovery involves a structured settlement. The basis for the calculation is the 'value' of the structured settlement. 'Value' is defined as the initial cash payments made to the client, plus the actual cost to the paying party of the deferred payment aspect of the structure. If the party paying the settlement is not the purchaser of the deferred payment component, then the actual cost is defined as the actual cost assigned by that party to the component.

The Rule further requires that the party making the settlement disclose the actual cost. If that party does not purchase the deferred payment aspect of the structured settlement, then the party must disclose the factors and assumptions used by it in assigning actual cost.

In 1985, the New York legislature added Article 50-A to its Civil Practice Law and Rules, and in 1986, the rules were amended to add Article 50-B. Together these articles mandate structured judgments in medical, dental and podiatric malpractice actions and personal injury, injury to property, and wrongful death actions. These articles created New York's structured judgment rules whereby future damages beyond

$250,000 are not paid out in one lump sum, but rather in structured payments over a period of years.

The structured payment arrangement gives the victorious plaintiff an immediate judgment in a lump sum in addition to periodic future payments. Prior to the enactment of Article 50-A, such structured payments were the product of only settlement agreements. However, after the enactment of the article, structured payments became mandatory if the parties were unable to settle outside of court, provided the judgment exceeded a certain sum. See the Commentary on Article 50-A in McKinney's Consolidated Laws of New York (Annotated).

Subdivision (c) of sections 5031 and 5041 pertain to the calculation of attorneys' fees. It states that attorneys fees payable out of judgments for past damages are to be paid in a lump sum. Attorneys' fees as a proportion of a judgment relating to future damages shall also be paid in a lump sum if the plaintiff is entitled to such payments in a lump sum. However, payment of that portion of attorneys' fees on future damages paid periodically to the plaintiff shall also be paid in a lump sum to the attorney. The attorney's fee will be calculated based on the present value of the annuity contract purchased to provide the periodically paid payments to the plaintiff.

Subdivision (e) to the respective sections provides that the value of the annuity contract shall be 'determined in accordance with generally accepted actuarial practices by applying the discount rate in effect at the time of the award to the full amount of the remaining future damages'. Defendants and their insurance carriers are required to offer to guarantee the purchase and payment of the annuity contract. The period of time over which the periodic payments are to be made and the period of time with which the present value of the annuity contract is calculated is to be determined by the trier of fact. The period of time over which periodic payments can be made and the period of time used to calculate the present value for damages attributable to pain and suffering shall not be greater than ten years.

The articles state that to supply the source of the periodic payments, an annuity contract must be purchased, executed by a qualified insurer, approved by the superintendent of insurance, and approved by the court.

As one can see, although there has not been a great deal of activity dealing with structured settlements, the rulings have been diverse. As is often the case in the US, location of the forum can govern the outcome.

6   NEW USES FOR THE STRUCTURED SETTLEMENT ARRANGEMENT IN THE UNITED STATES

6.1   Structured settlements and environmental clean-up

The structured settlement concept has recently been applied to environmental claims, and its use has been endorsed by the federal Environmental Protection Agency (EPA). The EPA is the regulating body for the removal and clean-up of contaminated or hazardous waste sites. It oversees the distribution of funds earmarked for the clean-up process. There are approximately 30,000 such sites as known to exist in the United States. The EPA has labeled more than 1,000 of these sites as national priorities.

Clean up costs average $25 million per site. Internal Revenue Code, section 107(c)(1) limits the liability for each site to $50 million. More than $8 billion has been allocated by the Comprehensive Environmental Response, Compensation and Liability Act (CERCLA), also known as the Superfund law, to clean up the sites. The fund is partially financed by monies collected from fines and penalties imposed upon parties responsible for contamination, as well as from taxes imposed on oil and on manufacturers and importers of certain chemical substances.

However, with tens of thousands of contaminated sites, the fund, if the only resource, would be depleted before the removal and clean-up process could be completed. Litigation can be complex and lengthy due to the number of parties involved, and disputes frequently arise over whether the potentially responsible party (PRP) is covered for clean-up costs. If an insurance policy includes a pollution exclusion provision, a dispute between the PRP and its insurer over coverage will usually result.

A 'policy buyout' can resolve a dispute and avoid the years of litigation usually involved. A policy buyout is a negotiated settlement between the insurer and its insured whereby each will contribute to the purchase of an annuity, which will be used to provide the funds needed to clean up a site, rather than litigating for years to determine whether a clean up is or is not covered under the policy.

In 1988, the EPA commissioned a study to determine ways to motivate PRP's to clean up the sites and to get their insurers to settle claims more quickly. The EPA concluded that 'structured settlements demonstrated the highest potential as an incentive to promote PRP settlements with the EPA'.

The EPA study also noted several advantages of using the structured settlement arrangement in environmental cases, including:

1 the settlement cost is lower as compared to a single lump sum payment;
2 it provides a secure source for funds;
3 the guarantee of available resources assures the timely completion of the clean-up; and
4 if actual costs exceed estimated costs, the additional funds generated by the investment are readily available.

When structured settlements are applied to environmental claims, the annuity is owned by the EPA and purchased by the PRP or its insurer. Annuity payments are deposited into the Superfund. These structured packages are well suited to environmental clean-ups because the cost to complete a clean-up easily runs into the tens of millions and the time to complete a clean-up usually runs into decades.

The design of the environmental structured settlement package does not differ greatly, if at all, from the usual structured settlement package found in personal injury litigation. It consists of an initial payout to cover the start up cost of the clean-up operation, and includes regular ongoing payments and intermittent lump sum payments to cover the cost of inflation, unforeseen events and the like.

Like any other structured settlement, the environmental package often pays out more over its life than the sum of an immediate lump sum settlement. The money generated by the annuity can easily be used, therefore, to offset any difference between the projected cost of clean up and the actual cost.

With the EPA's ringing endorsement, the use of structured settlements is all but guaranteed to increase in popularity in the environmental litigation area as it has in personal injury litigation.

6.2 Structured settlements and marital dissolution

Statistics show that less than one-half of all single parents who are awarded child support payments receive the full amount from their former spouse. One-fourth of such parents receive no payments at all.

Structured settlements provide a new method of funding and insuring spousal and child support payments. Structured settlements are used when current assets are large enough to purchase an annuity that will fund all future support or spousal payments. As with structured settlements in the personal injury context, payments may be for a limited term of years, such as until the child reaches the age of maturity, or may continue for the life of the recipient spouse.

Parties to a divorce mutually benefit from this creative financing technique. Because payments are guaranteed and the amounts set, the need to seek a court order to enforce support decrees or to increase the payment amounts are eliminated. Further benefit is provided in that payments are guaranteed even if the former spouse remarries. There is also a freedom of choice issue regarding lifestyle. For the recipient spouse, payments are guaranteed even if that spouse remarries or cohabits. The lifestyle of the paying spouse is not diminished or disrupted in the future as payments are funded by current assets and not future earnings.

The use of structured settlements to fund future spousal and child support payments eliminates the often emotionally traumatic need for future interaction between the parties. The burden, psychological or otherwise, attendant to making out monthly payments directly to or receiving directly from a former spouse is eliminated. The monthly payments are not subject to fluctuations in amounts, or other uncertainties, caused by changes in the paying spouse's economic or marital circumstances. Payments are timely and continuous even if the paying spouse dies or is disabled.

As stated above, the annuity is purchased by using current assets. The assets can be a home, cash or perhaps a pension plan. A qualified retirement plan — an asset often overlooked in dissolution matters — can be amended during divorce proceedings under a qualified domestic relations order, as defined by Internal Revenue Code, section 414(p), without incurring the usual harsh early withdrawal tax penalties.

The use of structured settlements in the marital dissolution context is a promising option, whose use can aid in negotiating and compromising during often emotionally taxing settlement discussions.

APPENDIX A

SAMPLE RELEASE AND SETTLEMENT AGREEMENT

For and in consideration of the amounts, terms and conditions stated herein, the terms and sufficiency of which are hereby agreed to and acknowledged by _____(Claimant/___Plaintiff)_____ (sometimes herein referred to as releasor), said claimant hereby releases and forever discharges ____(Defendant)_____ and ____(Insurer)_____(sometimes herein referred to as releasees), employees, representatives, agents, assigns and successors, and all other persons, firms or corporations liable or who might be claimed to be liable in any manner, from any and all claims, demands, actions, causes of action or suits of any kind or nature whatsoever, both known and unknown, to person and property, which have resulted in the past or may in the future develop as a result of the incident which occurred ___(Date)___ at or near ___(Location)_____. It is understood and agreed by the parties that the payments, as set out herein, are not to be construed as an admission of liability on the part of the defendant by whom liability is expressly denied.

In consideration of the release as set forth above, the sum of ($____) Dollars has been paid to claimant/plaintiff, on behalf of the defendant, the receipt and sufficiency of which is hereby acknowledged, as full accord, satisfaction and settlement of all claims as stated and referred to herein with the exception only as to future periodic payments as set forth in Addendum #1.

In the event that releasor dies prior to the date that is set for the last guaranteed payment, the balance of the guaranteed payments shall continue to be paid on the same basis outlined in Addendum #1 for the remainder of said guaranteed period to such person or entity as shall be designated in writing at the time of settlement by said claimant/plaintiff to the insurer. The following person(s) is/are designated as the beneficiary . . .

(NAME OF SPECIFIC BENEFICIARY OR BENEFICIARIES SHALL BE INSERTED HERE...IF THE ANNUITANT IS A MINOR THE RECOMMENDED BENEFICIARY IS AS FOLLOWS: ('The Estate of ————'). THIS MUST MATCH THE INFORMATION PROVIDED ON THE INFORMATION REQUEST FORM).

Payee may request in writing the life insurance company change the beneficiary designation under this agreement. The life insurance company will do so but will not be liable, however, for any payment made prior to receipt or so soon thereafter that payment could not reasonably be stopped.

(a)   accelerate said future payments to any time or vary in any respects the payments;
(b)   receive the present discounted value of future payments;
(c)   have any control of the investments or funds from which payments are made;
(d)   have any right to increase or decrease the monthly payments;
(e)   change or modify the manner, mode or method of meeting any payments or discharging any obligations set forth in this agreement.

Within the meaning of Section 130(c) of the Internal Revenue Code of 1986 as amended (the 'Code'), defendant and/or the Insurer (Assignor) may made a 'qualified assignment' to Insert here: (Life Insurance Assignment Company) (Assignee) of Assignor's obligation to make the future payments described in Addendum #1 hereof (the periodic payments). Claimant hereby consents to such an assignment and agrees (a) that claimant's rights to the periodic payments and against the Assignee shall be no greater than those of a general creditor, (b) that Assignee is not required to set aside specific assets to secure such periodic payments, and (c) that Assignee's obligation to make periodic payments shall be no greater than those of Assignor immediately preceding the assignment. Upon assignment, Assignee or its designee shall mail future payments directly to the claimant.

Upon making such a qualified assignment, Assignor shall be fully released from all obligations to make the periodic payments and only Assignee shall be obligated to make the periodic payments. Assignee's obligations to make each periodic payments shall be discharged upon mailing of a valid check in the amount due to the address so designated by the claimant.

Assignee may fund the periodic payments by purchasing a qualified funding asset, within the meaning of Section 130(d) of the Code, in the form of an annuity policy from Insert here: (Life Insurance Company) with claimant designated as 'limiting life' or 'measuring life' under the contract. All rights of ownership and control of such annuity policy shall be vested in the Assignee, but Assignee may have <u>Insert here: (Life Insurance Company)</u> make payments directly to the claimant for Assignee's convenience.   Payments made pursuant to said annuity contract shall operate as a pro tanto discharge of the payment obligations set forth in Addendum #1.

It is further understood and agreed that there will be no fees or charges made to recipients by the releasees or any of their employees or agents (including, without limitation, the issuing and owning insurance companies of the annuities described herein), for the purchase or administration of the annuities or payments described herein.

To procure payment of the aforementioned sums, the undersigned does hereby declare that he/she is competent and of the age of majority, that no representations about the nature and extent of said damages, loss or injury made by any attorney or agent of any party hereby released, nor any representation regarding the nature and extent of the legal liability or financial responsibility of any of the parties hereby released have induced releasor to make this settlement; that in determining said sum, there has been taken into consideration not only the ascertained damages and losses, but also the fact that consequences not now ascertained may result from said occurrence, casualty or event as hereinbefore referred to.

Releasor does hereby further covenant and agree that he/she will never institute in the future any complaint, suit, action or cause of action, in law or in equity, against the releasees; nor institute, prosecute or in any way aid in the institution or prosecution of any claim, demand, action, cause of action, suit or complaint for or on account of any damage, loss, injury or expense in consequence of the occurrence, casualty or event hereinbefore referred to, whether such injury, damage, loss or expense is known or unknown, past, present or future.   In connection therewith, releasor does hereby covenant and agree to indemnify and hold harmless the aforementioned releasees from any and all claims, demands, actions, causes of action, suits or complaints that may be brought by any person, persons, firm, corporation or other entity against the releasees, for injury, damage or loss of releasor arising out of the casualty, occurrence or event hereinbefore referred to.

Releasor hereby acknowledges receipt of a copy of this release before signing same. It is understood that the provisions of this Release and Settlement Agreement are contractual and are not merely recitals and that the undersigned has read the foregoing Release and Settlement Agreement, understands it and signs same as his/her voluntary act and deed.

By _____

Releasor (Claimant/Plaintiff)

Read, Witnessed and Approved by:

_____

Attorney for Claimant/Plaintiff

APPROVAL OF RELEASE AND SETTLEMENT AGREEMENT

The foregoing Release and Settlement Agreement is hereby approved by the undersigned authorized representative of the (Insert: Insurance Company) and the obligations of said company set forth therein are hereby acknowledged and accepted.

This _____ day of _____, 19__.

INSURANCE COMPANY

By:_____

Authorized Representative

ADDENDUM #1

Description of Future Periodic Payments:

APPENDIX B

UNIFORM QUALIFIED ASSIGNMENT

'Claimant'

'Assignor'

'Assignee'

'Annuity Issuer'

'Effective Date'

This Agreement is made and entered into by and between the parties hereto as of the Effective Date with reference to the following facts:

A. Claimant has executed a settlement agreement or release dated _____, 19__ (the 'Settlement Agreement') that provides for the Assignor to make certain periodic payments to or for the benefit of the Claimant as stated in Addendum No 1 (the 'Periodic Payments'); and

B. The parties desire to effect a 'qualified assignment' within the meaning and subject to the conditions of Section 130(c) of the Internal Revenue Code of 1986 (the 'Code').

NOW, THEREFORE, in consideration of the foregoing and other good and valuable consideration, the parties agree as follows:

1. The Assignor hereby assigns and the Assignee hereby assumes all of the Assignor's liability to make the Periodic Payments. The Assignee assumes no liability to make any payment not specified in Addendum No 1.

2. The Periodic Payments constitute damages on account of personal injury or sickness in a case involving physical injury or physical sickness within the meaning of Sections 104(a)(2) and 130(c) of the Code.

3. The Assignee's liability to make the Periodic Payments is no greater than that of the Assignor immediately preceding this Agreement. Assignee is not required to set aside specific assets to secure the Periodic Payments. The Claimant has no rights against the Assignee greater than a general creditor. None of the Periodic Payments may be accelerated, deferred, increased or decreased and may not be anticipated, sold, assigned or encumbered.

4. The obligation assumed by Assignee with respect to any required payment shall be discharged upon the mailing on or before the due date of a valid check in the amount specified to the address of record.

5. This Agreement shall be governed by and interpreted in accordance with the laws of the State of _____.

6. The Assignee may fund the Periodic Payments by purchasing a 'qualified funding asset' within the meaning of Section 130(d) of the Code in the form of an annuity contract issued by the Annuity issuer. All rights of ownership and control of such annuity contract shall be and remain vested in the Assignee exclusively.

7. The Assignee may have the Annuity Issuer send payments under any 'qualified funding asset' purchased hereunder directly to the payee(s) specified in Addendum No 1. Such direction of payments shall be solely for the Assignee's convenience and shall not provide the Claimant or any payee with any rights of ownership or control over the 'qualified funding asset' or against the Annuity Issuer.

8.   Assignee's liability to make the Periodic Payments shall continue without diminution regardless of any bankruptcy or insolvency of the Assignor.

9.   In the event the Settlement Agreement is declared terminated by a court of law or in the event that Section 130(c) of the Code has not been satisfied, this Agreement shall terminate. The Assignee shall then assign ownership of any 'qualified funding asset' purchased hereunder to Assignor, and Assignee's liability for the Periodic Payments shall terminate.

10. This Agreement shall be binding upon the respective representatives, heirs, successors and assigns of the Claimant, the Assignor and the Assignee and upon any person or entity that may assert any right hereunder or to any of the Periodic Payments.

Assignor: _____   Assignee: _____

BY: _____   BY: _____

Authorized Representative   Authorized Representative

Title: _____   Title: _____

SOURCES

Bayer, Barry D; Cohen, Benjamin J; Welch, Mark J, 'Computing a structured settlement', *Legal Times*, Vol 13, No 23, p 35, 5 November 1990.

Best's Review — Property-Casualty Insurance Edition, September, 1992, Vol 93; No 5, P 82, 'Structured settlements: panacea or placebo; Liability damage awards', Klingler, Peter J; Blonder, Leonard A.

Business Insurance, 19 March 1990, p 23, 'Using structured settlements; self-insurers need guidelines for settling claims', by Michael J Casey.

Business Insurance, 22 October 1990, p 51, 'Hazardous waste cleanup Structured settlements help reduce the cost', by Robert Bell and John Machir.

Carney, William J, 'Structured settlements: their benefits to claimants and their lawyers', *Trial Lawyers' Guide*, Vol 36, No 1, pp 44–64, 22 March 1992 Spring.

Coel, Mark A, 'Tax aspects of personal injury awards and structured settlements', *Florida Bar Journal*, Vol 66, No 5, pp 78–81, May 1992.

Danninger, Brent B; Johnson, Robert W; Jerue, Mary B, 'Legal malpractice and structured settlements', *Case & Comment*, Vol 93, No 2, pp 16(6), March 1988.

Fabry, Scott M; Herreman, Jon S, 'Tax consequences of accepting annuities as attorney's fees in structured settlements', *The Wisconsin Lawyer*, Vol 65, No 4, p 17, April 1992.

Fuchsberg, Abraham, 'Pitfalls in structured settlements', *Trial Lawyers Quarterly*, Vol 20, No 2, 22 September 1989 Fall.

Kess, Sidney, 'Attorneys' fees in structured settlements', *New York Law Journal inches*, Vol 206, No 116, p 3, 16 December 1991.

Mandel, Richard G, 'An ounce of prevention: some dos and don'ts. (Structured Settlements)', *Trial*, Vol 24, No 12, p 32, December 1988.

Mandel, Richard G, 'How to Evaluate Proposals; Avoid Fee Disputes (Structured Settlements)', *Trial*, Vol 24, No 12, p 38, December 1988.

Massachusetts Lawyers Weekly, 21 January 1991, 'Structured Settlement Tax Law Change', by Brent B Danninger.

Michigan Lawyers Weekly, 18 February 1991, p S3, 'Structure Settlements Applied To Environmental Claims', by Lawrence A Cohen.

Parsons, Chris, 'Structured settlements raise difficult questions on taxes, viability of annuity carrier', *Texas Bar Journal*, Vol 54, No 10, p 1141, November 1991.

Sinclaire, William T, 'A look at structured settlements', *Journal of the American Society of CLU & ChFC*, Vol 43, No 2, pp 70(3), March 1989.

The National Underwriter Company, Property & Casualty/Risk & Benefits Management Edition, 6 March 1989, p 7, 'Structured Settlements Cut Workers' Comp. Costs', by Robert G Knowles.

The National Underwriter Company, Property & Casualty/Risk & Benefits Management Edition, 5 February 1990, p 31, 'Structured Settlement Concept May Spread', by L H Otis.

Appendices

Appendix I — *Kelly v Dawes*

Queen's Bench Division
14 July 1989

MR JUSTICE POTTER: These proceedings arise from a road accident on 5 July 1986, in which the first plaintiff, Catherine Kelly (now a patient aged 25) suffered serious injury and her husband, Andrew Kelly ('the deceased'), was killed. The second plaintiff is the father and next friend of the first plaintiff and sues also as administrator of the deceased's estate. I have before me a summons issued on 24 November 1988 to approve a settlement arrived at on behalf of the first plaintiff.

So far as the first plaintiff's condition is concerned, suffice it to say that, as a result of the injuries she received, she was transformed from a lively young woman, qualified as a State Registered Nurse and recently married, into a bed-ridden invalid with grossly impaired neurological functions, almost wholly unaware of her surroundings, totally dependent on skilled nursing care and the devoted attention of her loving parents and family. Her condition will not improve for the rest of her life, in respect of which her life expectancy has been reduced to some 20 years. That figure is of necessity uncertain. It is the product of a 'compromise' medical view between doctors whose best guesses are on either side of the figure agreed.

The second plaintiff, who is the father of the first plaintiff and wholly concerned with her best interests, is a retired insurance company agent. He is particularly concerned with what may happen to the first plaintiff in the future, and in particular what funds may be available for her medical care, if she should live to the end of, or even beyond, the life expectancy period which I have mentioned, by which time it is unlikely that her parents will be living, or at least able to give active help with her care as they do at present.

In consultation with the plaintiff's legal and financial advisers and with an eye to future costs of care, the second plaintiff has on the first plaintiff's behalf agreed on terms of settlement with the first defendants (or in reality with the deceased's insurers), subject to the approval of the court which he now seeks. Those terms are in the nature of a 'structured settlement', that is to say that they do not provide simply for payment in traditional form of a lump sum, to be enjoyed outright by the plaintiff or to be invested or administered on her behalf by Trustees or the Court of Protection, but they provide also for payment by the insurers of annual sums, increasing in line with inflation under a form of agreement to which I shall turn in a moment.

In reaching such a settlement the plaintiffs seek to take advantage of provisions of revenue law, or at least the interpretation of those provisions which is currently acceptable to the Inland Revenue, which appear to render a structured settlement beneficial in actions involving large awards for future financial losses, in particular in relation to long-term care. This is because, under the terms of such a settlement, a defendant's insurers pay out somewhat less money than would be necessary to meet a single lump sum award, assessed on conventional lines and paid over to the plaintiff, while the plaintiff obtains the benefit of annual payments greater than the income which would have arisen from investment by the plaintiff of the lump sum award. Hitherto the position has been that, while the recipient of a lump sum by way of damages has paid no tax on the lump sum itself, he has faced the prospect of taxation on any income arising from it so that, for example, if he has used the lump sum in purchase of an annuity, the periodic payments have been taxable in his hands, and that would remain the position even if the annuity were purchased on his behalf rather than in his own name. It now appears that, by reason of an interpretation confirmed in July 1987 between the Inland Revenue and the Association of British Insurers, periodic payments to a plaintiff, funded by an annuity purchased *by the insurer* from a separate life office, may be treated as payments of capital rather than income, with the result that the insurers can buy for less than the lump sum he would originally have paid to the plaintiff, an annuity which yields higher benefits than the plaintiff could have expected to derive from such lump sum, the gain to both parties being financed from the tax saving resulting.

In these circumstances an appropriate and advantageous form of settlement in cases involving large awards for future loss may be to provide for two elements: a lump sum payment to cover the financial losses incurred to date of settlement, and what is in effect a pension in respect of future losses, designed to last for the remainder of the plaintiff's life and 'indexed' in respect of anticipated cost of living increases. It is such a settlement which is proposed in this case.

The terms of the settlement have been the product of careful thought by the plaintiff's advisers and have been arrived at after substantial correspondence and consultation involving also the Inland Revenue and the Master of the Court of Protection concerned with the plaintiff patient's affairs, both of whom have been kept informed and asked for their comments on the structure and intentions of the settlement proposed to be placed before this court. The terms proposed have also been the subject of helpful comment and suggestion so far as the mechanics of their approval are concerned, by Mr Registrar Gee, the District Registrar before whom the summons for approval was originally returnable. Mr Registrar Gee adjourned the summons for approval by a High Court judge on the basis that there are a number of 'structured settlements' in the course of negotiation as the result of various cases involving multiple and other serious accidents, but this is the first to come before the court. Accordingly the summons now comes before me for approval and any observations which may now be thought appropriate. It is in those circumstances that I give this short judgment recording my approval in terms which I hope will afford assistance in similar cases.

Since any general interest in my judgment lies not in the amount of the settlement but its machinery, I shall not recount the details by which that amount was arrived at. Suffice it to say I have satisfied myself that the proper sum for settlement of the first plaintiff's claim on conventional lines would be £427,500, the calculation of which has been carefully considered by Mr Machell, QC in written opinions placed before the court and by further elucidation on this summons. I am satisfied that the utmost care and good sense has gone into the exercise and that I should endorse the figure arrived at as correct in all the circumstances of this case.

The information placed before me has included all the important letters passing in the correspondence and consultation process which I have already mentioned, culminating in a long and careful letter to Goma & Co the plaintiffs' solicitors from Frenkel Topping & Co, chartered accountants of Manchester, the plaintiffs' financial advisers. That letter considers the rival advantages to the first plaintiff of the two alternatives of a conventional 'lump sum' payment or of a 'structured settlement', in the light of the investment alternatives available, to which I shall refer further below.

I would summarise the basis of the proposed structured settlement as follows:

The first feature to be observed is an unusual one. It has been agreed that, if the settlement proceeds, the total payment shall be £410,000, whereas, if it does not proceed the sum payable will be £427,500 (ie the appropriate figure for a conventional award). The 'discount' or 'differential' has been agreed on the basis that, since the benefits to the first plaintiff under the structure contemplated (as opposed to a single lump sum settlement) will considerably exceed £17,500, the defendants should be permitted also to participate in the benefits resulting from the reduced levels of taxation which will be payable. Of course it is the position that, in approving the settlement, I have to be satisfied that the interests of the first plaintiff are fully protected. Normally, no doubt, that involves ensuring that a plaintiff receives the highest possible payment on offer from the defendants; however, if it be that the first plaintiff's interests are better protected by receipt and/or expenditure of a reduced sum which will ultimately yield a greater benefit, I see no objection in principle to the differential proposed, which has been agreed by the parties in the course of an arrangement responsibly reached.

The essentials of the proposals from the first plaintiff's point of view are that, out of a total settlement sum of £410,000 the sum of £300,000 will be appropriated by the insurers to the purchase of an annuity payable to them against which to secure the annual payments to be made to the first plaintiff, while the sum of £110,000 will be paid over as a straightforward lump sum payment.

When added to the settlement moneys already paid by the first defendants' insurers in respect of the claim of the plaintiff's deceased husband and which will come to the first plaintiff as part of his estate, as well as the equity in the matrimonial home, that lump sum will make available a substantial contingency fund, in addition to the guaranteed income to be provided over the first plaintiff's lifetime by the structured terms, thus providing for a considerable measure of flexibility in handling the first plaintiff's financial affairs outside the confines of the structure provided.

The sum of £300,000 will be expended by the first defendants' insurers in the purchase of an annuity for the remainder of the plaintiff's life. The annual sum to be provided under the quotation obtained is £25,562 which annual sum is to be index-linked and guaranteed for a period of ten years, that is to say that payments will continue for a ten-year period even if the plaintiff dies before that period has expired. The calculations of Frenkel Topping & Co demonstrate that on an assumed inflation rate of 5 per cent, in 12 years time such an annual sum would have increased to a sum of £45,906 continuing (and increasing with inflation) for the remainder of her life, whereas a traditional lump sum investment in gilts or in mixed gilts and equities would yield very substantially lower figures. On the latter basis, provision of an annual rate of £25,562 index-linked at 5 per cent inflation would lead to total exhaustion of the fund in years 12 or 13, and, even given a return before tax of, say, 14 per cent, the period that the fund would last would be only 15 years.

Quite apart from the comparison of projected income levels, the advantages of such a settlement can be said to be:

(a) significant savings in the administration of the fund;
(b) guaranteed annual payments on an inflation-proof basis, so that all element of financial risk that the plaintiff will live beyond her life expectancy is removed.

The disadvantages may be said to be:

(a) that once the structure has been set up, there is a potential lack of flexibility in the opportunities for financial investment and management of the structured sum;
(b) there will be no residue of moneys due to the estate if the plaintiff dies after the ten-year guaranteed period.

I am not troubled in this case by either of the disadvantages I have mentioned. As to (a), in the plaintiff's case there is just short of £200,000 available as a contingency fund, so that flexibility will in fact remain to a large extent. As to (b), it is the protection of, and benefits to, the plaintiff in her lifetime which concern me and not the interests of future beneficiaries from her estate.

An additional aspect requires mention.

In a letter from the Public Trust Office before me, concern is expressed that the tax laws could change in the future so as to alter the present position and understanding which appears so conducive to the concept of structured settlements in large cases. That is certainly a risk which requires consideration. Indeed it might not necessarily require a change in legislation to reverse the present position; such a result might follow from a court decision in a revenue case which directly or indirectly invalidated the present favourable approach of the Inland Revenue; indeed that approach might alter for other reasons.

An explanation of the rationale of the approach is before me in the form of a letter to the plaintiffs' solicitors from the Insurers Specialist Division of the Inland Revenue, dated 12 January 1989. It is to the effect that the future payments to the plaintiff by insurers of sums equivalent to those received under the annuity taken out by them will be treated as the discharge of instalment payments of the capital debt brought into existence by the structured settlement agreement, those instalment payments being regarded as retaining a capital nature even though the quantum is linked to the Retail Price Index and the duration of the instalment payments is determined by reference to the claimant's lifetime. It is of course of the essence of the concession that the insurer is the person beneficially entitled to the annuity payments made by the life office from which the annuity is purchased, the obligation of the insurer to pay over annual sums of equivalent amount springing from the structured settlement agreement and not by reason of any beneficial interest in the annuity payments received by the insurer.

I have not heard argument on, let alone decided, the question of whether the present interpretation in fact represents a true application of the taxation provisions concerned. Nonetheless I feel justified in assuming that the interpretation will continue to apply for the time being. Even if it does not, it seems to me practically inconceivable that any future change in the law or in revenue practice which reverses its effect would be applied retroactively to settlements already entered into on the faith of the interpretation, let alone to payments already made.

On that basis and on the basis that the revenue have approved the form of agreement in this case as being within the concession referred to, I give my approval to this settlement.

As already mentioned, it appears that a number of structured settlements await the approval of the court in various parts of the country, and, assuming that the revenue position remains as now, such settlements may well become a preferred method of provision in substantial cases where the cost of long-term care is a prime concern. For the assistance of practitioners, as well as Masters and District Registrars who will in future be concerned with applications to approve such settlements, I append the relevant parts of the form of settlement agreement (as approved by the revenue in this case) at the end of this judgment. In making such applications in the future, it may be thought appropriate for the applicant to place at least the following information before the court:

(1) A detailed opinion of counsel assessing the value of the claim and its constituent elements on a conventional basis, and the appropriate lump sum figure or bracket for settlement on that basis. Careful consideration of the plaintiff's life expectancy based on the medical opinions should be included.

(2) A report by accountants or other financial experts as to the fiscal and investment advantages to the plaintiff of the structured settlement proposed, with particular regard to the life expectancy of the plaintiff and the likely future costs of care.

(3) A draft of the form of agreement proposed, together with confirmation that the Inland Revenue regard such an agreement as within the scope of any revenue provisions or practice on which the value of the structured settlement depends.

(4) Where appropriate, confirmation of the approved terms of the agreement by the Court of Protection conditional upon the approval of the settlement by the court.

(5) Material to satisfy the court that there are sufficient funds available outside the structured provisions to meet any foreseeable capital needs of the plaintiff, whether by means of a 'lump sum' element in the settlement or by reason of other resources available to the plaintiff.

(6) Material to satisfy the court that the agreement involves secure arrangements by responsible insurers, whether one of the well-known 'tariff' companies or one of the syndicates operating under the rules and protection of the Lloyd's market (which of course includes the availability of the Lloyd's Central Fund if the need arises).

Even where such information has been provided, it will of course be a matter for individual consideration in every case whether the settlement may be approved as in the overall interests of the disabled plaintiff, and it may well be that other queries and concerns of the court will need to be satisfied before it feels able to give such approval.

Finally, if the confirmation referred to in (3) above cannot be given to the court at the time application for approval is made, and if the proposed settlement involves a 'discount' on the appropriate figure for a conventional lump sum settlement, the court may well think it appropriate to withhold its approval unless the settlement agreement makes express provision against the contingency that the revenue does not recognise the agreement as giving rise to the tax advantage which has been assumed by the parties.

Appendix II — Practice Note (Structured Settlements: Court's Approval)

1. This Practice Note applies only to proceedings in the Central Office and the Admiralty and Commercial Registry of the High Court. It concerns settlements of claims in respect of personal injury or death where approval of the court is required and which include a structured element. The practice set out below, adapted as indicated, is appropriate whether or not the Court of Protection is involved. It will apply, on an experimental basis, until further notice. If the plaintiff is under mental disability then the additional steps set out in paragraph 6(viii) and 8 of this Practice Note should be taken.

2. By this Practice Note it is intended to establish a practice to overcome the present administrative difficulties caused by the short period over which life offices keep open offers of annuities at a given price. It has proved difficult for plaintiffs' solicitors to do all that is necessary to obtain the approval of the court within the period during which the annuity offer remains open.

3. As from 30 March 1992 all applications for approval in structured settlement cases will be listed for hearing on Friday mornings during term time.

4. After setting down, applications for the fixing of dates for these purposes should be made to the Clerk of the Lists in Room 547.

5. Once a hearing date has been obtained, documents should be lodged in Room 547 not later than noon on the Thursday immediately before the Friday for which the hearing is fixed.

6. The following are the classes of document which should be lodged in accordance with paragraph 5 above;
(i)   copies of originating process or pleadings, if any;
(ii)   an opinion of counsel assessing the value of the claim on a conventional basis (unless approval has already been given) and, if practicable, the opinion of counsel on the structured settlement proposed;

(iii) a report of forensic accountants setting out the advantages and disadvantages, if any, of structuring bearing in mind the plaintiff's life expectancy and the anticipated costs of future care;

(iv) a draft of the proposed agreement as approved by the Inland Revenue (and by the Treasury where the defendant or other paying party is a health authority);

(v) sufficient material to satisfy the court that enough capital is available free of the structure to meet anticipated future capital needs: particular reference to accommodation and transport needs will usually be helpful in this context;

(vi) sufficient material to satisfy the court that the structure is secure and backed by responsible insurers;

(vii) evidence of other assets available to the plaintiff beyond the award the subject of the application;

(viii) in cases where the plaintiff is under mental disability the consent of the Court of Protection.

The classes of documents required to be lodged should be separately bundled and clearly marked so that the presence of the appropriate classes of document (but not the adequacy of their content) may be checked by the clerks in Room 547.

7. If the proceedings are in the Admiralty and Commercial Registry application should be made to the Admiralty Registrar in good time for the transfer of the proceedings to the Central Office for the purpose of the application for approval only.

8. In cases where the plaintiff if under mental disability, the documents are set out in paragraphs 6(i)–(vii) (inclusive) should be lodged in the Enquiries and Acceptances Branch of the Public Trust Office, Stewart House, 24 Kingsway, London, WC2B 6JH, not later than noon on the Monday immediately before the Friday for which the hearing is fixed. Unless an application has already been made for the appointment of a receiver, there must also be lodged an application for the appointment of a receiver (form CP1) (in duplicate), a certificate of family and property (form CP5) and a medical certificate (form CP3). (Blank forms are available from the same address.) The Court of Protection's approval, if granted, will be available by 10.30 on the Thursday immediately before the Friday fixed for the hearing.

9.   This Practice Note is issued with the approval of Watkins LJ, Deputy Chief Justice, the judge in charge of the non-jury list, the Admiralty judge and the Master of the Court of Protection.

KEITH TOPLEY
Senior Master
Queen's Bench Division

Appendix III — The Model Agreement

A standard form of such an agreement, with four alternative forms of attached schedule to cater for the four main kinds of periodic payment arrangement likely to be required, has been accepted by the Inland Revenue as conforming to the principles which must apply in order to enable the claimant to receive the periodic payments in question without undergoing an income tax liability. However, the Inland Revenue have warned that as they have approved draft documentation rather than an actual case their agreement is of necessity provisional. The circumstances of a completed settlement might possibly introduce other factors which would cause the Revenue to take a different view.

Copies of the draft documents are enclosed. The four schedules would be for use in the following circumstances:

(a) *Basic Terms*

For use in cases in which, possibly because the claimant will be entitled to receive a retirement pension on reaching a certain age, he wishes the periodic payment part of the settlement to cease after a pre-set period and to consist of a series of pre-set amounts.

(b) *Indexed Terms*

To be used in the same circumstances as in (a) except that the claimant wishes the periodic payments to be inflation-proofed by having them increased in proportion to any rise in the Index of Retail Prices over the period in question.

(c) *Terms for Life*

This form of agreement will apply in what will probably be the more usual circumstances in which the claimant wishes the periodic payments, in pre-set amounts, to continue until the date of his death (but with the option to make this subject to a pre-set minimum number of payments being received).

(d) *Indexed Terms for Life*

For use as in (c) except that the periodic payments are inflation-proofed through linkage to the Index of Retail Prices. Given the inflationary environment ruling in the UK in recent years, it may well be that this proves the most popular of the four schedules.

Although it is possible that other forms of settlement conforming to the same basic principles might be acceptable to the Inland Revenue, these would need to be individually cleared with the Revenue, with the inevitable additional delay that would thereby arise.

This is the only documentation that should follow Inland Revenue recommended wording. However, it is advisable to 'test' the Annuity Market once the parties agree to consider structuring a part of the settlement. Basic rates will of course vary frequently with changing economic conditions, but what the parties (particularly defendant) need to establish is the degree to which the Annuity Office assess the plaintiff's impairment. That is to say, what is their current view of the plaintiff's life expectancy — this may well differ from the other medical views.

If preferential rates are not obtainable it is much less likely that structuring will have appeal based on figures alone. As settlement date approaches it will be essential to obtain an annuity quotation that will hold for longer than the 10–14 days to enable all parties to have time to complete.

MODEL AGREEMENT

PARTIES: (1)

('the Claimant')

(2)

('the Insurer')

WHEREAS:

(1)   The Claimant has made a claim against ....
('the Insured') arising out of ....
('the Claim').

(2)   It is agreed that the Claim shall be settled for £ ....

AGREED:

1   The Insurer shall be substituted for the Insured to the intent that any liability of the Insured to the Claimant in respect of the Claim shall

attach to and be the sole responsibility of the Insurer and that the Insured shall be discharged from any such liability.

2   By way of settlement of the Claim the Insurer shall pay or procure to be paid to the Claimant the sum of £.................. and the Claimant shall accept such sum in full and final settlement of the Claim, which is discharged.

3   Subject to the Claimant complying with clause 4 to the satisfaction of the Insurer, the debt of £.................. arising under clause 2 shall be discharged by payments by the Insurer to the claimant in accordance with the Schedule.

4.1   The Claimant shall forthwith take all necessary steps to discontinue any proceedings which have been begun or threatened against the Insurer or the Insured in connection with the Claim.

4.2   The Claimant shall not institute any proceedings against the Insurer or the Insured in connection with the Claim.

DATED:...

SIGNED: (1)   .... (the Claimant)

               (2)   ....(for the Insurer)

                                                    Form (a)

BASIC TERMS

THE SCHEDULE

Amount	Date for payment

[This form is for anticipated use in cases in which the plaintiff wants the periodic payments to run for a pre-set period and consist of pre-set amounts.]

INDEXED TERMS

THE SCHEDULE

Amount   Date for payment

Amounts payable under this Schedule shall be increased annually on or after the date of each anniversary of this agreement in proportion to the increase if any in the figure for the General Index of Retail Prices (all items) for the relevant month over the figures for the same month of the preceding year. For the first anniversary the relevant month shall be that for which the monthly Index was last published by the Department of Employment before that anniversary; for the second and subsequent anniversaries the relevant month in the year of the anniversary in question shall be the same as that used in calculating the increase due on the first anniversary. These increases shall take effect each year on the anniversary of this agreement, or on the date of publication of the Index figure for the relevant month, whichever is later.

In the event that in any year the figure for the General Index of Retail prices (all items) for the relevant month is lower than the figure for the same month of the preceding year (the 'Base Figure'), then:

(1)   In that year, the amounts payable under this Schedule shall be the same amount ('the fixed amounts') as were paid in the previous year.

(2)   In subsequent years, the amounts payable under this Schedule shall remain at the fixed amounts until in any subsequent year (a 'year of RPI increase') the figure for the General Index of Retail Prices (all items) for the relevant month is higher than the Base Figure.

(3)   In such a year of RPI increase, the amounts payable under the Schedule shall be increased on or after the date of the anniversary of this agreement in proportion to the increase in the figure for the General Index of Retail Prices (all items) for the relevant month over the Base Figure. Such an increase shall take effect in accordance with the terms of this Schedule.

[By this form, the periodic payments are inflation-proofed by having them increased in proportion to any rise in the Index of Retail Prices over the period in question.]

Form (c)

TERMS FOR LIFE

THE SCHEDULE

Amount

Date for payment

A minimum of £................. payments shall be made under this Schedule, regardless of the date of the Claimant, but subject to this no amounts shall be payable after the date of death of the Claimant.

[This form is for cases where the periodic payments, in pre-set amounts, continue until the date of the plaintiff's death.]

Form (d)

INDEXED TERMS FOR LIFE

THE SCHEDULE

Amount

Date for payment

Amounts payable under this Schedule shall be increased annually on or after the date of each anniversary of this agreement in proportion to the increase if any in the figure for the General Index of Retail Prices (all terms) for the relevant month over the figure for the same month of the preceding year. For the first anniversary the relevant month shall be that for which the monthly Index was last published by the Department of Employment before that anniversary; for the second and subsequent anniversaries the relevant month in the year of the anniversary in question shall be the same as that used in calculating the increase due on the first anniversary. These increases shall take effect each year on the anniversary of this agreement, or on the date of publication of the Index figures for the relevant month, whichever is later.

In the event that in any year the figure for the General Index of Retail Prices (all items) for the relevant month is lower than the figure for the same month of the preceding year (the 'Base Figure') then:

(1)   In that year, the amounts payable under this Schedule shall be the same amount ('the fixed amounts') as were paid in the previous year.

(2)   In subsequent years, the amounts payable under this Schedule shall remain at the fixed amounts until in any subsequent year (a 'year of RPI increase') the figure for the General Index of Retail Prices (all times) for the relevant month is higher than the Base Figure.

(3)   In such a year of RPI increase, the amounts under the Schedule shall be increased on or after the date of the anniversary of this agreement in proportion to the increase in the figure for the General Index of Retail Prices (all times) for the relevant month over the Base Figure. Such an increase shall take effect in accordance with the terms of this Schedule.

A minimum of.................. payments shall be made under this Schedule, regardless of the date of death of the Claimant, but subject to this no amounts shall be payable after the date of death of the Claimant.

[The periodic payments are inflation-proofed through linkage to the Index of Retail Prices.]

Dated the.................. day of.................. 19 ....

1993 A No 1234

IN THE HIGH COURT OF JUSTICE
QUEEN'S BENCH DIVISION
LIVERPOOL DISTRICT REGISTRY

Before the Honourable Mr Justice

BETWEEN:

AB

(a patient who sues by his father and Next Friend, BB)

Plaintiff

and

THE .... HEALTH AUTHORITY

<u>Defendant</u>

WHEREAS this action came before the Honourable Mr Justice.......at The Queen Elizabeth II Law Court, Derby Square, Liverpool 2 on the ....day of 1993,

AND UPON HEARING Mr X of counsel on behalf of the plaintiff and Mr Y of counsel on behalf of the defendant, and

AND UPON the plaintiff and the defendant agreeing to the terms set forth in the Agreement and the Schedule annexed hereto and such terms having been approved by the Court.

BY CONSENT IT IS ORDERED THAT:

(a)   the action of the plaintiff by his next friend be discontinued, and
(b)   the defendant do pay the plaintiff's costs of this action on the standard basis to be taxed if not agreed.
(c)   the plaintiff's costs be taxed on a standard basis in accordance with Regulation 107 of the Civil Legal Aid (General) Regulations 1989.

IT IS FURTHER ORDERED that all further proceedings in this action shall be stayed save for the purpose of carrying such terms into effect.

LIBERTY TO APPLY as to carrying such terms into effect.

Appendix IV — Guidance from The Law Society on structured settlements, practical and ethical considerations

1. *Consideration of structured settlements is vital*
    It is now absolutely essential that in any substantial claim for damages the solicitors (perhaps with other advisers) should consider whether the claim can be resolved by a structured settlement. It is impossible to define 'substantial' for these purposes, but to date virtually all structured settlements achieved have been in cases with a conventional value of six figures.

2. *Who is this guidance for?*
    This guidance is concerned with the general principles of structured settlements, and it is important to note that each case has to be dealt with according to its own circumstances. The guidance is intended to draw structured settlements to the attention of solicitors who deal with some personal injury work but who would not claim to be specialists. It is not intended to be a comprehensive text and readers are referred to the published literature, legal journals and case reports.

3. *Ethical and practical problems also addressed*
    This guidance is also intended to address the practical, ethical and financial services questions posed by some solicitors currently considering structured settlements. It is not feasible to give advice on every potential problem: each case must be dealt with according to its own circumstances. If necessary solicitors can consult the Ethics and Guidance Department (telephone 071-242 1222/ 0527 517141).

4. *What is a structured settlement?*
    A settlement involving receipt by the plaintiff of periodic payments for life, instead of a single lump sum.

5.   *What are the features of a structured settlement?*

(a)   The *periodic payments* may be agreed to the plaintiff's needs eg nursing, care, transport.

(b)   These payments are usually funded by (one or more) *annuities* purchased by the defendant or its insurers.

(c)   The use of annuities means the payments may be *indexed linked* to inflation.

(d)   Annuities also enable the payments to be stepped up if the plaintiff's needs so demand and may also provide for additional lump sums.

(e)   The periodic payments are treated as *payments of capital*, on the basis that the figure agreed at the time of the settlement is an antecedent debt which is then paid by instalments.

(f)   As the periodic payments are treated as capital payments they are *tax free* in the plaintiff's hands.

(g)   Usually there is an *insurer's discount*: the structured settlement costs the insurer less than it would have paid in a single lump sum settlement. In effect this is a trade off: the plaintiff trades some of the advantages accruing from the structure thus providing the discount which the insurer can use to cover the cost of administering the structure.

(h)   In certain circumstances it may be possible to agree a *guarantee period*. The annuity policy is always on the life of the plaintiff, but payments may be guaranteed for a minimum number of years irrespective of the premature death of the plaintiff.

6.   *When should a structure be considered?*
As soon as possible. The plaintiff's solicitor should discuss the concept with the plaintiff at an early stage and explain the advantages and disadvantages. If the plaintiff insists on a conventional lump sum the matter can proceed no further. If the plaintiff is interested in a structure the next stage is to ascertain whether the defendant wishes to explore settlement in this way. Costs incurred in exploring a structured settlement before confirming that the parties wish to consider resolving the claim in the manner might prove to be irrecoverable. In a legal aid case consider obtaining authority from the Legal Aid Board before proceeding.

7. *Can a structure be imposed?*
No. Both parties must consent. *Burke v Tower Hamlets Health Authority* [(1989) Times, 10 August].

8. *Does liability have to be agreed?*
No. If there is an issue on primary liability or contributory negligence it might prove possible to bridge the gap between the parties by agreeing a structured settlement. Alternatively, liability could be resolved by a split trial, and a structure could be negotiated thereafter.

9. *How is the structure arrived at, and by who?*
It is crucial to identify the plaintiff's needs and evaluate those in financial terms. The final details cannot be arrived at until it is possible to make a conventional evaluation of quantum. As with any claim for substantial damages the solicitor may require expert guidance from a specialist solicitor, counsel, a forensic accountant and/or other experts.

10. *There is more than one approach*
There are at least two distinct approaches. The more traditional approach has been to evaluate quantum in the usual way and use that figure as a starting point for negotiations on the structure. (The case is worth £X, how can £X be structured?) The other approach is to arrange a structure by concentrating on the plaintiff's needs and requirements. (The plaintiff wants an initial lump sum of £A and an annual income, index linked, commencing at £B per annum). These approaches might be referred to as 'top down' and 'bottom up' respectively. Either way, the solicitors for the parties will have to advise on the structure proposal against the benchmark of the conventional evaluation of quantum.

11. *Who advises about annuities?*
The defendant (or its insurer) purchases the annuity or annuities. Before settlement can be considered it is necessary to ascertain what is available on the insurance market to provide for the plaintiff's future needs, and at what costs. Advice can be obtained from a broker.

12.   *Is it necessary to obtain independent advice?*
Yes. This is the considered view of the Civil Litigation Committee of the Law Society on the basis of the research carried out by its working party over a period of several months. It is considered that the plaintiff requires independent advice on such questions as:

(a)   the benefits and disadvantages of the structure proposal compared with a conventional award;

(b)   the cost in the insurance market place of the structure proposed: what would be the cost of like annuities with a like return?

(c)   the brokerage fees, and how these affect the structure proposal;

(d)   the size of the discount, if any.

Of course, this list is not exhaustive.

13.   *Advice packages*
There are firms that can supply a package to structure an award. They are often prepared to act for both sides. advising the plaintiff on the merits of the structure and arranging the purchase of the annuity for the defendant. The remuneration is usually on a contingency arrangement whereby the package adviser receives a commission on the purchase of the annuity, but nothing at all if the matter does not proceed. In light of the preceding paragraph very serious consideration should be given to proceeding with an arrangement of this nature. It is the view of the Ethics and Guidance Department that the plaintiff needs independent advice, and hence such arrangements should be approached with great caution.

14.   *Costs and commissions*
Plaintiffs should note that, as in any case, the cost of independent expert's advice may have to be justified on taxation. Reference has already been made to obtaining prior authority in legal aid cases. Annuities are usually purchased from life companies who invariably transact their business through brokers on a commission basis; the brokerage commission or fee is a matter between the defendant or its insurer and the life office concerned (but see paragraph 12 (c) above).

15. *Financial Services Act 1986*
    An annuity is an 'investment' as defined by the Act. The annuity will be purchased by the defendant (or its insurer). The only investment business being undertaken is that being conducted by the authorised person acting on behalf of the defendant.

16. *Is there a model agreement for a structured settlement?*
    Yes. See *Kemp and Kemp* para 6A-053. Most solicitors will require expert assistance by this stage, and certainly if any amendment to the model agreement is contemplated. This model is not an universal precedent; great care is required to ensure that the correct form of words is used.

17. *Is Inland Revenue approval of draft structured settlements advisable?*
    It is essential in the case of a plaintiff under a disability. In routine cases it will probably suffice to have expert advice to ensure that the model agreement has been adhered to.

18. *Can a plaintiff under a disability have a structured settlement?*
    Yes. The approval of the court is required in the usual way. See the Practice Note, Structured Settlements; Court's Approval, by Senior Master K Topley dated 12 February 1992. Note that in the case of a plaintiff under a mental disability it will be necessary to involve the Court of Protection.

19. *Can a medical negligence claim be structured?*
    Yes, but there are difficulties, and this particular field is evolving quickly. It will probably be necessary to obtain approval from the Treasury and/or the Health Authority. Trust hospitals may require special consideration.

20. *Can a structured settlement be used in a fatal case?*
    Yes. See *Boobbyer v Johnson* [(1992) Times, 21 January].

21. *Some of the major pitfalls*

    (a) Failing to advise a client that a structured settlement might be appropriate. Numerous commentators have suggested that such a failure might amount to negligence.

(b)   Failing to give consideration to obtaining independent advice.

(c)   Failing to appreciate that a structured settlement must be entered into before any final judgment. An award cannot be structured once there has been a judgment, order or binding agreement for a lump sum.

(d)   Failing to give adequate consideration to the security of the investment. (There have been problems in the USA.) Note: the plaintiff's contract is with the defendant or its insurers, and not with the life office. Hence, the plaintiff's concern is as to the security of the defendant or its insurer and not the life office.

(e)   Failing to act quickly. The plaintiff's team must be able to respond rapidly to an offer: life offer quotations are only good for about ten days.

22.   *What are the leading cases?*
Many cases have now been reported, and there are numerous articles in legal journals. Leading cases include:

Dott v Brown [1936] 1 All ER 543, CA
Kelly v Dawes, (1990) Times, 27 September, Halsbury's
    Abridgement 1990, para 775
Grimsley v Grimsley and Meade [1991] PMILL vol 7 no 9 p 67.

Appendix V — Schedule of damages

The following schedule, reproduced by kind permission of Frenkel Topping, sets out the net damages for the plaintiff Raymond Everett, based on a structured settlement with indexation of 5% per annum.

Notes:

1 All payments are guaranteed for life
2 Annuities 1 and 2 are guaranteed to pay out for at least 15 years
3 Annuity 3 on the lump sums will only be paid if Mr Everett is alive
4 Payments indexed — 5% pa compound
5 No need to include receipts on Income Tax Return as tax-free
6 If Mr Everett actually lives to 80 years then total payable — £14,399,370
7 Cost of structure is £799,683 if purchased by 17 July 1991

Years from Settlement	Age of Plaintiff £	Annuity 1 Annual Sum	Annuity 2 Annual Sum £	Annuity 3 Annual Sum £	Total Annual Sum £	Monthly Equivalent £	Lump Sums £	Cumulative Net Damages
1	30	25,000			25,000	2,083		25,000
2	31	26,250			26,250	2,188		51,250
3	32	27,563			27,563	2,297	25,000	103,813
4	33	28,941			28,941	2,412		132,753
5	34	30,388			30,388	2,532		163,141
6	35	31,907			31,907	2,659		195,048
7	36	33,502	22,500		56,002	4,667		251,050
8	37	35,178	23,625		58,803	4,900	31,907	341,760
9	38	36,936	24,806		61,743	5,145		403,502
10	39	38,783	26,047		64,830	5,402		468,332
11	40	40,722	27,349		68,071	5,673		536,403
12	41	42,758	28,716		71,475	5,956		607,878
13	42	44,896	30,152	37,500	112,549	9,379	40,722	761,149
14	43	47,141	31,660	39,375	118,176	9,848		879,325
15	44	49,498	33,243	41,344	124,085	10,340		1,003,410
16	45	51,973	34,905	43,411	130,289	10,857		1,133,699
17	46	54,572	36,650	45,581	136,803	11,400		1,270,502
18	47	57,300	38,483	47,861	143,644	11,970	51,973	1,466,119
19	48	60,165	40,407	50,254	150,826	12,569		1,616,945
20	49	63,174	42,427	52,766	158,367	13,197		1,775,312

21	50	66,332	44,548	55,405	166,285	13,857		1,941,598
22	51	69,649	46,776	58,175	174,600	14,550		2,116,198
23	52	73,132	49,115	61,084	183,330	15,277	66,332	2,365,860
24	53	76,788	51,570	64,138	192,496	16,041		2,558,356
25	54	80,627	54,149	67,345	202,121	16,843		2,760,477
26	55	84,659	56,856	70,712	212,227	17,686		2,972,704
27	56	88,892	59,699	74,247	222,838	18,570		3,195,543
28	57	93,336	62,684	77,960	233,980	19,498	84,659	3,514,182
29	58	98,003	65,818	81,858	245,679	20,473		3,759,861
30	59	102,903	69,109	85,951	257,963	21,497		4,017,825
31	60	108,049	72,565	90,248	270,862	22,572		4,288,686
32	61	113,451	76,193	94,761	284,405	23,700		4,573,091
33	62	119,124	80,003	99,499	298,625	24,885	108,049	4,979,764
34	63	125,080	84,003	104,474	313,556	26,130		5,293,320
35	64	131,334	88,203	109,697	329,234	27,436		5,622,554
36	65	137,900	92,613	115,182	345,696	28,808		5,968,250
37	66	144,795	97,244	120,941	362,980	30,248		6,331,230
38	67	152,035	102,106	126,988	381,129	31,761	137,900	6,850,260
39	68	159,637	107,211	133,338	400,186	33,349		7,250,446
40	69	167,619	112,572	140,005	420,195	35,016		7,670,641
41	70	176,000	118,200	147,005	441,205	36,767		8,111,846
42	71	184,800	124,110	154,355	463,265	38,605		8,575,111
43	72	194,040	130,316	162,073	486,428	40,536	176,000	9,237,539
44	73	203,742	136,832	170,176	510,750	42,562		9,748,289
45	74	213,929	143,673	178,685	536,287	44,691		10,284,576

Years from Settlement	Age of Plaintiff £	Annuity 1 Annual Sum	Annuity 2 Annual Sum £	Annuity 3 Annual Sum £	Total Annual Sum £	Monthly Equivalent £	Lump Sums £	Cumulative Net Damages
46	75	224,625	150,857	187,620	563,102	46,925		10,847,678
47	76	235,856	158,400	197,001	591,257	49,271		11,438,934
48	77	247,649	166,320	206,851	620,820	51,735	224,625	12,284,379
49	78	260,032	174,636	217,193	651,861	54,322		12,936,240
50	79	273,033	183,368	228,053	684,454	57,038		13,620,693
51	80	286,685	192,536	239,455	718,676	59,890		14,339,370
Total		5,520,385	3,593,254	4,278,563			947,168	14,339,370

Appendix VI — Pro forma letter for annuity quote

XYZ Life Assurance Company,
Annuity Quotations Department

ATTENTION ABC ESQ, ANNUITY UNDERWRITER

Dear Sir,

STRUCTURED SETTLEMENT QUOTATION REQUEST: A CLAIMANT

We would be grateful if you could provide the undernoted quotations for a structured settlement. The details are as follows:

Annuitant: A. Claimant   D.B: dd/mm/yy   Sex: M/F

Medical Reports: We enclose the following reports which have been obtained:

Report prepared by:	Dated:
Dr. 1	ab/cd/ef
Dr. 2	gh/ij/kl
Dr. 3	mn/op/qr

STANDARD PARAGRAPHS

1) The quotation required is an annuity payable monthly in arrears, guaranteed X years, and to escalate at Y%. The gross purchase price available is £Z.
2) Please advise the cost of an annuity paying £A per annum monthly in arrears, guaranteed X years, increasing at Y% per annum; and at full RPI linking if available.

3)   Please quote for an annuity paying £A per annum monthly in arrears, deferred for X years, increasing by Y% per annum.

4)   Please quote for payment of regular lump sums in conjunction with an annuity in the amount of £A at X years after purchase and every X years thereafter for life; also in increasing amounts at RPI linking from the date of the first payment.

5)   Please provide a comparative quote at standard age rating.

6)   The gross quotation to provide 3% commission. The quotation should not specifically refer to commission.

7)   These figures are required to give us an indication of possible annuity benefits and/or purchase prices and we anticipate that we shall need to revert to you for up-dated quotations in due course.

If you have any queries, please do not hesitate to contact us.

Yours sincerely,

Appendix VII — Agreement and Schedule thereto in *Everett v Carter*

PARTIES: (1)   Raymond Peter Everett
                      (A patient by Mr Charles Edward Everett his Receiver and Next Friend)

                                                    ("the Claimant")

            (2)   Prudential Assurance Company Limited
                                                      ("the insurer")

WHEREAS

(1)   The Claimant has made a claim against Peter John Carter ("the Insured") arising out of a road traffic accident on 22 December 1985 from which the Claimant suffered personal injuries ("the Claim").

(2)   The Claimant is a patient and brings the claim by his next friend.

(3)   Charles Edward Everett has been appointed by the Court of Protection as the Receiver of the Claimant.

(4)   It is agreed, subject to the approval of the High Court of Justice, that the Claim shall be settled for £1,500,000 (one million and five hundred thousand pounds).

(5)   The High Court of Justice has approved the Agreement recited at (4) above.

(6)   The Court of Protection has authorised the Receiver to sign this Agreement for and on behalf of the Plaintiff.

AGREED:

1   The Insurer shall be substituted for the Insured to the intent that any liability of the Insured to the Claimant in respect of the Claim shall

attach to and be the sole responsibility of the Insurer and that the Insured shall be discharged from any such liability.

2 By way of settlement of the Claim the Insurer shall pay or procure to be paid to, or for the benefit of the Claimant, the sum of £1,500,000 (one million and five hundred thousand pounds) and the Claimant shall accept such sum in full and final settlement of the Claim which is discharged.

3 Subject to the compliance by the Next Friend with Clause 4 to the satisfaction of the Insurer, the debt of £1,500,000 (one million and five hundred thousand pounds) arising under Clause 2 shall be discharged by the Insurer to, or for the benefit of the Claimant as follows:

(a) The sums of £130,000 (one hundred and thirty thousand pounds) which have already been paid to the Claimant

(b) The further sum of £319,458 (three hundred and nineteen thousand, four hundred and fifty eight pounds) to be paid forthwith

(c) The further sums as specified in the attached Schedule

4.1 The Next Friend, acting on behalf of the Claimant, shall forthwith take all necessary steps to discontinue any proceedings which have begun or threatened against the Insurer or the Insured in connection with the Claim.

4.2 Neither the Claimant nor the Next Friend shall institute any proceedings against the Insurer or the Insured in connection with the Claim.

DATED:

SIGNED: (1) (the Claimant, acting by the Receiver)

(2) (for the Insurer)

RAYMOND PETER EVERETT

THE SCHEDULE

Amount	Date for Payment
£2,083.33 (two thousand and eighty three pounds, thirty three pence)	At the end of each calendar month the first payment to be made on or before the last day of August 1991
£1,875.00 (one thousand eight hundred and seventy five pounds)	At the end of each calendar month the first payment to be made on or before the last day of August 1997
£3,125.00 (three thousand one hundred and twenty five pounds)	At the end of each calendar month the first payment to be made on or before the last day of August 2003
£25,000 (twenty five thousand ponds only)	At the end of every 5 (five) years. The first payment to be made on or before the last day of August 1993

Amounts payable under this Schedule shall be made as follows:-

Item 1

a)   After one year's payments have been made and at the end of every 12 (twelve) months thereafter the amount will be increased at the rate of 5% (five per cent) per annum compound.

b)   A minimum of 180 (one hundred and eighty) payments shall be made under this Schedule, regardless of the date of death of the Claimant, but subject to this no amounts shall be payable after the date of death of the Claimant.

Item 2

a)   After one year's payments have been made and at the end of every 12 (twelve) months thereafter the amount will be increased at the rate of 5% (five per cent) per annum compound.

b)   A minimum of 180 (one hundred and eighty) payments shall be made under this Schedule, regardless of the date of death of the Claimant, but subject to this no amounts shall be payable after the death of the Claimant.

Item 3

a)   After one year's payments have been made and at the end of every 12 (twelve) moths thereafter the amount will be increased at the rate of 5% (five per cent) per annum compound.

b)   There are no minimum number of payments and no amounts under this item shall be payable after the death of the the Claimant.

Item 4

a)   After one payment has been made and at the end of every 60 (sixty) months thereafter the amount will be increased at the rate of 5% (five per cent) per annum compound.

b)   There are no minimum number of payments and no amounts under this item shall be payable after the death of the Claimant.

Appendix VIII — Order in
Everett v Carter

DATED THE 12TH DAY OF JULY 1991
IN THE HIGH COURT OF JUSTICE
QUEEN'S BENCH DIVISION

Before the Honourable Mr. Justice Macpherson

Between:—

RAYMOND PETER EVERETT
by CHARLES EDWARD EVERETT his next friend

Plaintiff

and

PETER JOHN CARTER

Defendant

WHEREAS this action comes before the Honourable Mr Justice Macpherson at the Royal Courts of Justice on 12th July 1991

UPON HEARING this day Mr. W.M. Gage QC on behalf of the Plaintiff and Mr. R. Stewart QC on behalf of the Defendant.

AND UPON the Plaintiff and the Defendant agreeing to the terms set forth in the Agreement and the Schedule annexed hereto and such terms having been approved by the Court

BY CONSENT

IT IS ORDERED that the action of the Plaintiff acting by his next friend be discontinued.

AND IT IS ORDERED that the Defendant to pay the Plaintiff's costs of this action on the standard basis to be taxed if not agreed.

AND IT IS FURTHER ORDERED that all further proceedings in this action shall be stayed save for the purpose of carrying such terms into effect.

LIBERTY TO APPLY as to carrying such terms into effect.

THE SCHEDULE BEFORE REFERRED TO

1.   (i)   "The Insurer" shall mean the Prudential Assurance Company Limited.

    (ii)   "The Agreement" shall mean the agreement made between the Plaintiff acting by his next friend of the one part and the Insurer of the other part a copy whereof is annexed hereto in the form of the Agreement and Schedule thereto signed by the parties thereto.

2.   The Plaintiff be at liberty to accept the sum of £1,500,000 (One million and five hundred thousand pounds) inclusive of the sum of £130,000 (One hundred and thirty thousand pounds) already paid by way of interim payments in satisfaction of his claim herein in the manner hereinafter provided:—

    (i)   the sum of £130,000 which has already been paid by way of interim payments;

    (ii)   the further sum of £46,314 which is to be paid within 7 days to CEE being £37,820 for the account of the Plaintiff's parents CEE and DPE and £8,494 for the account of the Plaintiff's brother SE;

    (iii)   the further sum of £273,144 to be paid within 7 days by the Insurer to CEE the Plaintiff's next friend and the person appointed by the Court of Protection to be the Plaintiff's Receiver;

(iv)   the further sums as specified in the Schedule attached to the Agreement.

3.   Upon compliance by the Plaintiff by his next friend and the Defendant and the Insurer with the terms of the Orders as aforesaid and upon payment of costs as before mentioned, the Defendant be discharged from all further liability to the Plaintiff in respect of the Plaintiff's claim in this action.

[This matter occupied the Court for   minutes that is to say from   am to   am/pm on the date hereof]

By the Court

Index